PELÉ

Harry Harris is a double winner of the British Sports Journalist of the Year award and was presented with the British Variety Club of Great Britain Silver Heart for 'Contribution to Sports Journalism'. He is also the only journalist ever to have won the Sports Story of the Year award twice. In all, he has garnered a total of twenty-four industry awards.

For some three decades, writing the most influential football columns in the country, Harry worked for the *Daily Mail*, *Daily Mirror*, *Daily Express*, *Daily Star*, *Sunday Express* and *Star on Sunday*, as well as BT Sport and ESPN SoccerNet, for which he was football correspondent. He has appeared regularly as a football analyst on all major TV sports, talk and news programmes, including *Richard & Judy*, *Newsnight*, BBC News and ITV *News at Ten*, Sky and *TalkSport*, and he featured in Sky's Christmas 2017 *Sunday Supplement* 'Legends' edition.

Harry is a prolific writer of bestselling football books. Among his eighty books are biographies of José Mourinho, Terry Venables, Franco Zola and Alex Ferguson, and of Roman Abramovich, while he collaborated on a number of autobiographies, including those of Gary Mabbutt and Kerry Dixon, as well as George Best's bestselling last book, *Hard Tackles and Dirty Baths*.

He is also a founder and director of footielegends100, and co-founder and director of H&H Sports Media Ltd/Zapsportz.com/Football30.

PELÉ

HIS LIFE AND TIMES

REVISED AND UPDATED EDITION

HARRY HARRIS

jb

Published in the UK by John Blake Publishing
an imprint of Bonnier Books UK
4th Floor, Victoria House
Bloomsbury Square,
London, WC1B 4DA
England

Owned by Bonnier Books
Sveavägen 56, Stockholm, Sweden

www.facebook.com/johnblakebooks ⦿
twitter.com/jblakebooks ⬛

First published by Robson Books in 2000
This revised and updated edition first published in paperback by
John Blake Publishing in 2018

Paperback ISBN: 978-1-78606-882-8
Ebook ISBN: 978-1-78946-010-0

British Library Cataloguing-in-Publication Data:
A CIP catalogue record for this book is available from the British Library.

Design by www.envydesign.co.uk

Printed and bound in Great Britain by Clays Ltd, Elcograf S.p.A.

3 5 7 9 10 8 6 4

John Blake Publishing is an imprint of Bonnier Books UK
www.bonnierbooks.co.uk

To Pelé and the Beautiful Game

AUTHOR'S NOTE
to the revised edition

This book was first published in 2000, and was the first biography of Pelé to receive the player's full cooperation. This new edition brings his extraordinary story up to date in the last two chapters, but to maintain the immediacy of the original edition, the preceding text has been left as originally published. Pelé, after all, belongs to the history not only of football, but of Brazil and the wider world; it seems apt, therefore, that the first part of his journey should be described in the words of the time.

HARRY HARRIS

CONTENTS

ACKNOWLEDGEMENTS

P elé personally has helped me over the years with numerous interviews in numerous locations from Rio to Dusseldorf. But this book could not reflect the true nature of the man or the footballer without the undiluted and freely given contributions of those who know him well, and of course of many high-profile personalities, past and present, within the game. Special thanks are due to FIFA head of communications Keith Cooper.

Of all these contributors I am most indebted to Sir Bobby Charlton, England's own global ambassador, who has played against Pelé and with whom Pelé has a special rapport. In Rio, I had the privilege and the pleasure of interviewing Jairzinho, Gerson and the mastermind behind the greatest team, coach Mário Zagalo, whose mind is as alive and active as ever at the age of sixty-eight.

My thanks, too, to the late George Best, for describing his feelings of forever being in the top five Best of All Time list without ever being able to dislodge Pelé from pole position.

Fascinating insights into Pelé as a player and a person have been provided by Kevin Keegan, Craig Brown, Ossie Ardiles, Gary Lineker, Trevor Brooking, Tony Banks MP, Ken Bates, Andy Roxburgh, Alan Mullery, Alan Hudson, Gordon Taylor, Doug Ellis, George Graham, Garth Crooks, Russell Osman, Jimmy Armfield, Terry Butcher, Gordon Hill, BBC Radio 5 Live's Alan Green and Mike Ingham, and Henry Winter of *The Daily Telegraph*.

Special appreciation goes to a dear friend from New York, Tony Signore, who has worked closely with Pelé since 1991 when his public relations company, Alan Taylor Communications, first began to deal with the MasterCard account. Through Tony I have been privileged to have met Pelé socially, which has enabled me to interview him in a relaxed and amenable atmosphere. Tony, Ryan Mucatel and Rick Liebling were instrumental in arranging for me to see Pelé at the 2002 World Cup draw in Tokyo in December at a crucial stage of my research.

Peter Draper, Martin Prothero, Simon Marsh, and Tim and Gillian at Umbro International have also organised on my behalf a number of interviews with Pelé during which I have got to know the great man and to enjoy his company both socially and professionally. Peter has moved on to become commercial manager at Manchester United.

Available details of Pelé's life and career are fragmented, and books such as Brian Glanville's authoritative *Story of the World Cup*, David Yallop's investigation into João Havelange in *How They Stole The Game*, *The Beautiful Team: In search of Pelé and the 1970 Brazilians* by Garry Jenkins, Bobby Moore's authorised biography (written by his close friend Jeff Powell and first published by Everest Books in 1976), and Pelé's own autobiography published in 1977, have been invaluable to my quest to produce the definitive biography.

INTRODUCTION

As Manchester United prepared for the inaugural World Club Championships at the Maracana Stadium, I posed proudly for a picture with Jairzinho outside the Intercontinental Hotel in Rio. Here in the spiritual home of the game, Jairzinho delivered a remark as profound and as memorable as one of his brilliant goals. 'Nobody has an opinion about Pelé – we just thank him for being such a wonderful player and for bringing so much happiness to the Brazilian people.'

Pelé has talked about the joy of playing with Jairzinho, and Jairzinho confirmed that the feeling was mutual. 'I feel the same,' he said through an interpreter. 'It was wonderful to be able to play with Pelé. He is the best in the world.'

The dawn of the twenty-first century established Pelé not only as the greatest footballer of all time, an honour he unarguably held already, but also as the planet's outstanding athlete. In the inevitable profusion of awards to mark the millennium, Pelé vied with Muhammad Ali for the highest possible accolade. The

National Olympic Committee voted Pelé Athlete of the Century even though he never competed in the Olympic Games, while Muhammad Ali, Olympic light-heavyweight champion of 1960, came second. The highly respected French sports daily *L'Equipe* also nominated Pelé Athlete of the Century and Ali second, with Carl Lewis third. Reuters, too, put Pelé at the top of their list.

In Britain, Pelé topped all the football polls and featured prominently in the BBC's Sports Personality of the Century award, won by Ali. After Ali collected his prestigious trophy in December 1999, Alan Hansen, *Match of the Day*'s pundit, wrote in his column in the *Express*:

> It is only natural to celebrate our sporting heroes as the end of the millennium approaches. The BBC honoured the man who will always be the greatest: Muhammad Ali. And in football too there remains no contest. It will take someone very special indeed to usurp Pelé from his throne. Diego Maradona went close, but nobody has ever seriously challenged Brazil's most famous number 10. And when it comes to the finest teams of the century, on the international stage it can only be Pelé's 1970 World Cup winning side. I can vividly recall those late nights sat in front of the telly watching them play in Mexico. For a fifteen-year-old with a head full of dreams it was wonderful to see. The magic of Jairzinho, the brilliance of Rivelino, the intelligence and creative genius of Gerson, and the revolutionary skills of Carlos Alberto. And then, of course, there was Pelé. No other side has ever had the ability to match the confidence of scoring three if the opposition struck twice.

INTRODUCTION

Brian Glanville, for many decades recognised as one of the world's leading football writers, described Pelé in one of his *Times* articles on the sporting icons of the century as 'probably the finest footballer of all time, a remarkable compound of athleticism, skill, flair and opportunism. We saw the best of him in the 1958 and 1970 finals; a maker and taker of goals.'

George Graham, one-time manager of Tottenham Hotspur, says:

> One of the big regrets of my football career was that I was never on the same pitch as Pelé. I played for Scotland in the Maracana when we were beaten 1–0 but Pelé never played. That was such a pity. I've no idea to this day why he was not in the side – perhaps he was injured. I've never seen him 'live', either, although I have studied many videos of his games. He had everything. All the great players had power allied to their enormous talents, and Pelé could look after himself, all right. As he got older and more experienced, he was able to do it far more subtly. I would liken Pelé to Nureyev: grace allied to power.

Kevin Keegan's assessment is that Pelé has made an enormous contribution to sport, and still does. Not that he knows him personally. Though he played against him once, for England against Team America when Pelé was close to forty, Keegan has not had the good fortune to have spent long enough in his company to engage in any meaningful conversation. Yet the England coach's affection for Pelé the player is unlimited, and he has no hesitation in placing the Brazilian as the pivotal figure in the advancement of the game in terms of promoting its aesthetic qualities. He did so as the world's best footballer and continues to do so as its worldwide ambassador. 'When he walks into the room, the king or queen of that country couldn't make more of an impact,' says Keegan. 'For me, he is the man of the century. Some great players have come and gone, but Pelé has stayed around from the time he started, in the late fifties, until right now. At the draw in Japan for the 2002 World Cup the whole place stopped when he entered the forum. Everyone looked round, as if to say to each other, "There he is". Just getting a look at him was enough. He has a royal status.'

Everyone has a favourite Pelé moment, and Keegan is no exception.

He is remembered in this country for the goal he didn't score, when Gordon Banks made that save from his tremendous header. It was unstoppable, but he stopped it. I still don't know how he did it, no matter how many times I have watched it rerun on TV. But it's typical of Pelé. Another memorable moment was from the World Cup in 1970, that shot from inside his own half. Had that gone in, it would have made David Beckham's goal from the halfway line against Wimbledon look like a tap-in. In that game he also dummied one way past the keeper, but missed – that was once in his life when he proved for a minute he was human. That would be my favourite memory of Pelé. I also recall how he was kicked out of the World Cup here in '66, and that is remembered for all the wrong reasons. I was just fifteen at the time and I watched it on TV. I had just got into my football six months before and I was eagerly awaiting the opportunity to see Pelé, but he was injured and it was such a shame. It was like going to watch a top West End show only for the big name to have the night off:

you felt cheated being forced to watch the understudy. The World Cup in '66 was not the same when Pelé was out of it. People like me who were interested in seeing the greatest player felt the tournament was robbed of its jewel. And that goal he scored in the World Cup final in 1958. It had about it a touch of Gazza's goal against Scotland in Euro '96, when he flipped the ball over a defender and then struck it on the volley. But in Pelé's case we're talking about a boy of seventeen in a World Cup final. Pelé is just special, very, very special. The mind boggles at what he might be worth in today's inflated transfer market. He would be priceless. Absolutely priceless. Even in those days it would have been cheaper to have bought the whole of Brazil than to have tried to buy Pelé from Santos. It's a difficult one to assess whether it is a great thing for the game or a sad development that players do move on far more now than they used to. But it was certainly great for Brazil that they were able to keep Pelé in their country for his entire career, apart from late on, when he returned from retirement to play in the States for Cosmos. The country is fortunate to have reared a legend who retained that status even when he finished playing. He was the official Minister of Sport in Brazil for only a short period, but in reality he has been Football Minister for the entire world for the past twenty years.

Pelé is not merely the twentieth century's greatest athlete, but one of its most famous names in any sphere. *Time* magazine named him among its top twenty 'Heroes and icons' of the twentieth century. On that list were Princess Diana, Marilyn Monroe, Anne

Frank, Muhammad Ali, Che Guevara, Emmeline Pankhurst and Mother Teresa. Now that is some accolade.

Pelé scored nearly 1,300 goals, an average of almost one goal per game; a record that will stand for all time. In a career which began when he was sixteen he played 1,363 games and scored 1,281 goals (he later added two more in special appearances), including 97 for his country. In Nigeria in 1967 a two-day truce was declared in the Biafran war so that both sides could watch him play. The Shah of Iran once waited three hours at an international airport just to speak to him. Frontier guards in Red China left their posts and came into Hong Kong to pay their respects to him. He has had audiences with three popes, dozens of kings, five emperors, nearly a hundred presidents and fifty chiefs of state. He is an honorary citizen of more cities and countries than any other person in history. In his prime, *Sports Illustrated* magazine voted his the most perfect physique of any athlete in the world.

The sportsman who became an actor, a poet, a musician and obtained a university degree speaks fluent Spanish, more than passable French, Italian and English as well as his native Portuguese. Many times I have watched him glide from table to table to be interviewed by journalists from several different countries, switching from one language to another with ease.

His charisma lies not in the fact that he was once a sex symbol in the George Best or David Beckham category, nor even because he attained the world-class stature exemplified latterly by Diego Maradona, Johan Cruyff or Ruud Gullit. It does not lie in his membership of the elite new breed of soccer multi-millionaires. He may be in a healthy financial position owing to his commercial links with Coca-Cola, MasterCard and Umbro, but the likes of David Beckham can command £8 million a year – of which only a small proportion comes from his football earnings and the remainder from endorsing products such as Brylcreem – more than Pelé has earned in a lifetime in the game.

No, it lies in the fact that Pelé has survived generation upon generation of World Cup performers of the highest calibre to remain number one, the undisputed greatest footballer of his or any generation. It is almost impossible when seeing Pelé not to instantly recall those images of 1970, the Gordon Banks save, the handshake with the sadly departed Bobby Moore, and the golden moments of Brazil's world dominance with a brand of football that ensured universal approval – although those brought up on Michael Owen, David Beckham and Ronaldo have only video evidence of his dazzling brilliance.

Ronaldo, the latest in the long line of potential pretenders to Pelé's crown, moved to PSV Eindhoven under Bobby Robson, then on to Barcelona and Inter Milan – and all this while still in his teens. By contrast, Pelé played for just two clubs: Santos for his entire top-class career, then New York Cosmos, ending up with a testimonial game in which he played one half for Santos and the other for Cosmos.

At the age of twenty-one, Ronaldo earned £20 million in World Cup year alone, including a share of Nike's $200 million sponsorship deal with the Brazilian FA. Yet Pelé displays not the slightest hint of bitterness at the fortunes earned by some of the high flyers of the game with not a fraction of his talent. The richness of this man is in his achievements for football as a whole, not in the augmentation of his bank balance.

While England invented the game, it was the Brazilians and Pelé who elevated it to another level of fine artistry and ideology. No one felt the departure of that philosophy more painfully and personally than Pelé when his beloved Brazil joined the mere mortals of world football and met with defeat in the last World Cup.

PELÉ: HIS LIFE AND TIMES

When I set out to compile Pelé's life story, I knew it would be a mammoth task to piece together one of the most fulfilled football careers of all time. Of all the research, of all the people close to him I interviewed, of all those who have a profound view of him from a position of strength within the sport, it was imperative to reach the man himself, because I wanted this to be a work that would meet with his approval. Not in the sense that it would be sanitised, or hide any part of his life that he would rather not discuss or linger upon: he has made mistakes and he has been open about them. So Pelé himself has made a major contribution and approved the manuscript.

The main part of this book is a tribute to the life and times of Pelé as he reached his landmark sixtieth year. Please note that this section was written in 2000/2001 and some of the people referred to are no longer with us, and references to their jobs and situations were current at that time and are likely to have changed since. However, the final part of the book is an up to date appraisal of his life since then. Astonishingly, prior to 2001, there had been no appraisal of his career since an autobiography published in the UK in 1977, so it is the first definitive life story of a player who represents all that is good about a sport tarnished by corruption, avarice, drugs and vice. Appropriately, the first year of the new millennium was also the thirtieth anniversary of his last World Cup, when, with Pelé at his majestic, magical best, Brazil won the world title for the third occasion with perhaps the best national team of all time. It was certainly the team closest to Pelé's soul, playing the game as it did in the way it ought to be played.

CHAPTER 1

FROM SHOESHINE TO GOLDEN BOOT

*'Of all the records I hold from my career, including 1,283 goals
as a professional, there is one of my father's I never equalled.
He is, I believe, the only player to have scored five goals in
one game all front headers.'*

Pelé

Pelé was born Edson Arantes do Nascimento on 23 October
1940. At least, that is what the records show. In fact, as he has
confirmed, he was born two days earlier than that, on 21 October,
though he celebrates his birthday on the 23rd. Among the poor
families of the town of Três Corações ('three hearts') in the state
of Minas Gerais, it was not uncommon for there to be confusion
about exact dates of birth.

Edson Arantes was the first of three children born to João
Ramos do Nascimento and his wife, Dona Celeste. His father was
an average professional footballer. He played for the local team,
Minas Gerais, where everyone knew him as Dondinho. He was

the star of the side, but earned such meagre wages that he could barely make ends meet. His big break came in 1942, when he was spotted by a scout for Atlético Mineiro in Belo Horizonte, the state capital. During his first match for the club, against São Cristóvão in Rio, he collided with the giant Augusto, later to captain Brazil in the 1950 World Cup. Dondinho fell so awkwardly that he was left with severely torn right knee ligaments and a permanent limp. The team doctors informed him that he would never play properly again. Atlético Mineiro dispensed with his services and paid for his return ticket to Três Corações. Afraid to have surgery, he continued to play for the local side, packing his knee with ice between games. Pelé has said: 'It was the only way he knew of making money at all.'

Dondinho's eldest son, *moleque* (black street urchin), first nicknamed Dico, was brought up surrounded by his extended family, which included his paternal grandmother Ambrosina, and Uncle Jorge, his mother's brother. Now the street where he lived is named after him, and the ramshackle house which was his first home bears a commemorative plaque. The house forms part of a shabby row of dwellings built of used bricks and held together by cracked plaster and peeling paint. Dico, later to become Pelé, knew little else of what life had to offer. When he was growing up, he thought everyone lived in houses like it.

It was only when Dondinho was offered a place with FC Bauru in the state of São Paulo, and a public service job to go with it, that his wife finally stopped complaining that he should forget the 'nonsense', as she called it, that was football. Pelé recalls: 'My first real memory begins with the train ride to Bauru when I was about four years old. I vaguely recall being taken to the railway station in an old wagon drawn by a pony.' He vividly remembers being clipped around the ear by his mother on the train for leaning too far out of the window to get a better view of the steam engine pulling it when the carriage rounded a sharp curve.

But in Bauru ill luck continued to dog Dondinho. The football club was restructured and became the Bauru Athletic Club, and its new directors, while honouring his playing contract, conveniently denied any responsibility for getting their new player a job as well. Now Dondinho found himself in a strange city with a family of seven to support, the household having expanded to include Dico's brother Jair and sister Maria Lucia. There were continued arguments as Dona Celeste, Dondinho's wife, nagged her husband about his obsession with the game while his family was in such dire straits.

Dico's Uncle Jorge cut wood for a time and sold it door-to-door, but as just about everyone else in their situation was doing the same, he made little money. Then he found work with a wholesaler, which helped to support the family. Aunt Maria took a job as a maid with a rich family in São Paulo. On her day off she would come to Bauru bringing fruits her relations had never seen or even heard of, such as pears and apples, plus hand-me-down clothes from her employer.

'And so we existed,' Pelé recalls. 'But as I grew up I began to learn what poverty was. Poverty is a curse that depresses the mind, drains the spirit and poisons life. When we didn't lack things, simple things like enough food in the house, or the small sum needed to pay our rent, we were very happy. There was a great deal of love in that small house; love that overcame much of the hardship. But there were also many bitter arguments, virulent recriminations, painful battles over the lack of necessities, things that Dona Celeste stubbornly maintained were our birthright because Dondinho had been promised that job.'

Their house was made of wood with a tiled roof that leaked,

and so haphazardly that it was impossible to know where to drag a mattress for a dry night's sleep during some of the torrential rains so characteristic of Brazilian weather. On cold nights – it's not always hot in Brazil – the family huddled together in the tiny kitchen to try to keep warm.

Yet despite the family's poverty, the young Dico was happy in Bauru. He played from dawn to dusk with the other kids, white, black, Japanese – it didn't matter. They played with whatever was to hand, constructing a trapeze which they hung from a mango tree in Dico's backyard – until his mother caught them and dealt him the customary clip round the head, and the rope came down. As for football, 'We couldn't afford a ball, so we did what most other kids did: we would stuff the largest man's sock we could find with rags or crumpled-up newspaper, roll it into as close a ball shape as we could manage, and tie it around with string.' The socks occasionally had to be purloined from clothes lines. The pitch was the street where Pelé lived, Rua Rubens Arruda, and the goalposts were the two ends of the street. It took some skill just to keep your balance on the surface, to control a ball of variable weight, depending on how much it had been kicked already and how many times it had run through the puddles of mud. 'But it made no difference; the pleasure of kicking that ball, making it move, making it respond to an action of mine, was the greatest feeling of power I had ever had up to that time.' Dondinho lovingly taught him the tricks of the trade.

Indeed, his father was Pelé's greatest influence. He was convinced that Edson had inherited the spirit of an uncle he had never known, Dondinho's elder brother Francisco, who had died at the age of twenty-five. Dondinho told Dico he hoped he would inherit his uncle's skill.

Dona Celeste, on the other hand, did not want her boy to fall into the same trap as his father. However, she wasn't too worried at first, because – to Dondinho's surprise – he had announced his firm intention of becoming a pilot, not a footballer, when he grew up. He would often sneak off to the Aero Club, where he would fantasise about wearing the goggles and leathers of the pilots he saw there. In the meantime, the price he had to pay for his football was taking care of his younger brother Jair, nicknamed Zoca. So he carried on playing in front of his house with Zoca trying to get in on the act and often ending up hurt. That meant another clip around the ear.

Dico had also inherited his mother's inner strength. Despite her appearance – she was blessed with a full head of beautiful brown hair, a beguiling smile and weighed less than seven stone – Dona could be fearsome. Pelé recalls: 'Anyone who made a judgement about Dona Celeste based on her lovely smile or petite figure was in for a surprise. She ruled the house with an authority that was absolute.' The family might have been poor, but they behaved. 'We didn't steal, we didn't beg, we didn't lie, we didn't cheat; we didn't use swear words, regardless of the provocation; we believed in God and prayed to him regularly, although we didn't expect him to solve our problems for us; we treated people older than ourselves with respect; and above all, we obeyed our parents – or else.'

Dona Celeste's immediate concern was her eldest son's lack of success at school. With hindsight, Pelé doesn't think it was because he was particularly stupid, just that he didn't see eye to eye with his teachers, particularly Dona Cida, a new teacher who arrived in his third year at the Ernesto Monte Primary School, whose disciplinary standards he failed to reach. 'For talking in class she would make me stuff my mouth full of balls of paper until my cheeks hurt. But after a while I discovered that by chewing the paper when she wasn't looking, I could eventually end up with a small wad that wasn't uncomfortable at all.' There was a far more painful punishment for throwing spitballs, pinching girls or fighting in class: you had to kneel on uncooked corn beans in a corner of the room. When the teacher's attention was diverted, Dico would pocket the beans to alleviate the discomfort.

By the time he was ten, the animosity he felt towards Dona Cida would have completely put him off school. As it was, by the age of seven he had already abandoned homework in favour of earning a little money as a shoeshine boy, or from selling discarded peanuts he picked up from passing trains. A friend helped him build a rough approximation of a shoeshine kit from an old box and Uncle Jorge financed the initial supplies. He thought it would be a wonderful excuse to make a legitimate daily visit to the Aero Club, where the pilots would naturally want their shoes shined, but his mother insisted he restricted his work to the streets nearer home. He knocked on doors for a full week before a neighbour finally took pity on him and became his first customer. He also polished his father's football boots, and his own pride and joy: a pair of proper shoes that had belonged to his Aunt Maria's employer's youngest son, who had outgrown them. These were reserved for church on Sunday, so of course Dico was heading for yet another ear tug when he wore them to play football. 'But I had to know how it felt to kick a ball with shoes on,' he explains.

After his failure to drum up custom on doorsteps, Dico persuaded his mother to let his father take him to the football club on match day, to ply his trade among the crowd. As Dondinho earned a crust on the field, he made two cruzeiros himself, and the pair of them went home happy. Next Dico was allowed to venture to the railway station, where most of the shoeshine boys congregated, and to the nearest football stadium, where the Noroeste Club, BAC's bitter rivals, played.

Dondinho finally got the job he had been promised when Dico was about eight; a job with the state, as an assistant in a health clinic, which involved sweeping the floors, cleaning bedpans, loading and unloading supplies. At last the friction within the house was relieved. When the last train had left the station and there was no more shoeshining to be done, Dico would often help his father make the coffee and listen to his reminiscences of his football career and of Uncle Francisco. These chats brought them closer and Dico now wanted no more than 'to be like my dad, a footballer'. This was compounded by a macabre experience when Dico and his pals accidentally saw an autopsy being performed on a dead pilot who had been brought into the local hospital. He and his friends had been playing football on some adjacent scrubland when the ball bounced away and came to rest next to one of the hospital's windows. As they retrieved the ball and glanced through the window, Dico's romantic view of flying quickly turned to horror as he saw an image that gave him nightmares for months afterwards.

Dico evolved into Pelé at the age of about nine or ten. 'I have no idea where the name came from, or who started it, because it has no meaning in Portuguese, or any other language as far as I know,' he says. 'I've been back to Bauru many times, and have asked all my old friends from those days, but they don't have a clue as to its origin or exactly when it started, either. They say it just began one day and after that it stuck because it seemed to fit, whatever it means.' It could have come from his own mispronunciation of the name of one of Minas Gerais's most famous players at the time, Belé; it might have been a half-Portuguese, half-Turkish concoction.

'One friend said it may have been given to me inadvertently by one of the many Turks who lived in Bauru. He thought it possible that whenever I accidentally touched the ball with my hands, they would shout "Pe-le!", meaning "foot" in Portuguese, and possibly "stupid" in Turkish – or maybe what they thought the word for stupid was in our language.' All he recalls for certain is that as a nine- or ten-year-old he hated it so much he would get into fights with those who used it. 'I must have lost most of them, because the name stuck. All I know is that from then on I was Pelé to everyone I know, except for my family, who continue to call me Dico to this day.'

By ten he was playing with much older children in a neighbourhood team called September 7, formed by his street football gang and named for Brazil's Independence Day. September 7's headquarters was Pelé's backyard. They craved a real ball, proper kit and even boots. Pelé came up with the idea of collecting football cards, putting them into albums and selling them to get the money for a ball. Raising the funds for shirts, shorts and socks was more of a problem. One of the gang suggested stacking firewood for neighbours, another collecting tobacco from cigarette butts to make up cigarettes to sell. Salvaging scrap metal to sell to a dealer was another idea. None of these scams worked. Back at the drawing board, one boy formulated a plan to steal peanuts from the railway warehouse and sell them outside the cinema, or when the circus came to town. Pelé feared his mother's retribution, and stuck to swapping cards. But getting his hands on the rare ones needed to complete the albums proved no easy task, and he was finally persuaded to join the peanut-stealing operation, now switched to the freight cars, deemed to be a softer target than the warehouse. The haul from the two-boy raid paid for the shirts and enough flour sacks for their mothers to make shorts from. That left the boots. A second peanut mission was planned, this time involving the entire gang.

It was to end in tragedy. The raid itself was successfully accomplished, but the gang needed somewhere to hide their contraband. They decided on some caves in the hills where they played. The smallest boy was assigned the job of stashing the peanuts in the cave. While he was inside, a storm broke, torrential rain began to lash the hillside and the boy was engulfed by a mudslide. The horrified boys ran for help, but it was too late. 'One of the men wrapped the small body in his jacket and started towards the boy's house, with all of us behind him, like a funeral procession.' The child's mother broke down. 'Her whimpers were accusing stabs I can still feel. When I finally got home, trembling from the shock of the experience and soaked from the rain, I was given a stern lecture on playing in such a dangerous place. But the stolen peanuts remained a secret, locked in the hearts of all who had participated.' His punishment was the endless nightmares in which he was himself trying in vain to escape from that muddy, clinging tomb.

Not surprisingly, after this terrible disaster the schemes to fund the purchase of boots were abandoned and September 7 opted instead to call themselves 'The Shoeless Ones'. It was not particularly original: every team in the vicinity seemed to have the same nickname. However, Pelé did eventually complete two of his football-card albums, which were traded for a ball of sorts. Pelé kept it in his house, and thus became the team's captain.

Naturally Pelé played centre-forward, but he also played in defence at times, and occasionally in goal as well. His father took him to the abandoned Noroeste field and impressed upon him the necessity to use both feet. Dondinho would instruct, coach and drill him constantly in all the skills of football, endlessly practising heading, passing and all the other arts of the game.

Most of the rest of Pelé's spare time was taken up with September 7 – either that or with fighting. There would be scraps with all sorts of boys, even his brother Zoca. When Zoca wasn't picked for September 7, he would assemble his own team, calling it Rubens Arruda after the street they lived in, sometimes challenging Pelé's team to a match. If Zoca's team won, Pelé would say that September 7 hadn't been trying and the pair would end up rolling on the floor, fighting. Even a game of 'button football' could end up the same way. Pelé also got into a scrap watching his father play, after a fan shouted abuse at Dondinho for missing a chance. When Dondinho got home and asked for an explanation, he told Pelé that if he expected to be a professional footballer he had to control his temper. It was the first indication from his father that he thought of him as a potential professional; it was also an important lecture. Dondinho said that Pelé must learn that fans could be aggressive, but they must be ignored. More pertinently, losing your temper on the field could result in a sending-off. The idea of becoming a professional footballer was taking root in the young Pelé's mind.

After that incident Dondinho took more interest in Pelé s September 7 team and would discuss his game as they walked home after matches. He also set an example in the matter of fitness by not drinking or smoking. He once caught Pelé smoking – albeit only a *xuxu*, a tasteless Brazilian vegetable which the impoverished kids rolled in paper to smoke – with his gang. He said nothing in front of the other boys, but waited until Pelé got home before giving him another lecture. 'He told me that smoking or drinking would impair my physical condition if I wanted to play football. But more importantly, "don't borrow" was his message, and he opened up his painfully thin wallet to offer me money to buy cigarettes rather than borrow them.' Pelé felt enormous shame at that, and never touched another cigarette.

It was not long before September 7 got their coveted boots. The boys were desperate to enter a football tournament sponsored by the mayor of Bauru, and the father of three brothers in the side, a salesman, offered to provide them with boots in return for becoming their coach. He fulfilled his promise by persuading the Noroeste club directors to part with their old boots. In honour of this improved status, September 7 changed its name to Ameriquinha, which in Portuguese means Little America. So the team accustomed to playing on potholed streets had their first outings on grass with proper kit. They trained every day, between their chores and schooling. As the tournament progressed, Ameriquinha remained unbeaten and the crowds were treated to a wonderful brand of football. Nicola Avallone Junior, the mayor, also owned the *Bauru Daily*, so the team were assured of plenty of publicity as they won through to the final of the Nicola Avallone Junior Victory Cup at the BAC stadium, packed for the occasion to its 5,000 capacity. Pelé, at twelve, the youngest boy in the side, scored in Ameriquinha's victory, full of pride that his father was present to see his goal.

'Of all the many memories I have of that glorious day, two things stand out,' he says. 'The crowd calling my name, Pelé, Pelé, in a constantly growing chant, until I found myself no longer hating the name but actually beginning to like it, and my father holding me tightly after the match and saying, "You played a beautiful game, Dico. I couldn't have played any better myself." When we got home and Dondinho triumphantly reported the news, my mother smiled for the first time at something involving football.' Dona Celeste had stayed at home, beginning a habit that was to last a lifetime. Throughout Pelé's illustrious career, she never went to see him play. Haunted by the injury that cut short Dondinho's career, she was terrified that the same fate would befall her son, and couldn't bear to watch.

Pelé came home from the junior Victory Cup with his first football earnings: 36 cruzeiros. It was a tradition for appreciative fans to throw money on to the pitch, and because Pelé had been the winning goalscorer, his teammates had given it all to him. Although the collection was a small fortune to his family, his mother insisted he shared it with the rest of the team. Shortly afterwards, Ameriquinha's coach and his three sons left the area and the team started to disintegrate. Happily, at about the same time, Bauru Athletic Club formed a youth team, Baquinho, or Little BAC. Pelé, dreaming of emulating his father and playing in the senior side, was quick to join, along with many of his friends. They were surprised to find that their new coach, Waldemar de Brito, was an inside-forward in the 1934 World Cup side. Coincidentally, he had also coached a state championship team Dondinho had played in. De Brito was a marvellous teacher, and helped Pelé to develop many of his crafts, notably his leaping ability for headers and the bicycle kick. People somehow have the idea that Pelé originated this kick, but he himself attributes it to Léonidas, who played for Brazil in 1934 with de Brito. Even by Latin standards, de Brito was a loud and opinionated coach, 'a shouter', according to Pelé. But he was astounded by his pupil's natural ability and introduced discipline into his game. 'He kept on to us continually about our mistakes, and was very good for me and four or five of my friends.'

De Brito, who had been posted to a civil-service job in Bauru, eventually became restless with life away from the more vibrant political centre of his native São Paulo; and decided to return there to coach professionals. With his departure, Baquinho's inspiration dwindled. Pelé, approached by the Radio club team Radium, joined them as the club's only non-professional at the age of fourteen. In spite of his tender years he led the scoring table with forty goals. He was also asked to play for Noroestinho (Little North-West) when the Noroeste club decided to start a youth side and organised a tournament played as a curtain-raiser to their professional night games.

Outgrowing the shoeshining game, when he wasn't playing football Pelé graduated to selling meat pies at the station to passengers through the windows of the train. He had to return the money and any unsold pies to Senhor Rosalino and his wife, who made them. They always suspected that the skinny kid had eaten a few. His thin excuse for any missing pies was that someone must have stolen them when he wasn't looking. Surely that cannot be where the ditty 'Who Ate All the Pies?' originated? Who knows.

Pelé finally managed to finish school, taking six years instead of the usual four. Then he took a job in a shoe factory, sewing welts on to boots. To earn extra cash he helped a Japanese friend in his dry-cleaning store and the friend's family in their vegetable market – mainly because he fancied his sister.

There was great excitement when Senhor Tim, who had played for Brazil in the 1938 World Cup and was now coach of the prestigious Bango club in Rio, arrived in Bantu, having heard of the exploits of the youth teams Pelé had played in and of Pelé himself. Pelé's head whirled with the thrilling prospect of playing in the Maracana. His father readily gave his blessing; his mother, however, dug in her heels.

A year later, when Pelé was fifteen, Waldemar de Brito reappeared in Bauru and visited Pelé's father. As a result of their discussion, de Brito approached a friend, Athie Jorge Couri, a member of the state legislature who also just happened to be president of Santos, a club with ambitions to break the stranglehold on the São Paulo regional championship, the Brazilian national championship and the Silver Cup held by upper-class sides like Corinthians, São Paulo FC and Palmeiras. He felt it had been the right decision not to let Pelé go to Rio, but now a year on, he felt Pelé was ready to try Santos. Dona Celeste was still reticent. She pointed to Pelé's short trousers and said that he was still her baby. De Brito returned a week later and invited Pelé's parents to his hotel to take a call from the Santos president. Dona Celeste returned in tears, but at last gave her permission for Pelé to go to the club to get some experience. But she was not happy about it, having lived with the sacrifices her husband had made for football, only to emerge virtually penniless. 'To me you are still a little boy, but everyone else seems to think you're grown up,' she complained to Pelé. But deep down she also knew that football was his only real chance of escape from the poverty in Bauru. 'You were never a good student,' she told him, 'and I don't want you sewing boots for the rest of your life.'

Santos, just south of the big industrialised city of São Paulo, was at the time a town like Bauru, although its large port gave it a more important air, and the club were the first division state champions. This made the town an acceptable size for Dona Celeste and the club suitably ambitious to satisfy Dondinho.

Despite the jealousy of her neighbours, who believed Santos's big shots would make a fool out of Pelé, Dona Celeste's mind was made up. His mother insisted he should graduate to long trousers for the journey. With the help of a loan from Pelé's excited boss at the shoe factory and advances on his father's and Uncle Jorge's salaries, they scraped together enough money for shirts, new shoes and his first visit to a tailor to make up two pairs of denim trousers to equip him for the adventure.

The night before his departure, Pelé's father had a message from Noroeste. They wanted Pelé to stay. They offered him a small salary as a professional, and warned Dondinho that he would lose many friends if he let his son go to Santos. Dona Celeste was heartened by this glimmer of hope that Pelé might be able to stay in Bauru, but his father, for once, was adamant: Pelé must go, and the loss of fair-weather friends was no loss at all.

So Pelé went with his father and De Brito by train to Santos. From the station they took a bus straight to the stadium to watch his new club in action against Comercial de Ribeirão Preto. De Brito had arranged excellent seats for the three of them. Pelé had seen on TV matches at the Maracana and at Pacaembu in São Paulo, and in comparison the stadium was disappointing, but by the end of the game he was enthralled by the quality and style of Santos and found himself cheering with the rest of the fans. After the game, which Santos won, Dondinho took the boy to the dressing rooms, where he was introduced by de Brito to the coach, Luis Alonso, known to all as Lula. 'So you're the famous Pelé,' said Lula. He then introduced the new boy to the players, some of whom knew Dondinho, and asked them to look after his son. Pelé felt shy and tongue-tied in the company of so many famous players, and already he was homesick. He wished he was going back to Bauru on the bus with his father, regardless of the prospect of training with the top stars of this wonderful Santos team.

Pelé moved into the Vila Belmiro, the *concentração* where the team was billeted before big games. Many of the players lived here, particularly the single ones. There were two or three bunk beds to a room, a nail on the back of the door for your clothes and a chair or two, and that was it. On his first night it took him some time to get to sleep, but he still woke early. He walked the mile to the beach. If nothing else, he would get the chance to look at the ocean.

Two days later he trained with the stars for the first time. He had feared he would be unwelcome, but he couldn't have been more wrong. The players couldn't have been more accommodating to the fifteen-year-old. In the practice match, Lula played him at centre forward – for the first team! Initially Pelé was gripped by nerves, but after a bad start he loosened up and it was as if he was back in Bauru playing for Norestinho. He didn't score, but he felt at home.

However, on the training pitch one difference between Pelé and his new teammates was instantly apparent. The coach was concerned by his lack of weight and height. Until he grew a bit more and filled out, he was too small to play with the professionals. It was time for massive meals. He was put on a special high-protein diet and told to build himself up in the youth sides. As one of the club's unofficial errand boys, he was given the nickname Gasolina, no doubt from the phrase, 'Get me a coffee, kid, and don't spare the gasolina'.

Engrossed in his football, his mind was occupied during the day, but at night, alone in a room, Pelé would cry himself to sleep. No matter how much he was being fed, he was paranoid about being small and skinny. After five nights of this, his worries and his homesickness got the better of him. His father had left him the money for his fare home and so, waking at 5 a.m., he packed his bags and crept downstairs and out of the Vila Belmiro. But for a chance meeting with the Santos odd-job man, Sabu, known as Sabuzao or Big Sabu, Pelé's career might have taken a very different turn – he might never have come back. Sabuzao was on his way to the market to buy fresh fish and rolls for his mother, who ran the kitchen, when he spotted the boy carrying his tell-tale suitcase. He told Pelé not to worry about being small, that he would be the fattest man in Santos in six months at the rate he was eating. Reassured, Pelé returned to his room.

After two weeks the Director of Sports offered him a pre-contract, a 'contract-in-the-drawer' as Pelé called it. This was a commonplace unofficial arrangement as he was too young to sign a proper contract. De Brito came to Santos to advise him and then Pelé went home to Bauru to discuss this with his parents, as the final decision rested with them. Although he had been away only a fortnight, he was delighted to be back home. But there was sadness, too. The contract offer shattered the illusions of his mother, who had been led to believe he was at Santos just for training experience. However, the deal meant a much-needed 5,000 cruzeiros a month. It was agreed that he would take it, signing on 8 April 1957, keeping 1,000 cruzeiros for himself and sending the rest to his father to put towards buying a house.

'My first contract was for ten dollars a month,' says Pelé. 'Nine months later, when I was sixteen and I was told I had been picked for Brazil, I got a rise. My wages went up to fifteen dollars.' He was to be on that same contract during the World Cup finals in Sweden in 1958.

Pelé concentrated on his football and made an immediate impact for Santos's *juvenil* (youth) and *amadores* (amateur) sides, scoring the vital goals which brought them state championship. He put three into the net the first time he wore the club's colours, in a youth game. It wasn't glory all the way, however. He played one important junior game, in which, for a change, he was the oldest on the field. Yet instead of dominating, he had a stinker. He even missed a penalty. To cap it all he was booed off. To lose against boys much younger than himself was a humiliation he couldn't take. He ran straight to his room and cried himself to sleep, still wearing his sweaty kit. When he woke in the middle of the night he packed his bag again. For the second time he intended to run away and go home. And for the second time, he was caught and persuaded to stay on by Big Sabu.

If Pelé feared the ridicule of the senior players, there was no need. They never mentioned his off day. There were more pressing problems to worry about, namely his failure to gain enough weight. Despite his special diet and callisthenics programme designed to build up his slight frame, he was still too lightweight to make any mark with the senior side.

Even so, when he finally pulled on the black-and-white strip of the Santos club for the first time in a first-team game, albeit a friendly against a local side, Cubatão, he scored four goals in a 6–1 win. It didn't count for the records, but it gave him the chance to consign the nickname Gasolina to history.

As so often happens, the misfortune of another player was a significant factor in Pelé's eventual breakthrough. He had been in the stands when Santos's main striker, the stylish Vasconcelos, known as Vasco, broke his leg in gruesome fashion in a match against São Paulo. Pelé discovered the news when he went to the dressing room at the end of the game. So it was then, at the age of fifteen, Pelé took over the number 10 shirt.

His first game as Vasco's replacement was a tough friendly against AIK Club of Sweden, in which Pelé was disappointed not to score. But the debut that counted was against Corinthians of Santo Andre on 7 September 1956. This time he was replacing Del Vecchio, one of the big star forwards the coach was saving for a more important match, and managed to put his name on the scoreboard. 'My first professional goal was enough to keep me walking on air for days,' he says. It was a goal to celebrate Independence Day, and a new house in Bauru for his parents.

In eleven games Pelé scored fifteen goals and began to get wider coverage in the newspapers. He was now sixteen and ready for a proper contract. He signed his first official contract with Santos on 8 April 1957, to run to 8 August 1958. But it was not going to bring him in line with the first-team players: he was awarded a rise of only 1,000 cruzeiros.

CHAPTER 2

THE WORLD CUP BOY WONDER ON FIFTEEN DOLLARS A MONTH

'We have neither rice nor bread, but we have Pelé,
and we have the Cup.'
João Goulart, President of Brazil

When the teenaged Pelé – at only five ft and 145lb still a scrawny kid, but an exceptional talent, even then, and with a temperament to match – first emerged on the world scene, football seemed such a simple game. In England there was the First Division title, the FA Cup and the Charity Shield; internationally, the World Cup was all. Nowadays there is a profusion of contrasting international events, from the FIFA Coca-Cola Cup and FIFA Futsal World Championship to the Under-17 World Championship for the FIFA/JVC Cup; there was even a Sepp Blatter proposal for a World Cup every two years. The European Champions League has superseded everything else with its £60-million reward for the winner of the revamped, enlarged European Cup, no longer the prerogative of the champions only.

In the 1950s, Brazilian football's principal problem was violence on the pitch. The 1954 World Cup held in Switzerland as FIFA celebrated its fiftieth anniversary, marked the birth of televised football. The quarter-final between favourites Hungary and Brazil, which Hungary won 4–2, was known as the Battle of Berne. Two of the goals came from penalties, and three players were sent off by English referee Arthur Ellis, two of them Brazilians. Even after the final whistle the violence continued on the touchline and in the dressing rooms. Amid the fracas Hungarian coach Gustav Sebes was punched and Brazilian captain Pinheiro was struck in the face by a bottle which, many observers insisted, had been wielded by the injured Ferenc Puskás, who had watched from the sidelines but was eager to join in. The brawl involved the majority of the players, police, photographers and even members of both camps' delegations. And again, during their tour of Europe in 1956–7, the Brazilian team and officials attempted to attack the referee after a match in Vienna.

In 1956, João Havelange was elected vice-president of the CBD, or the Brazilian Commission of Sports, the body responsible for overseeing twenty-three different sports in Brazil. He became president two years later, his appointment coinciding with a spectacular sporting event for Brazil – the 1958 World Cup.

Havelange made an immediate impact. In a visionary move, he appointed a new coach, Vicente Feola, team doctor Hilton Gosling and team psychologist Professor João Carvalhais, all from São Paulo, to the national side, all under the direction of Dr Paulo Machado da Carvalho. The England team did not even have a dedicated doctor until Alf Ramsey took charge in 1963. Havelange explained his thinking:

> I had the security of a comfortable environment to grow up in. For me to travel abroad to Berlin, Helsinki

or Melbourne was not a problem. Many of these young footballers came from humble homes, from the favelas, from backgrounds of great deprivation. They had to make tremendous adjustments, sometimes in a very short space of time. They had to channel their natural violence, to understand and accept discipline. Before I took control no thought had been given to these problems, and we could not continue towards the 1958 World Cup in Sweden in the same manner. I was determined that what had happened at Berne and in Vienna would never happen again. One of the first things that I did was to produce, with the help of these professionals – doctors, psychologists and the rest of the experts – a highly detailed, very secret report on every single potential member of the national squad. Those who, in our opinion, could not or would not make the necessary adjustments were dropped from the squad. The psychologist played a vital role in all of this. There is no point in sending out a team that is only physically prepared. They must also be mentally fit.

Meanwhile, in Santos, the young Pelé was proving himself on the field and finally settling down off the pitch, too. He had found himself surrogate parents in the form of a well-known ex basketball player, Raimundo, and his wife Dona Georgina, who ran a boarding house. Pete left the lonely Vila Belmiro and moved in with them, much to the delight of Dona Celeste. In fact Raimundo and Dona Georgina became Pelé's second family. He had been playing regularly for Santos for the best part of a year, alternating with Del Vecchio, the team's regular centre-forward, and even though he didn't make the side in every game he finished top scorer, not only for his club, but leading State of São Paulo's goalscorers' chart with thirty-two.

In June 1957, at the age of sixteen, he played at the Maracana for the first time. It was a tournament that ended abruptly and was never completed, but it brought him to the attention of the Brazilian national team.

Santos and Vasco da Gama of Rio were playing as a composite team and Pelé was selected at centre-forward. He got a hat-trick in a 6–1 win over Belenenses of Portugal and scored his side's goals in three 1–1 draws: against Dinamo Zagreb, Flamengo and São Paulo. Santos-Vasco da Gama were in first place, with Pelé the top scorer, when the tournament came to its premature end. Pelé recalls: 'I am sure this had much to do with Silvio Pirillo selecting me to play with the Brazilian team against Argentina in the Copa Roca that followed shortly afterwards.'

In the Copa Roca, a traditional fixture between the two countries, the Brazilians lost the first game 2–1 and won the second 2–0. Pelé scored in both. After the tournament, Pelé went home to Bauru to visit his family. When the Brazilian World Cup squad contenders were due to be announced, he anxiously switched on the radio. Though he was still only sixteen, and had been a professional for only a year, he still hoped. Deep down, however, he didn't think it possible, not yet. As the news came through he moved closer to the radio. Then the announcer read out his name. He had to sit down; he was trembling. His mother walked in and asked him, 'What's the matter with you, Dico?'

Brazil had been fortunate to qualify for the finals. In their last tie, against Peru, they had scraped through 1–0 thanks to a Didi banana kick. Debate raged in Brazil as to whether the precocious talent of Pelé should be exposed so early to the harsh realities of World Cup football in Sweden in 1958, or whether he should be held back until he matured for the finals in Chile in 1962. João Havelange was among those who argued that Pelé should go to Sweden to help his country in its bid to win, for the first time, the coveted Jules Rimet Trophy.

Pelé had won through to the initial selection, but he still had to make it to the final twenty-two. All the players trained hard and the competition was fierce. Finally, Dr Paulo Machado da Carvalho called them all together to make the nerve-wracking announcement of the names of those who had failed to make coach Vicente Feola's final squad.

Pelé's name was not on the list. His own joy was indescribable; by contrast, around him some gifted players were weeping openly. Feola and Dr Paulo, deeply upset themselves, left the room and those left out boarded the bus back to São Paulo.

The omission of Corinthians favourite Luisinho caused a particularly heated debate, especially in São Paulo. Ironically, the final practice match before the squad left for Europe was against Corinthians. It gave the rejected Luisinho a chance to make a point. In the Paecambu Stadium in São Paulo the Brazilian team were booed as they ran on to the field. In the event, Luisinho was kept in his place by Orlando and Brazil's display won over a sector of the partisan crowd. Brazil were leading 3–1, Pelé having scored the second, when their new star embarked on a dribble which was ended by a vicious challenge from Ari Clemente. Pelé's right knee was twisted. He tried to continue, wanting to take the free kick, but when he made contact with the ball the knee gave way. In the dressing room an anxious doctor and masseur applied the traditional ice pack. Mario Americo, the masseur, talked to him all the time he was treating him. 'Don't worry about it, kid,' he said reassuringly. 'Leave it to Daddy. I'll have you chasing girls again in no time.'

But it wasn't until Pelé was actually on the plane that he believed he would make it to Sweden. Dr Hilton Gosling and Mario were sure he would recover in time to make a contribution, and they were clearly prepared to take the risk.

For the first time Brazil planned their World Cup campaign with precision. Instead of accepting whatever base was on offer, they sent Dr Gosling and psychologist João Carvalhais on ahead of the main party to find a suitable training camp outside Gothenburg. En route the team stopped in Italy, where they won exhibition games against Internazionale and Fiorentina. The atmosphere in the camp was always a good one and everybody got on. As with all teams, the jokers supply the laughs, and in Brazil's case these came from Mario Trigo, the dentist. Pelé, however, was in no mood for fun, confined to the bench and becoming very worried about his injury. He was not encouraged by the memory of the knee injury that had cut short his father's career. Before the team left Italy for Sweden, Pelé went to see Dr Paulo. Acknowledging that his knee was not getting any better, he offered to return to Brazil rather than leave his country a man short for the finals. The verdict was that his knee had not healed as rapidly as they expected, but they could prescribe some 'tough' treatment, if he was prepared to go through it.

Pelé agreed. The treatment consisted of Mario Americo and his assistant Chico de Assis dipping towels in water as hot as they thought Pelé would be able to bear and wrapping them around the knee.

The coach could at least afford to take his time with Pelé because, alongside the established faces of Didi, Nilton Santos and Djalma Santos, the squad was strong in exciting new talent in the shape of the 'Little Bird' Garrincha, Vava, Zito and Zagalo. Brazil were drawn in Group 4, where they were to meet Austria,

England and the Soviet Union. Neither Pelé nor Garrincha was selected for the first match, against Austria. Although Brazil won 3–0, Feola thought they should have scored far more. For the next game, against England, he again left out both Pelé and Garrincha. England's 1958 World Cup squad had been deprived of some of its finest players by the Munich air tragedy, among them Duncan Edwards, Roger Byrne and Tommy Taylor, who would have been certainties. Yet Brazil missed several chances against this rebuilt England side in the first half and were lucky not to concede a second-half penalty when Derek Kevan, the England centre-forward, was brought down by Bellini. Although the crowd were treated to some exciting football from both sides, the match ended in a 0–0 draw.

Before Brazil's third match against the Soviet Union, the team psychologist counselled against giving Pelé a game. The basis of this advice was bizarre, to say the least. At their woodland retreat, Dr Carvalhais liked the players to express themselves through drawings. Pelé remembers him as 'a pleasant enough person who wandered about, studying us all day, usually dressed in a grey sweater and either forgetting to shave, or unshaven because he preferred it that way. He explained that he was not in favour of addressing the players as a group, as little was ever accomplished in this manner. On the other hand, to talk to the players as individuals often made them nervous, increased their problems, and made any diagnosis unreliable. Instead, his method was to have the players all draw pictures of a man.' The theory went that the most sophisticated players would draw the most complicated figures, while the least sophisticated would draw less detailed, even stick-man, childlike figures. Carvalhais felt that one of each of the two types would work well in the wing positions. On the evidence of these drawings, he concluded that

Garrincha's lack of sophistication would make it advisable not to play him, while Pelé was 'infantile' and lacked the essential fighting spirit required in a forward and the responsibility needed in a team player.

The players had a private meeting and sent a deputation to see the coach, calling for the selection of Garrincha against the Soviet Union. In the event Feola not only brought in Garrincha but also selected Zito, another newcomer who had not been picked to date, and Pelé. He took no notice whatsoever of the psychologist's interpretation of the sketches, telling the players that Pelé would come in when his knee was right rather than on the basis of his artistic ability.

In his autobiography, *My Life and the Beautiful Game*, Pelé discussed his country's chances against the key Soviet players: Simonian, the agile Armenian centre forward; the outstanding keeper Yashin; left-half and captain Igor Netto and the highly intelligent inside-left, Salnikov. He referred to the Soviet Union as 'the big red team', a nation for which there was enormous respect in their first-time World Cup competition. He was of the opinion that if they had participated in previous tournaments they might well have won three by then. Of his debut, he wrote:

> The Nya Ullevi Stadium is jammed to capacity, crowded with people who have come to see the Soviet Union demolish Brazil ... Many think Russia might well win the championship, although they concede that Wales is also strong, and one cannot discount West Germany, the champions in the previous World Cup games, nor Sweden who, although present without having to qualify, is known to be dangerous. Other than the Brazilians present, nobody really expects too much from the South

American team. True, they beat Austria 3–1 in their first game, but those who saw, and reported it, knew it was far from being as one-sided as the score seemed to indicate. And the best the Brazilians were able to do against a weak English team playing without men like Matthews, their great outside right by then retired, or Lofthouse, the squat powerful centre forward; bringing to the games, in fact, only twenty players although entitled to twenty-two, had been a scoreless tie, and the Brazilians had to play their hearts out to gain that.

Pelé was not impressed with Brazil's previous failures. He was not very complimentary about their defeat in the 1950 World Cup final – 'playing in their own country, on their own field, before their own fans and against an admittedly weaker team, they had ignominiously lost' – and their performance four years later was so bad that he couldn't bring himself to talk about it much. Given this background he concluded that in 1958 nobody was expecting any miracles from them.

The skinny black kid was dwarfed by his teammates as he took the field for the first time in the tournament. Since no mass produced team sheets were handed out in those days, he was certain that no one would recognise him as a part of the side until he lined up for the national anthems wearing the number 10 on his back. He jokes that most of the people in the stands would have assumed he was either the team mascot or the son of a friend of the coach: he couldn't have been the son of the coach himself because the coach was white. He envisioned the newspapermen and the radio and television broadcasters all consulting their lists to see who the devil was playing at centre-forward, saying that:

I am sure that some of those in the stands are faintly amused to see a child on the field in a World Cup match and some are probably outraged that as important event as a World Cup match should be reduced to parody by having an infant on the field. The more sentimental, however, probably feel pity for a team so reduced in talent as to face the need to bring children along with them. The entire Brazilian team is young as teams go; everyone knows that, but they undoubtedly feel that this is ridiculous.

Pelé's self-effacement is of course rooted in humour. In truth he was a confident kid, very much like the young Michael Owen in the 1998 World Cup. Neither showed any nerves on the pitch. He was ready, all right, and he knew it. He continues:

When the band strikes up the first chords of the Brazilian national anthem, all of us Brazilians feel a strange force with us. I cannot describe it; I doubt if any of us could describe it. If the people in the stands are amazed to see me down there on the field, I am far more amazed. All of us are living in a dream, but none more so than me. I try not to waste time trying to analyse this strange feeling. I know this is no time to be distracted.

Pelé looked at their opponents, all bigger than the Brazilians, particularly the keeper, Yashin, who, it seemed to him, would have only to spread out his arms to cover the entire goal. Getting the ball past this monster, he thought with a sinking heart, was going to be almost impossible. But once the game started he was relaxed, both physically and mentally. The Soviet Union were no longer monsters, just another set of opponents to be beaten.

In the first minute an inspired Garrincha had the crowd on their feet as he took on the defence and struck a shot on the run that had Pelé shouting 'Goal!' But it hit the bar. A minute later, Pelé caught the bar as well. He had read the pass from Didi, slipping between two defenders to receive the ball ahead of him and, without breaking stride, had hit the ball on the run. Once again the scream of 'Goal!' rose in his throat, but once again the ball found the crossbar and bounced back on to the field, where Yashin grabbed it in relief. Pelé glared at the goalposts. Didi, trotting past him, laughed. 'Relax, son, it'll go in. Give it time.'

Pelé's suspect knee was beginning to throb now, but two minutes later, he spotted Didi in possession again and, expecting a pass, made a burst forward. But Didi directed his pass in the opposite direction, where Vava had anticipated it, and the Russian defence had not. He brought it under control with one light touch, even though he was running at full speed. Vava's shot was unstoppable.

The Brazilians celebrated the goal as only Brazilians could. 'We are all over Vava, screaming, thumping him, pummelling, jumping in the air, waving our fists hysterically,' he wrote. 'Yashin is stretched out on the ground, looking at us sadly, as if we were bad children who had somehow disappointed a permissive parent.' This was the sort of fantasy football the whole nation of Brazil had been yearning for, and which captured the imagination of the entire world.

Pelé might have lived up to all the lavish expectations heaped on to his young shoulders for the best part of the year leading up to the World Cup finals, but he was not happy with his performance at half-time. 'I wanted to wrap the game up and go back to the hotel where I could hug the memory of it, as a child hugs a favourite toy. My dribbling was good; my evasions, my feints, my tackles brought shouts of approval from the crowd, now strongly behind us. But I had lost two sure goals through not being relaxed enough at the moment of kicking.'

The second half continued on much the same lines until late on, when Pelé saw Didi preparing to launch one of his pinpoint long passes. Pelé took it, and dribbled through, so mesmerising the defence with his skills that they failed to notice Vava coming in for a pass. It was perfect, and so too was Vava's finish. He wept at the poetry of the last-gasp goal.

Brazil had come through the qualifying stages unbeaten, and this 2–0 victory over the Soviet Union left them topping the table in Group 4. After a celebration meal with his teammates, Pelé retired to his room, unable to sleep at first as he relived the game in his mind's eye. 'I realised that I had been over-anxious. I flinched when I thought of the lost opportunities, but I also knew that I hadn't played badly and had nothing to be ashamed of.' He lay awake wondering what everyone at home in Bauru was thinking at that moment – his parents, his brother, his sister, Uncle Jorge and Dona Ambrosina, his grandmother, his friends. He imagined the elation in the streets, the people all talking about Pelé, the little *moleque* who not long before was being punished for kicking a football into the first streetlight on his street, breaking the bulb and plunging the neighbourhood into darkness.

I bring my thoughts back to the game. I promise myself that if I am scheduled to play in the next match, I will be calmer, more relaxed, like Garrincha, or Didi, or Vava, or Zagalo. I will be more professional. I promise. I still cannot sleep. My thoughts once more return to the incredible steps that have brought me to this point, where I am playing with the Brazilian team in the World Cup matches in such a short space of time. It had to be God who did it, but why? Why has He chosen me? What could have been His motive? I knew it was futile to consider His motives. Whatever the reason, though, it had to be a miracle.

Brazil were to meet Wales in their quarter-final. In the run-up to the next stage it was back to training, more boiling-towel treatment and endless interviews. The world's media was fascinated by the young Brazilian team, and especially by the youngest player in the tournament. Once again Feola rotated his squad. With two-goal Vava injured, back came Mazola, and Pelé was thrilled to be picked again. Brazil were strong favourites against the unfancied Welsh, who were without the injured John Charles. However, the South Americans had begun to believe the media hype, and an heroic Wales side mounted such a formidable defensive operation that for the first time Brazil suddenly felt the title slipping from their grasp. Wales held out for more than seventy minutes as Brazil missed chances and Kelsey saved those they did take. Then Pelé took a perfect pass from Didi.

He passed it to me on the run with that incredible accuracy of his when I was only a few feet from the goal area. I was about to kick when I saw a foot swooping down to the ball. I touched the ball lightly, bouncing it towards me as the foot passed beneath; I let the ball fall and then kicked it. To my disappointment I saw Kelsey dive to intercept, but just as he seemed sure to block it, the ball struck the foot of another defender and skidded past Kelsey into the net. I have no idea how many times I ran and jumped, ran and jumped, all the while screaming, 'GOOOOOOAAAAAAAALLLLL!' like a maniac. I had to get rid of that tremendous pressure of relief, of joy, I don't know what that was inside me. I was crying like a baby, babbling, while the rest of the team pummelled me, almost suffocating me. That was certainly my most unforgettable goal – my luckiest, but definitely my most unforgettable. It was the goal that was the most decisive for our team, for it ensured our continuing in the World Cup games. It was one of the most important goals I ever scored. Not one of the best, but it settled me. Calmed me.

It sure did. With that goal, Pelé had become a celebrity. Interviewed as often as the older, more established stars, he was a touch intimidated by the attention, but at the same time he loved it, knowing how his family would be relishing it back home. He was astounded by the number of Swedish girls who came to talk to him, ask for his autograph and at times to rub their hands on his arms and face. 'Some seemed surprised, as if they found it odd that my colour didn't run.'

One girl in particular, called Lena, would go to the team's hotel and go out walking with Pelé. 'We were both seventeen, a very romantic age. We would go out hand in hand, thrilled with each other's different colour, happy to be together. I remember she cried when I left, and I remember what a big man it made me feel to have a girl, a beautiful girl, crying because I wouldn't be there.'

He has fond memories, too, of his first encounter with British players in the shape of the gallant Welsh. 'It will be hard ever to forget the excellent play of men like Hopkins and Owen, of Stuart Williams and Sullivan, or the truly inspired goalkeeping of Jack Kelsey, and those magic hands of his.'

France, the tournament's highest scorers with fifteen goals

in four games, stood between Brazil, who had yet to concede a goal, and the final. Fontaine, Kopa, Piantoni, Vincent ... it was a formidable array of attacking strength to test the Brazilian defensive barrier. But Feola was sure of victory, and told his players so.

Just a minute into their semi-final at the Rasunda Stadium in Solna, Didi, Garrincha and Pelé combined with devastating effect to lay on the opening goal for Vava. Seven minutes later Raymond Kopa and Just Fontaine matched Brazil's inventiveness as Fontaine conjured an equaliser – the first goal conceded by Gilmar in the competition to date. Pelé followed the ball into the Brazilian net, picked it out and ran to the centre circle, shouting, 'Let's stop wasting time, let's get started.' He recalls: 'The rest of the team stared at me. The action was certainly out of place for the newest and youngest member of the team, but it was completely automatic on my part.'

In any event it did not have the desired effect as Brazil, Pelé included, hit a poor patch and a Garrincha goal was ruled offside. Pelé was upset, but his captain, Bellini, calmed him down before he voiced his protests to the referee.

Then, at last, Brazil got their break. The game turned on a thirty-fifth-minute clash between Robert Jonquet and Vava. The French defender was carried off with a serious injury to his right knee, returning gamely as a virtual passenger, limping along the wing. Effectively down to ten men, the French were no match for such a brilliant Brazilian team. Indeed, Didi had put them ahead before Jonquet made it back to the pitch.

Pelé took over the show in the second half, scoring a wonderful hat-trick, of which his third goal came from a spectacular volley from the edge of the area, and what had begun as a close game ended in a 5–2 win for Brazil. They had made it to the final.

The Brazilians were determined not to make the same mistake as they had with Wales and underestimate the host nation, Sweden, in the battle for the ultimate prize. And though they considered themselves the favourites, the Swedish media were tipping the home side. As the tournament had progressed the Swedish football authorities had become increasingly concerned by the apathy of the home fans. Even when Sweden had been making stunning progress there had been a definite lack of atmosphere, of substantial backing for their country from a reserved footballing following. So for Sweden's semi-final with West Germany, cheerleaders had been summoned to whip up some fervour and enthusiasm. It worked. Amid a profusion of flags and chants, Sweden had beaten West Germany 3–1. The big question-mark against Brazil now was how they would keep their Latin temperament in check in front of this newly animated partisan crowd.

As the final approached, João Havelange, who never missed a trick, was back in Rio on urgent business for the CBD. Over the phone from CBD headquarters, he sought assurances from the World Cup Committee as to the impartiality of the referee, fearing the possible influence on him of a suddenly vociferous home audience. Amazingly, Havelange won the point and an important psychological advantage. It was announced that the Committee had banned any manifestation of biased home support. The cheerleaders were consigned to the sin bin, and the law-abiding Swedes returned to their previously subdued demeanour. Not so the Brazilians who had made the trip, of course. They would make as much noise as ever.

Within the Swedish camp, however, expectancy remained high. 'If the Brazilians go a goal down, they'll panic all over the place,' remarked manager and coach George Raynor.

Lining up for the World Cup final was, of course, a moment of supreme pride for the young Pelé.

When the Brazilian national anthem was played, I felt even more moved than when I heard it standing in my place ready to start the game with the Soviet Union. I trembled as I stood and listened. I suddenly thought of Dondinho, back in Bauru at this exact moment, sitting before the radio, straining not to miss a sound or a word. And my mother. I knew she would be out of the room, determined not to listen to the game, although I was equally certain that as soon as the game was over she would be deluging Dondinho with questions as to how I was physically and how I had done.

In only four minutes, Sweden were a goal up after Liedholm beat Brazil's keeper, Gilmar, with a low shot into the right-hand corner, and for the first time in the tournament the Brazilians were trailing. Yet the Swedish coach's prediction that this would have a devastating impact on the South Americans didn't materialise. In fact, if anything, it had the reverse effect. Pelé himself says he felt a strange calmness, as if he could take on the opposition at will. Sure enough, just five minutes later came the equaliser as Garrincha beat two to cross for Vava to score. Brazil were the masters now, but their second goal was a long time coming. Eventually, Garrincha again flew down the wing to cross for Vava, who put them into the lead.

It was in the second half that Pelé made his indelible mark on World Cup history. With his back to goal, ten minutes after half-time, he controlled a high cross with his thigh, hooked it over his own head and the Swedish defender, twisted and manoeuvred around the centre-half, completing the whirlwind move by volleying past keeper Svensson.

With thirteen minutes left Zagalo burst away from the defence and swept past four opponents to score a brilliant fourth. He knelt down on the pitch, crossed himself and shed tears of joy. The carnival atmosphere among the samba-dancing Brazilian section reached a new crescendo. Clearly they had not been told of the World Cup Committee's decree.

Simonsson pulled one back, despite looking suspiciously offside, but the final word rested with Pelé. Leaping to meet Zagalo's cross, he directed a perfect looping header over Svensson's hands to take the score in the 1958 World Cup final to 5–2.

As the final whistle blew, and the realisation that Brazil were the world champions began to sink in, Pelé had 'a strange feeling that I was going to faint. I felt my knees collapsing under me and reached out to prevent myself hitting the ground. And then I was being lifted, raised to the shoulders of my teammates, and being carried around the field. Everyone was crying. Tears streamed from my eyes as I hung on wildly. Gilmar reached up and squeezed my leg. "Go ahead and cry, *moleque*, it's good for you."'

The Brazilian players were ecstatic. Reporters, photographers, fans, all rushed on to the pitch as the victorious team waved their national flag over their heads on their lap of honour. Mario Americo had rushed into the goal to retrieve the ball and refused to give it up to the referee. A Swedish flag appeared. Bellini caught the players' attention, and they scooped up their hosts' standard and raised it above their heads as they marched round the field to the cheers of the crowd. The Brazilian national anthem struck up again, and the Brazilian flag was hoisted high above all the others in the stadium. The tears flowed anew. King Gustav of Sweden came down to shake the players' hands. In the dressing room it was bedlam, and the team had to fight their way to the bus.

They couldn't wait to get home, but in those pre-jet days it was a long haul from Sweden to Brazil aboard the Panair do Brasil plane. At last, during a stop to refuel on Brazilian soil at Recife, the players climbed down the aluminium steps to be mobbed by a massive crowd. Then it was on to Rio and to an even more rapturous reception: carnival in the streets, traffic diverted, avenues jammed with people, and sheer noise: honking horns, shouting, screaming, laughter, fireworks. Then came reunion with their families in the offices of the magazine *O Cruzeiro*. For Pelé there were hugs from his father and mother, and plenty more tears.

The team moved from reception to cocktail party to presentations before Pelé was finally able to return to Bauru. Two years earlier he had left the town with a second-class train ticket; now he returned on a plane with the press swarming around him and the whole town waiting to greet their local hero. He describes:

> I could see the crowds jammed against the railings and the police standing in front of the terminal building ready to hold the people back from storming the plane. I began to feel the excitement building up in me as I hadn't felt it in Recife, Rio, São Paulo or even Santos. This was my home. Every place we passed reminded me of some scrape or two I had been in, the Ernestoi Monte Primary School, the railway station where I had shined shoes and stolen peanuts and sold meat pies.

The importance to the country of its status as champions of the world was immeasurable. When the Korean War broke out, it took a back seat to a front-page report on the World Cup. And it was in Bauru, Pelé's home town – where he had shined shoes, stolen peanuts and sold meat pies – that it counted the most. Banners everywhere proclaimed: 'Welcome Pelé, son of Bauru, champion of the world'.

CHAPTER 3

THE PAIN AS WELL AS WORLD CUP GLORY

*'When I was a boy I grew up watching Pelé play and it was
my dream to one day play alongside him or against him.'*
Roberto Rivelino

João Havelange took enormous credit upon himself when he
maintained: 'Pelé owes me a great deal, and his debt to me began
in the 1950s when I gave him the chance of going to Sweden.' But
there can be no question that Pelé was a national hero. To show
their appreciation, the townspeople of Bauru clubbed together
and presented him with a car. A car! That was really something in
those days, for they cost more than the average man could expect
to earn in a lifetime. It was a Romisetta, a modest three-wheeler
that opened at the front to accommodate two people, but it was a
car all the same, and he was proud of it. Pelé eventually managed
to force his father to accept it, in spite of Dondinho's vehement
protestations. Dondinho probably wished he hadn't after taking
his wife for a spin and ending up in a ditch.

And it was not only at home in Brazil that Pelé was a celebrity.

His exploits in Sweden had a profound effect on players in England, even at that time. The England side had left the 1958 World Cup finals early, despite not having lost a game, even to the ultimate world champions. Bobby Charlton watched the final back in England on television – black-and-white, in those days, of course. The image of Pelé's first goal of the match, the spectacular volley, was very vivid in the minds of Charlton and his England teammates as they prepared to meet the world champions again shortly after the World Cup. Sir Bobby has followed Pelé's football career closely, and has some fascinating observations to make, many quite unexpected.

I didn't play against him very much, perhaps just twice in fact. The first time was in the Maracana shortly after Brazil failed to beat England in the 1958 World Cup finals. It's a trait of the Brazilians that they want to put things right, and quickly. So because they hadn't beaten England in Sweden, when they first won the World Cup they wanted to do something about it. So a game was arranged in Rio. I was standing in the centre circle in the Maracana and I looked round behind me. There is the entire England team, back in defence. They're all there, in position. I said to myself, 'OK, Pelé, if you're such a good player, let's see what you can do.' A few seconds later, he scored. And before he allowed the ball to leave his feet he had already shouted, 'GOOOLLL!' They beat us by five, and Pelé was just unbelievable the way he scored that goal, going right through our entire team.

Sir Bobby – well, just plain Bobby in those days – did not meet Pelé on the field again until the 1970 World Cup finals in Mexico.

THE PAIN AS WELL AS WORLD CUP GLORY

While Sir Bobby respects and admires Pelé, he is one of the rare breed, highly respected himself in world soccer circles, able to be objective about the Brazilian. 'He's not perfect,' Sir Bobby ventures, as if no one else would dare, continuing to say:

> You know, he should have been sent off once. There was a tournament in São Paulo in 1964 involving Argentina, Brazil, Portugal and ourselves. In Brazil's match against Argentina, Pelé nutted an opponent. It was fully intentional, but he was not sent off. Argentina beat them by 2–0 or 3–0 that day – it was at a time when Argentina seemed to have a hold over Brazil. We watched from the sidelines and we were all shocked by Pelé's actions. We all looked at each other as if to say, "What's he done?" No one could believe it.

Jimmy Greaves is another who felt Pelé could be more aggressive than his reputation might suggest. He believes a lot of myth surrounds Pelé. All we see are the great moments – we never saw him warts and all. In those days, without the benefit of modern technology, we were never able to properly judge the player for ourselves. Greaves, too, remembers the incident with the Argentinian in 1964. 'All hell broke loose on the pitch and in the stands, and it is the first time I can remember four teams being on the field at once. We were watching from the sidelines and we had to run to the centre circle to be safe. I'm not going mad and suggesting Pelé was not a great player, for he undoubtedly was a true great. But were we all truly able to judge completely for ourselves the extent of his greatness, as we were, say, with Maradona?' The colour of Brazil, the stories, the lads playing on Copacabana Beach, all contribute to give us a much more powerful image of Pelé than the one we have of Maradona, he argues.

I don't believe the Brazilian league football Pelé played in can be compared to the testing nature of European football, either. Pelé ran riot, but Maradona excelled in the world's toughest leagues in both Spain and, most notably, Italy. Diego is the best I ever saw, without doubt the greatest footballer of all time. I believe Brazil would have won the World Cups of 1958 and 1970 without Pelé. Indeed, they did win in 1962, with his involvement curtailed due to injury. But Argentina would not have won in 1986 without Maradona, nor would they have got to the final four years later in Italy. Maradona was kicked out of games more often than Pelé. He battled on after some of the most vicious treatment dished out to a footballer by opponents, treatment that often went unpunished by refs who were weak or biased against the great man. I know what it is like to enjoy great moments in football and then hit rock bottom. That is why, as Maradona struggles to recover from a drugs overdose, I feel nothing but sympathy for the man.

Jimmy Armfield, now an FA consultant, missed out on the World Cup of 1958 as he didn't make his debut for his country until the following year, though he went on to play in the 1962 finals. He says:

To think Pelé was just seventeen and he reduced Sweden to a team of nothings when they were actually a very good team at that time. I made my debut against Brazil in Rio, and although Pelé didn't score in that match, his team scored before I had even touched the ball! It must have taken them only about ninety seconds. But I did manage to swap shirts with Pelé after the game. I've still got his shirt somewhere, but I've no idea whether he kept mine.

In 1962, I thought Brazil had an even better team, arguably their strongest, when you think that Pelé was injured early in the tournament and they had such a fantastic replacement in Amarildo. To think they could have a forward line that would include either Pelé or Amarildo meant they had so much going for it.

As for England, we didn't lose and ended up going out, but I have always felt if the Munich air crash hadn't deprived the England team of so many good players we would have been World Cup champions in 1958 and maybe even 1962.

Armfield concurs with Sir Bobby Charlton and Jimmy Greaves on the matter of Pelé's aggression:

He was an aggressive player, and no one really makes much of that aspect of his game. But he could look after himself. Some of the lads I played with in the England team told me how Pelé went for one of the England players during a Little World Cup tie. But he is the best player I've ever seen coming late in the box. In fact I wouldn't be able to name a better one. He could play up front or just behind the strikers and perhaps that was his best position as he could time his runs so perfectly. When he was young he had all this ball brilliance, but later in his career he played with enormous intelligence. He matured into a really terrific player. He had the lot. He played off the right foot, he could play off the left foot, he was great in the air. He was out of this world in chest control; he would jump up and hold the ball on his chest no matter how fast it came at him. He also had a marvellous physique, powerful legs. All great players have got body strength.

Terry Butcher, England's tenacious defender of the 1980s, agrees with Jimmy about Pelé's best position being playing off the front strikers, a role he would be suited to in the modern game. However, he takes a different view from Jimmy Greaves in the Pelé versus Maradona debate. 'I played against Maradona, of course, in the 1986 World Cup finals, and from personal experience I can vouch for how good the Argentinian could be. I have always rated Maradona very highly – at least, in his pre-cocaine days – but when you think about what Pelé achieved and what he stands for, he cannot be surpassed.'

Notwithstanding Pelé's subsequent success, still his greatest achievement remains having been a World Cup-winner and goalscorer at the age of seventeen. Yet had he been born English it is unlikely ever to have happened. Although in recent times England have had Michael Owen playing in the World Cup in France, and Joe Cole has emerged as another promising young international, in general England has not been renowned for bringing on young players. Even in Brazil in the late fifties, it was staggering for someone of his age to make such an impact so soon. As a result of his fame, Pelé was on his way to becoming the richest sportsman in the world.

At the end of his teens, Italy offered $1 million, an enormous amount of money – the equivalent of £30 million today – to lure him to Europe. The Brazilian Congress went into emergency session, the Italians were politely told to 'forget it' and Pelé was declared a 'non-exportable national treasure'.

By the age of nineteen, Pelé's earnings were remarkable, too. Santos raised his salary from 6,000 cruzeiros to 13,000 as soon as he returned from Stockholm. In the August of that year, when his contract ended, a new deal elevated him to the realm of the big-time earners. His monthly salary was increased to 15,000 cruzeiros plus win bonuses – and with Santos becoming a world-class club and playing so often, he was collecting those more and more frequently.

After 1959 his contract was adjusted to 80,000 cruzeiros per month with a 60,000-cruzeiro cost-of-living allowance, while his bonuses came to almost 1 million cruzeiros a year. The new contract included a $27,000 signing-on fee, a $10,000 house for his mother and a new Volkswagen for his father.

The modest house on 7 September Street in Bauru was now paid for, and the constant worry of finding the rent was long over for his family. Instead, his father now had the money to make the improvements Dona Celeste had nagged him to make for years, and for them to make regular visits to see their son. On receiving one bonus, Pelé felt so rich that he decided to splash out on some modern technology for his mother. Remembering all those hard winter days loading the firewood to keep everyone warm, he bought a gas stove and had it shipped immediately to Bauru. His mother thanked him in a letter and would profusely reiterate her thanks whenever she came to visit. But on her instructions a deep, dark secret had to be kept from Pelé at all costs: Bauru at that time had neither piped nor bottled gas, and the brand-new stove, admired as it was, was merely a conversation piece in the house.

There was precious little time to sit back and glow in the

aftermath of the success in Sweden. Instead it was straight back to work with Santos a mere seventeen days after winning the World Cup. Pelé's first match since Stockholm was against Jabaquara on 16 July, and within days of that game it was back to the old routine of fixtures virtually every three or four days. Del Vecchio had accepted a European offer and the club released him, so Pelé was now the recognised, full-time, first-choice centre-forward.

Some time after the 1958 World Cup, Pelé met a young girl, Rosemeri, who several years later became his wife, explaining:

> We were sitting around in our camp the night before a big game, bored with each other's company, when somebody suggested we go downstairs to the gym and watch a girls' basketball game that was to be played that night. One girl, who was sitting on the bench as a reserve, caught my eye. After we had stared at each other for a while, I waved to her and motioned for her to come up and join me. Our conversation was brief – she merely instructed me not to beat Corinthians (our opponents the next day), and returned to the bench.

A few days later, Pelé discovered that, despite Rose's support for Corinthians of São Paulo, she actually lived in Santos, and tracked her down to a local record shop. They agreed to meet at Rose's house the following Saturday.

> So that was how I met and wooed Rose. At least that was how we met; the wooing went on for many years and was an extremely slow process. Rosemeri's parents were very nice, considering I was probably the first boy she had invited to her home, and almost certainly the first black

boy. It was only the first of many visits to her home, nor were our meetings limited to those, although whenever we met away from her home it was always in an offhand manner and with the connivance of her aunt, who always came with her. After all, Rose was just fourteen (though I was also still only seventeen myself) and we were both very sure her parents would not be pleased if the newspapers began to speculate on the relationship between a young black football star and an under-age white girl.

In a very short time I became aware that the fame of the name Pelé meant very little to Rosemeri. I think in that regard she is quite a bit like my mother; they both think it very odd that people will pay money to see grown men in short pants kick a ball around a field.

In the year after the World Cup he played forty-four games for Santos, of which they won thirty-one, drew eight and lost five. He was top scorer with fifty-eight goals in thirty-eight games in the state championship. It was to be the best scoring season of his career – a total of 126 goals in all matches.

Pelé was the heart and soul, the inspiration, the undisputed brightest star of the star-studded Santos team as it travelled the world through the 1960s and his reputation as the best footballer on the planet grew. With world champions in Zito, Pepe and Pelé, the team was considered the best in Brazil, and offered a brand of exciting, entertaining football that filled stadia around the world.

There was a gruelling tour of South and Central America, with games in Peru, Ecuador, Costa Rica, Guatemala, Mexico, Curaçao and Venezuela: sea-level one day, 8,000ft the next, a non-stop regime where the players would play, eat, sleep, catch a train, week-in, week-out. In six weeks they played fourteen games in seven countries, winning thirteen and losing only to a Czechoslovakian team in Mexico. On his return, Pelé was selected to play for the São Paulo state team in a game against a side representing Rio de Janeiro and then against the World Cup teams of Peru, Chile, Bolivia, Paraguay and Argentina.

With Santos's reputation now assured, the club attracted a tour of Europe, on which it was scheduled to play almost daily. There was no time to soak up the atmosphere. Sightseeing consisted of a few glimpses of the world outside from a train or coach window. Sometimes sleep was snatched on a train, from which the players would emerge half-asleep with bags in one hand, occasionally trousers in the other. Pelé observed: 'It was a brutal schedule, designed to make Santos rich and with small regard for the players.' He and his teammates were astonished when, on the last leg of this exhausting tour, they discovered that an extra game had been added to the schedule for the first day they arrived in Spain.

And not just any game. Real Madrid. The only club side to dispute Santos's claim to be the best club in the world. Not only were the players in desperate need of rest, but they had stomach upsets from the change of water, and some of them slept badly, unable to get accustomed to European-style bedding. But that mattered little to the directors, who saw another financial killing. Those with injuries played because they knew their absence would have meant loss of earnings. There were no such problems for Real Madrid, on the other hand. As soon as they knew of the fixture, they dropped some of their games to concentrate on training and getting into shape.

So it is perhaps not altogether surprising that Real won 5–3. It was a defeat that rankled with Pelé, and one he has never forgotten.

He says that some time later in a tournament in Argentina, Real Madrid withdrew rather than face a return match with a fresher and better-prepared Santos.

After two months away, Pelé was glad to be back home, weary, but with plenty of cash in the bank. Before the end of 1958, he reached his eighteenth birthday, a milestone which had come to the attention of the Brazilian Army before he embarked on his first European tour. So on his return he spent a year doing his national service in the itchy uniform of the armed forces. He was called up to the 6th Group, Motorised Coast Artillery, stationed at Santos under the command of Colonel Osman, who happened to be a director of the football club. Of course Pelé's first thought was that all the mind-numbing chores of drilling, peeling potatoes or making beds would be set aside to free him up to play in the barracks football team.

He was partly right. Naturally, the Colonel did indeed expect him to play in the barracks team. And the Brazilian Army international games, and for Santos, and for Brazil. But at the same time he gave Pelé's commanding officer, Captain Aurino, the go-ahead to treat him just like all the other new recruits. So much for special privileges.

The coach of the barracks team was Lieutenant Falcao. Discipline in army football was a touch easier than in the real world: any fooling around meant extra guard duty. Even so, picked for the Military XI against an Argentinian team, Pelé was sent off for fighting. He explained:

People have often mentioned how pleasant I am on the field, how I smile at the opponent who bumps into me, accidentally or on purpose, how I help him to his feet. They ask me, "Don't you ever lose your temper?" People who ask this question haven't followed my career very closely. I lose my temper very often, but I try my best not to show it, especially not to an opponent during a game. It gives him an advantage to know you're angry, and he may well make you pay for showing your temper.

Pelé preferred to react in a positive way, making his opponent feel foolish by outwitting him with his skills, often provoking him to retaliate instead.

But on this occasion Pelé had had enough. He caught his tormentor on the shin, and when the Argentinian swung his fists, Pelé responded in kind. Both of them were sent off. As he trudged towards the dressing room, Lieutenant Falcao warned him that if his team lost, it would mean a week in detention. Fortunately for Pelé, the Brazilians won 2–l.

The next day Pelé was in Porto Alegre, where Santos were defending the Brazil Cup against Gremio. He was to perform in more than a hundred games that year.

After his year in the army, it was back on the tour circuit, first with Brazil to South America and a slightly less hectic schedule in Europe. In Egypt he was able to visit the pyramids and shop in the bazaars, even to take a camel ride. From Egypt the Brazilians moved on to Malmo, their first time in Sweden since the World Cup, and then to Copenhagen before Pelé linked up with Santos and a much more heavy-duty schedule.

In Paris he was introduced to Kiki, a fashion model who showed him the town. Posing for photographers with her seemed a good idea at the time, but when the pictures hit the front pages and were wired back to Brazil with a caption stating that marriage was imminent, it didn't go down too well with Rose, his girlfriend at home. It was a salutary lesson in the pitfalls of being public property, and he was far more careful about who he was pictured with on subsequent trips.

A total of seventy-two goals in eighty-two games in 1960 was followed by one of the greatest of all time, scored on 5 March 1961, back in Brazil at the Maracana, where Santos beat Fluminense of Rio. This was the goal known as the Goal of the Plaque, scored after Pelé beat the entire team, having collected the ball in his own penalty area. To commemorate 'the most beautiful goal ever scored in the Maracana', the sports newspaper *O Esporte* of São Paulo had a plaque cast and mounted at the entrance of the stadium. 'It was a great honour,' says Pelé, 'and one of which I am very proud.'

The Brazilian team for the 1962 World Cup finals in Chile retained much of the nucleus of the successful squad in Sweden, including Gilmar, Nilton Santos, Djalmar Santos, Zito, Didi, Garrincha, Vava, Zagalo and Pelé. Coach Vicente Feola, however, was in poor health and replaced by Aimore Moreira, the brother of Zeze Moreira, who had managed the 1954 side. Bellini was still involved in the squad, but his position had been taken by Mauro. Orlando, now playing in Argentina, was replaced by Zozimo, while Mazola, whose name was actually Altafini, and who held dual Italian-Brazilian nationality, played for Italy. Pepe, who had missed out through injury in 1958, finally made it. Castilho, a survivor of 1954, was in the squad, although he had no real chance of playing a part. There were also some fresh young faces: Pelé's Santos teammate, the outstanding Coutinho, was selected, along with Amarildo, Jair da Costa, Mengalvio, Zequinho, Jair Marinho and Jurandir. Pelé, now twenty-one, considered himself one of the old boys. Dr Paulo Machado de Carvalho remained the head of the delegation, assisted by Carlos Nascimento. The backroom staff were trainer Paulo Amaral;

Mario Americo, head masseur; dentist Dr Mario Trigo and Dr Hilton Gosling.

Brazil, who qualified as the holders, joined Czechoslovakia, Spain and Mexico in Group 3, playing their group games in Vina del Mar. Amaral's ethos was that everyone would train on equal terms: if you could walk, you train; if you couldn't, then talk to the doctor. It was a philosophy contrary to modern thinking, which is to devise schedules tailored to the individual.

As they had no qualifying games to warm them up, the team played four training matches in the build-up to the finals, two against Portugal and two against Wales, all of which they won. After the first game against Portugal, Pelé left the field with a slight pain in his lower abdomen. Having no argument with the trainer's philosophy, he did not complain and carried on the next day with training. It was a grave mistake. He compounded it by playing in all the practice games, scoring four goals, two of which clinched the result. The pain was still there, but he kept quiet.

In May 1962 the Brazilians travelled to Chile. Their match was against Mexico, whom they beat 2–0 with goals from Zagalo and Pelé. Pelé was exhausted from the extensive training and his groin was getting worse. At last he faced the fact that he had no choice but to consult Dr Gosling. The doctor's advice was simple: if it continued to hurt he would have to be excused from training, and that, under the current regime, meant from the games as well.

So Pelé lined up for the second game, against the Czechs at Vina del Mar. In good spirits, raised by the samba band in the crowd and the local fans behind Brazil, he forgot the pain and began playing with complete confidence. Collecting a pass from Garrincha, he dribbled past several defenders as his run took him into the area. He beat the remaining defender and cracked a shot against the post. It rebounded to him and he struck the ball again, with even more power. This time he felt a searing pain in his groin. He collapsed on the ground. Mario Americo raced to his aid. There were no substitutes, so he had to continue, a crippled player being better than no player at all.

Pelé was very grateful for the sportsmanship shown by Masopust, Popluhár and Lala, who did not inflict any tough tackles on a player clearly in distress. Indeed, he described the exemplary attitude as 'one of the finest things that happened in my entire football career'. For while Pelé no longer posed any threat that day, he might have done later in the tournament: it was on the cards that the two sides might meet again in the final, as they eventually did.

The game ended goalless. Back in the team hotel, Pelé could hardly walk. Nonetheless he was convinced the injury would heal, despite Dr Gosling's pessimism. He underwent intensive treatment, and then, the day before the Spain game, he asked to see the doctor. He told him he was willing to take a painkilling injection to play. The doctor replied that it might cripple him for life, and that he was not prepared to do it.

So Pelé watched Brazil beat Spain 2–1 on television. His replacement, Amarildo, a twenty-four-year-old from Botafogo, was outstanding, coping excellently with Puskas at centre-forward and Paco Gento at outside-left. He scored both goals after Spain had taken the lead ten minutes before half-time. Although Pelé was delighted for his country, he couldn't help but wonder, as he lay there in bed, whether Amarildo would be the new Pelé and would take his place in the team. Having already missed the start of the previous World Cup in 1958, he worried that he might be injury prone when it came to the important games.

Brazil, topping the Group 3 table, went into the quarter-finals to meet England – still without Pelé. England newcomer Bobby

Moore was convinced his side were ready for Brazil, even though he had never yet seen them play, and the fact that Pelé was missing gave him cause for greater optimism. It was misplaced. Garrincha scored in the first half, the tiny forward outjumping the massive Tottenham centre-half Maurice Norman from a corner. Gerry Hitchens clawed a goal back, but when one of Garrincha's famous free kicks struck Ron Springett in the chest, Vava reacted instantly to the rebound to put Brazil back in front. As England pushed for another equaliser, Garrincha scored again. England went home without waiting to watch Brazil play the hosts, Chile, in the semi final and Czechoslovakia in the final. As for Pelé, he was still in pain, but praying he would recover in time.

Then one morning he woke and suddenly realised the pain had gone. He continued with the hot-towel treatment and even trained, though he still missed the semi-final because he was not in top condition, watching from the stands as Vava and Garrincha scored two each in a 4–2 win over Chile. It was a tough game, and Pelé, still nursing the recovering muscle, conceded that it was better he was not involved. The clash of Latin temperaments came to a head when Garrincha was sent off six minutes from time for kicking Rojos. As a result there was some doubt as to whether Garrincha would be allowed to play in the final. The prospect of defending the World Cup without Garrincha or Pelé caused some anxiety in the Brazilian camp, but Pelé was positive he would make it.

Three days later he went to practise corner kicks, Paulo Amaral beside him. At the first kick he felt a sickeningly familiar wave of pain in the groin. The muscle had gone again. Pelé broke down in tears. He knew he was going to miss the final. He just couldn't come to terms with the fact that he could play almost a hundred games a year – for his club, the army, the national side, on tour for both club and country – yet miss out on the last four vital World Cup games.

So Pelé again watched from the stands as Brazil beat Czechoslovakia 3–1, with goals from Vava, Zito and Amarildo. It was a very difficult time for him. He was haunted by the kind of self-doubts one would not have believed. With Pelé in their line-up in the group match against Czechoslovakia, Brazil had managed only a goalless draw; without him they had beaten the same side by a two-goal margin, and in the final.

It was two months before Pelé was able to play again. Back on the field, all the subconscious doubts evaporated as he concentrated on the future, determined to blot out the agonising disappointments of the recent past. That year Santos took the World Inter-Club title, winning twenty-seven of their thirty-four games, drawing six and losing just one. In the final, against Benfica, Pelé collected a hat-trick to add to two from Coutinho in a 5–2 win over the great Portuguese side. He played in every one of the World Inter-Club games and finished the highest scorer with fifty-two goals. But only two games in Chile.

CHAPTER 4

THE GREATEST AT TWENTY-ONE ... BUT NOT IN BUSINESS

*'Some people wanted to touch him, some people wanted
to kiss him. In some countries they kissed the ground he
walked on. I thought it was beautiful, beautiful.'*
Clodoaldo

By 1963, Pelé had been hailed as the greatest footballer in the world. Santos's outstanding coach, Lula, described Pelé at the age of twenty-one thus: 'Pelé can no longer be compared to anyone else.' Later he expanded: 'He is fast on the ground and in the air, he is strong, has a good shot, good ball control, an ability to dictate play, a feeling for the move, he is unselfish, good-natured and modest. He is also the only forward in the world who always aims the ball at a precise point in the opposition's net at the moment of shooting for goal.'

By the mid-sixties Santos had superseded Real Madrid as the most formidable club side in the world. The all-whites of the Vila Belmiro included three double World Cup winners in Gilmar, Zito and Pelé, two 1966 squad members, Orlano and Edu, and two new

Brazilian national stars, Joel and Carlos Alberto. With two World Club championships, in 1961 and 1962, under their belts, the glamour club everyone wanted to see embarked on a fresh round of lucrative whirlwind non-stop tours.

Garth Crooks, who went on to play for his home-town club, Stoke City, before making his name with Spurs and latterly as a television interviewer for the BBC, was just eleven years old when Pelé came to the Victoria Ground at Stoke to play for a Rest of the World side in Stanley Matthews's testimonial. Garth couldn't afford the admission price, but football had taken such a grip on his life that he just had to see Pelé. So he waited until the gates were open to let the first paying customers out and he was able to get into the ground. He managed to catch the last twenty minutes of the game. 'I also saw him play for Santos at the Victoria Ground in the late sixties. Gordon Banks was playing for Stoke then, but Pelé scored a fantastic goal, beating Banks from twenty yards.'

The Midlands, too, were treated to the chance to see Pelé in action. In 1969, Doug Ellis, then the ambitious young man newly in charge at Aston Villa, succeeded in luring the greatest club side in the world to Villa Park. He arranged a fee of £10,000, an awful lot of money in those days, for Santos to play. But at the last minute there was some doubt as to whether Pelé would turn out. Ellis was told that Villa had failed to account for the additional £5,000 fee for Pelé, and that he would not be turning out unless they did. 'Well, there was no way we couldn't pay the fee for Pelé,' says Ellis. 'We had sold 53,000 tickets and they had all come to see one man.'

That issue was sorted out amicably, but the bright new boy in the Villa chair had to go to extraordinary lengths to circumvent the effects of an electricians' strike. If the floodlights didn't work the whole event was in jeopardy. He sent out a total of twenty-three telegrams all over the Continent to try to find a generator of the right size to work the floodlights. You couldn't buy a generator in England for love nor money, because they had all been snapped up owing to the strike. He managed to find two, at £5,000 apiece, and weighing around two or three tons each, in Düsseldorf. The scheme was to ship them to Rotterdam, where they would be transferred to a ship bound for Lowestoft. The unions found out about this and planned to block the arrival of the generators. When that news reached Ellis the course had to be secretly changed and the ship switched to Hull, with its cargo camouflaged. From Hull, the generators were transported by a low-loader to Birmingham, checked over and whisked to Villa Park, where a security guard was mounted, with dogs patrolling outside.

The game went ahead, and Villa were delighted to have pulled it off. But after all that, the generators turned out not to be big enough, and there was a flashback during the first half. Advised that they couldn't risk using all four floodlights for the second half, they shut one of them down. Deciding that if one team should be put at a disadvantage it should be Santos, they switched off one of the two lights illuminating the Brazilians' goalmouth.

But they had reckoned without the astute Pelé. 'Smart lad that he is, he called a meeting of his team by the dugout and got the agreement of the players that they would refuse to continue unless they switched ends and Villa had the gloomy goalmouth,' remembers Ellis. 'Of course, we all had to agree. There was hardly much of a choice. We had a capacity crowd, paying two shillings in those days, and we were still making an enormous profit, despite all the match guarantees we had to pay and the cost of the generators. And of course, Pelé scored a great goal.'

For Ellis it was a marvellous thrill to have Pelé in Birmingham.

The day before the game he took the Brazilian on a private sightseeing tour of the city – 'I stuck him in my Rolls Royce and drove him round the area' – and after the match he went to chat to Pelé in the dressing room.

> I said to him, 'You know, Pelé, you and I both come from very humble backgrounds, and yet we have done everything we have wanted to in our lives. Is there anything you haven't done already that you would like to do?' He turned to me in all seriousness and said, 'Yes, Mr Ellis, I'd like to own another bank.' Another bank, mind you. I just had to laugh.

Ellis enjoyed meeting up with Pelé many years later when Pelé was the guest of honour at Wembley for the Umbro Cup. He recalls: 'I had Franz Beckenbauer on my left with his wife and Pelé with his wife on my right. He was very quiet, but I said to him: "Remember playing at Villa Park?" He said: "Yes, Mr Ellis." He never mentioned the floodlights!'

By the end of the 1960s, Santos's commitments were so demanding they make the current crisis over fixture congestion, notably in England, seem a trifle tame. In one tour lasting just over two weeks, the club squeezed in seven matches in four countries, criss-crossing Europe to play in Yugoslavia, Spain, England and Italy. The final leg of their tour involved leaving Sarajevo at 5 a.m. for Manchester, arriving at 11.45 p.m., travelling to Stoke for a match there the following evening, then on to London and a 3 a.m. flight to Genoa. Nevertheless, they returned unbeaten, of course.

In 1965, a new physical training instructor had arrived at Santos from Palmeiras in São Paulo. Professor Julio Mazzei was to prove a major influence on Pelé. He had studied at the Michigan State University and spoke many languages, and he was also innovative in the way he understood the players' personalities and their problems. It was as a result of Mazzei's encouragement that Pelé decided to return to his studies after the 1970 World Cup and obtained a university degree.

Pelé's new contract with Santos in the same year included a huge house a few blocks from the beach, which had once belonged to one of the directors. His income was increasing rapidly, not least because he had endorsement deals for everything from soft drinks to trousers. His brother Zoca had moved to Santos and was living at the house of a Spaniard called Pepe Gordo (real name Jose Gonzales Ozoril) who was also a friend and business adviser to Pelé's old friend and teammate, Zito. Pelé needed someone to invest his money and put Gordo in charge of his financial affairs, forming a company along with Zito to do so. The company was called Sanitaria Santista. Zoca was also playing with the Santos club, although he never allowed his football to interfere with his studies to become a lawyer. Despite Pepe Gordo's advice that it would be a distraction, Pelé brought his entire family to the big house: Dondinho, Dona Celeste, Dona Ambrosina (his maternal grandmother), Uncle Jorge, Maria Lucia and Zoca.

Next he told Rose that he wanted to get engaged, and although she protested that he ought to keep on waiting, he had had enough and planned to tell her father on a fishing trip they had arranged. But Sr Guillerme Cholby would neither approve nor disapprove until he had the opportunity to discuss the matter in front of Dona Idalina, Rose's mother. After a frustrating full day's fishing, Rose's parents approved and they got engaged. There was a dual celebration with Pelé's twenty-fifth birthday. Unfortunately at that party a photographer snapped Pelé with

Rose's sister, and it was published as his bride-to-be. It should have been nothing more sinister than something to giggle over, except Rose's sister's fiancé was convinced something was up and broke off the engagement. Pelé pondered if the real reason was that the fiancé didn't want a black brother-in-law!

Months before the wedding, Pepe Gordo approached Pelé for more money for the business. Pelé queried that surely the banks were open. He knew that they were, as Rose worked as a secretary to the bank manager and was working that day. Pepe Gordo confessed with a shrug that Pelé's account was depleted, that there had been some poor investments and several small reversals in the business.

The truth was that there had been many bad investments for some time and nobody had told Pelé. Well, Rose had raised her concerns, but Pelé thought little of them, having complete faith in Pepe Gordo. Zito had left Sanitaria Santista some months earlier after several disagreements with Pepe Gordo, as he didn't like his methods, and wanted to concentrate on a dairy farm he had bought as his sole interest outside of his football and study. Pelé had not really asked him in any detail why he wanted to leave and had been blind to the warning signs, like so many footballers before him and afterwards, who had not paid enough attention to their business investments or to the men who were running them.

Pelé recalled: 'It seems that properties had been purchased that were unsuitable for construction. Construction materials had been purchased from fly-by-night outfits who took payment for their shoddy goods and then either went into bankruptcy or disappeared before they could be brought to account. Apartment buildings had been built at sites where nobody wanted to live. Roofs leaked from bad materials and poor workmanship, sanitary facilities were of poor quality and had to be replaced while practically new.' The bills piled up and creditors threatened to sue him.

Everyone in Brazil thought Pelé was wealthy. Pepe Gordo recommended bankruptcy. Pelé was sickened. 'I thought of the punishment I had taken on the football field, the target of kicks from every defender who wanted to be a hero to his fans and put me in hospital. I thought of playing those two forty-five-minute halves without a second's rest, running myself ragged, just to build for the future. The future? What future? It was all in some set of accountant's books I could not pretend to understand, and it wasn't a future at all. It was a past, and a painful and expensive one at that.'

Worse, his reputation, the good name of Pelé, was under threat. Not knowing who to turn to, he went for advice to Rose's boss, Sr Jose Bernardes Ferreira, who in addition to being a banker, was also a member of the Santos Club. He conducted a full search into Pelé's position and later declared that it was worse than he imagined. Even the possibility of a loan to pay the creditors of the company Sanitaria Santista was remote. His bank would not be able to accommodate a loan.

Pelé was forced to go begging to the Santos board. He sat down with the directors at Vila Belmiro. In return for coming to his financial rescue, putting up the money to cover his debts, Santos demanded that he sign a new three-year contract – he had just one year left on his existing one – in which he played the second season without any increase in pay or bonuses, and the third free of charge. Pelé had little choice other than to accept.

But he refused to let it spoil his wedding plans, and despite the grandiose venue suggested in the media, he had always planned a very small religious ceremony at his parents' home in Santos. He had invited Pepe Gordo some time earlier to be his 'best man' despite Gordo's vocal opposition to a black Pelé marrying a white Rosemeri – this on top of being responsible for Pelé's financial mess. Nevertheless, he still retained the honour at Pelé's wedding. The wedding took place at the house, with police holding back the crowd beyond the garden wall. After a small reception, confined to family and close friends, Pelé and his bride waited for the fans to disperse and return to Carnival, before they made their escape.

The honeymoon came courtesy of a wealthy German industrialist from Munich, Roland Endler, a fan who travelled throughout South America watching Santos, and who was president of a large football club in his home town. He offered Pelé a present, but when it was refused he insisted they come to Europe for the honeymoon. They travelled from Munich to Paris, and on to Switzerland and the Alps, and then Vienna, where the couple were surprised when an old-fashioned carriage drawn by six horses pulled up outside their hotel and ferried them through cheering crowds to the residence of the Mayor, who performed a 'second' marriage ceremony. Next stop Italy and the Vatican for a meeting with Pope Paul VI, where the press ran a story suggesting the Pope was more nervous of meeting Pelé than Pelé was of meeting the Pope – Pelé had met Pope John XXIII in 1961 when travelling with the Santos team.

His lifelong association with Santos transformed them into the most glamorous, sought-after club in the world. Santos embarked on world tours built around Pelé's presence, and almost all the exhibition match contracts stipulated that he should play for a minimum of sixty-five minutes. There are similarities with Manchester United, who travel as far as Australia, the Far East and China to promote their image and sell merchandise. Players such as David Beckham are star attractions, particularly following his marriage to pop star Victoria Adams. Beckham has of course developed into a world-class player, admired by none other than Pelé himself.

But he is nowhere near the attraction that Pelé was. The whole of Brazil adored Pelé. His enormous humility endeared him to the entire nation. He was more than a footballing hero – he was a vision of hope. In return, the people supported him on the field. 'Player No. 12' he called his fans. Streets, brands of coffee, sweets and thousands of babies were named after him. Worldwide, he became Brazil's most recognisable export, and also became the first black man to appear on the cover of America's *Life* magazine, at a time when racial prejudice in North America was endemic.

Even his marriage to Rosemeri Cholby, a white woman, was accepted, even held up as an example of Brazil's new enlightenment in racial integration. Pelé's stature was equivalent to that of any politician or statesman and there was even concern over how Pelé would meet royalty when the Duke of Edinburgh was present before a game in São Paulo in 1994. Who would be introduced to whom? As it turned out the Duke came to Pelé. In Paris he was greeted by a French Minister at Orly and swept into the capital in a motorcade like a visiting president.

On the pitch Pelé was king. That was never better illustrated than in a rather bizarre, brutal match in Bogota in 1969. Santos's Colombian opponents were attempting to kick and bait Pelé and his black co-strikers Edu and Lima out of the game with racist insults. Pelé was never afraid to launch into a confrontation on the pitch, and he launched into the referee after Edu had retaliated. Pelé was sent off for dissent and was in the dressing room taking off his boots and getting ready for an early bath, when a match official raced in demanding that Pelé should return to the pitch immediately. A bemused Pelé emerged from the tunnel to discover play suspended, the stadium filled with smoke, and the perimeter of the pitch lined with armed police. The dismissal had so enraged the Colombian crowd that they were on the verge of attacking the referee and a stream of flaming cushions were hurled on to the pitch. The police ordered Pelé back into the game fearing a full-scale riot, and also escorted the referee out of the stadium. The referee was sent off – not Pelé – by popular demand.

When, also in 1969, he scored his famous 1,000th goal at the Maracana, he publicly wept and said: 'Remember the children, remember the poor children.' Despite his enormous fame, he never forgot his humble roots, and the people loved him for his sincerity.

King on the pitch, even a god, but the human frailties off the field somehow made him even more endearing. Despite his enormous earning capacity, Pelé was twice on the brink of bankruptcy.

Sometimes women were just as problematical for Pelé. His first wife Rosemeri was white, and naturally it caused a stir when they got engaged and then married. Pelé had not experienced racism, as his country was relatively free of such a disease, but the newspapers made quite an issue of his mixed marriage as 'regardless of the Brazilian's boast of being prejudice-free, underneath there is a well of racial prejudice waiting to be tapped'. But Pelé, at least at that time, felt it would remain untapped.

CHAPTER 5

THE BRUTALITY AND THE BOYS OF '66

*'There is only one way to describe Brazil's 1966 World
Cup effort, and that is to declare that from beginning to end it
was a total and unmitigated disaster.'*
Pelé

E ngland's sole World Cup triumph, by contrast, was to be a grim
affair for Pelé and his brand of the beautiful game. Brazil were
bidding to become the first nation ever to win the World Cup three
times, and their fans were confident of success. Many Brazilians
came to England for the World Cup games, more, in fact, than
made the far shorter trip to Chile for the 1962 tournament. 'And
these people paid in advance – many, many months in advance
– for their tickets without receiving them until their arrival in
England,' Pelé said. 'There are few places in the world where a
Brazilian has enough confidence and trust to pay out his money
months in advance and have any hope of arriving and finding
the tickets waiting for him. It is difficult for a Brazilian to pay a
country a higher compliment than this.'

Yet behind the scenes, all was not as it should have been. Familiar backroom men such as coach Vicente Feola and Dr Gosling travelled to England, as did many of the 1962 team – astonishingly, even two veterans of 1958, defenders Bellini and Orlando survived, plus Djalmar Santos and Zito, who had been new boys then along with Pelé. But there was one significant change to the delegation. The man who had organised the triumphant trips to Sweden and Chile, Dr Paulo Machado de Carvalho, was replaced by Carlos Nascimento, his deputy in 1962. Nascimento had opposite views from the coach on which players should be selected. Pelé was concerned that the coach no longer wielded the same sort of authority that he had in the past, and observed that perhaps he didn't want to. In addition, CBD president João Havelange decided it was time he travelled personally with the squad to oversee the entire organisation.

The inevitable indecision over selection created problems. Initially forty-four players were selected as possibles, divided into four separate teams to train in four different locations. Even when they left for Europe, they did so with far too many players. Worse still, Pelé and other senior players were consulted about who should not be selected for the squad, and that of course led to friction within the camp. There was also a great deal of debate in Brazil over whether a large number of the team were too old, while Garrincha, though selected, was still recovering from the effects of a car accident and his fondness for alcohol, a problem that eventually led to an early death.

Even the trainer had changed. Paulo Amaral, who had coached in Italy, had thought of himself as part of the technical party. The new man, Bruno Hermany, who did not have a footballing background, took control of the training, and Pelé felt that the side suffered as a result. He thought that the Santos trainer, 'the best in the world', Julio Mazzei, should have been put in charge.

Warm-up games in Madrid, Scotland and a series of matches in Sweden added to the confusion when surprise decisions were made to send home key players. Confidence in the coaches evaporated. Finally, the players' anxieties filtered through to the management and a meeting was called to pacify them. It served only to increase the divisions and Pelé's suspicion that it would all end in grief. He observed: 'I wouldn't have minded being cut myself, since I was ready to concede our not winning a single game.'

Yet in the eyes of Brazil, all these problems and political intrigue did not apply to Pelé, in whom they saw their best chance of an historic hat-trick of World Cups. Little did they know that Europe's hatchet men would be given the licence to hack their star out of the tournament.

At the heart of Brazil's failure in 1966, Pelé believed, lay complacency, fed by the hype originating from Brazil's sports federation and eagerly seized upon by the media. He pinpointed the errors of judgement. 'There had been the over-invitation of players, the divided training in Brazil, the ridiculous selection of our European pre-tournament schedule, with endless travel and constant changes in climate and food, there had been the inadequate physical preparation, the ever-present and continuing uncertainty as to who might still be cut, the continuing squabbles between our two coaches and between our head coach and the head of the delegation.'

The psychological well-being of the players, their morale and relaxation, was no better managed. Brazil, who were playing their group matches at Goodison Park, were based on Merseyside. An intermediary approached Pelé and told him that the Beatles, who had by then been established as the most famous pop group in the world, would like to entertain the Brazilian team in honour of their having won the two previous World Cups. The players were obviously excited at this offer. 'Besides our native love of music, the truth was that being in football *concentração* for a month or more leaves a lot to be desired as far as entertainment is concerned. This is especially true in a country where language presents any kind of problem and we are weary of trying to make sense of the films which we are occasionally allowed to see. But music is an international language, and we looked forward eagerly to seeing the Beatles.' The directors, however, thought differently. To them the Beatles, with their long hair and anti-establishment attitudes, were the epitome of decadence and posed a serious threat to the peace and security of the impressionable young men in their charge. So the fabulous offer was refused. 'One wonders what the directors' children had to say to their fathers when they learned that they had turned down the chance of a private performance by the Beatles,' marvelled Pelé. 'My own feeling when I later had to pay a king's ransom for a ticket for one of their concerts was that I should have sent the bill to my directors. I have never since had an opportunity to meet the group in person, either as a functioning band or as individuals, and I blame my directors for this.'

On the field, as England moved comfortably, if not convincingly, into the quarter-finals, it was a sorry tale for Brazil. Drawn in Group 3 with Bulgaria, Portugal and Hungary, by far the best group in the tournament, they won their first match, against Bulgaria, 2–0, with two exquisite goals from free kicks from Pelé and Garrincha. Pelé, tired from the six-game pre-tournament schedule, was in addition a victim of intimidation by Bulgaria's Zhechev. Pelé has since heard it suggested that Sir Stanley Rous, in control of the selection of referees, had instructed them to go easy on the Europeans' aggressive style against the South American sides, 'with the result that Zhechev did everything he could to physically cripple me, and the West German referee, Kurt Tschenscher, gave neither me nor any of the others on our team the protection we had a right to expect from an official in a game.'

It was decided to rest Pelé for the next game, against Hungary. Pelé himself felt this was a mistake. Although his legs had taken a battering, he was confident he was fit to play. The decision was taken, he thought, because Brazil considered it a foregone conclusion that they would beat Hungary and reach the quarter finals. This proved to be more overconfidence. Feola selected Garrincha for his second game within a few days, against medical advice, and the weakened Brazilians were humbled 3–1 by an exhilarating display from Hungary. Pelé watched from the stands, and it was a bitter experience indeed for him to see Brazil lose a match for the first time in twelve years of World Cup football.

Now Brazil had to beat Portugal, led by Eusebio and their black captain and left-half Mario Coluña, by an impressive score if they were to qualify. It has been said of this match that there were attempts to bribe the referee, offers mooted but quickly abandoned, though there is no evidence to support this allegation apart from that of an unnamed source.

Pelé, still suffering the effects of his injury, returned to a jittery side as one of nine changes. He was staggered by the indecision over who would play and a final selection showing so many alterations. Pelé felt that the directors had relied far too heavily on the old dictum that God was a Brazilian, and that therefore everything would work out.

After twenty-five minutes Brazil were two goals down and looking like going out of the tournament. The only hope of salvation rested with Pelé. He finally gathered possession and moved forward threateningly, only to be hacked down by defender Morais, who gave no sign of attempting to play the ball. Pelé staggered on, his huge heart and determination refusing to succumb to the brutality, but again Morais chopped him down, this time to the ground. English referee George McCabe took no action. With Pelé a forlorn, limping figure after such a horrendous assault, Portugal ran out 3–1 winners. Dr Gosling and Mario Americo had to help Pelé from the field.

Pelé recalls:

> Morais had a field day fouling me, and eventually putting me out of the game. He tripped me, and when I was stumbling to the ground he leaped at me, feet first, and cut me down completely. For sure he should have been sent off. I was so intent on getting us back into the game that it was only afterwards, when I saw it on film, that I realised just how bad those fouls really were, what a terribly vicious double-foul it was.

Morais was unrepentant. 'Oh, it looked much worse than it really was. What made it look so bad was that Pelé was already injured, so he was already moving with pain.'

Gordon Taylor, now the highly influential players' union leader, was a player with Bolton during the tournament, which afforded him the privilege of gaining access to the venues, where he was especially keen to watch Pelé. He says: 'I was heartbroken during the World Cup in 1966 that Pelé had been manhandled out of the tournament. It was a tragedy to see Pelé kicked out of the competition.'

The ramifications were immense. Not only had the holders been kicked out of the World Cup at the home of world football, but it strengthened the South American cartel's theory that there was a conspiracy to enable England to win the tournament. The knock-on effect was an increased determination to end the European domination of FIFA. As for Pelé, he was so broken, physically and mentally, that at the time he vowed never again to play World Cup football. 'I don't want to finish my life as an invalid,' he said.

The pervading stench of inept refereeing and thuggery having crippled the world's best player, the later stages of the tournament only increased the tension between Europe and South America. Uruguay had two players sent off in their 4–0 quarter-final defeat by West Germany at Hillsborough, refereed by another Englishman, Jim Finney. At Wembley a German referee, Rudolf Kreitlein, was appointed for what turned out to be the infamous clash between England and Argentina in the quarter-finals, after which England manager Alf Ramsey described the Argentinians as 'animals'. The ugly game had prevailed over the beautiful one.

Back in Brazil, the national side suffered a cruel media backlash – or at least, the players did. Those who were actually responsible escaped. 'I was completely disgusted with what happened,' said Pelé. 'I have been the target for attacks many times, but seldom as often or as viciously as in those games.' He had made up his mind to continue with Santos, but said that he would consider whether to continue to play for Brazil in matches other than World Cup ties. In any event, 'the thankless job of playing for the Jules Rimet trophy under the inept leadership of a technical commission such as we suffered could be left to others. I had competed in three World Cup tournaments, that was enough.' He was completely disillusioned about the refereeing that had left him with injuries that might have threatened his career.

In England, meanwhile, Brazil's humiliation was submerged by the national side's semi-final glory against Portugal and

Eusebio and then, of course, we thought it was all over. And it was when Geoff Hurst completed his hat-trick and England won the World Cup.

As for Pelé, he didn't get to meet the Queen until a couple of years later, at the Maracana Stadium in Rio in November 1968. It was at a game between Carioca, the crack Rio de Janeiro team, and Paulista, the leading São Paulo side, for whom Pelé was playing. The Queen had expressed an interest in seeing a match between two top Brazilian teams, and the fixture had been named the Queen's Game in her honour. Before the kick-off Pelé was told that the Queen had asked to meet him.

To make sure that I committed as few gaffes as possible, behaved correctly and did not embarrass Brazil in the eyes of the world, a representative of the Brazilian equivalent of the British Foreign Office came to see me first to give me advice. 'Protocol is extremely important,' he said sternly. 'One does not come barging into a room with one's hand out, saying something like, "Hello, Queen, how have you been?" Everything must be done properly. Now, do you know how to bow?' 'Bow?' I said. 'Forget it,' he said, looking at his watch. 'There isn't time. Try to remember a few simple rules. A representative of Her Majesty will approach you and take you to the Queen and introduce you. When you are in front of Her Majesty, stand perfectly still. Do not squirm. Do not scratch. Do not put your hand out until Her Majesty puts her hand out. When the Queen does put her hand out, take it, hold it lightly for a very short time, and bend your head respectfully. Then release her hand, straighten up your head, and wait for Her Majesty to speak. When she does, answer with short, polite answers. And always refer to Her Majesty as "Your Majesty". Is that clear?'

He did not wait for me to answer but looked at his watch again. 'Let's go,' he said, 'or we'll hold up the game.' The room where visiting dignitaries are entertained at the Maracana Stadium is a very beautiful salon, quite impressive. I must admit that I was rather preoccupied on my way to the meeting. I had met many other heads of state, many presidents and even a few dictators, but this was my first queen. Besides, this was the first time I had been so thoroughly instructed in proper protocol, and it made me a bit nervous trying to remember exactly what those instructions had been. Was I to speak first or wait to be spoken to? Was I to approach the Queen or wait to be approached? I knew I was to do one thing first and wait for the other, but I had forgotten which was which. When I entered the room, however, it made no difference. Protocol went out of the window. Queen Elizabeth walked over to me, put her hand on my arm and said, 'I'm very pleased to meet you at last. My husband has told me many things about you; he's quite a fan of yours.' And we fell into an animated conversation about football, England and other subjects. When I excused myself and went down to change into my uniform for the game, I looked around for my instructor in protocol, but he was staring at the floor and refused to meet my eye. After the game, which we won 3–2 and in which I was fortunate enough to score a goal, I returned to the salon to be presented with the trophy. On my return, Her Majesty's ease of manner was exactly as it had been in our previous meeting, and the impression it left on me made that a memorable day in all respects. I had a feeling that the Queen was a woman who cared about many things, but mainly about people. It was an occasion I shall never forget, and one that has bound me to Great Britain with ties that shall endure throughout my life.

When Pelé returned to Brazil in 1966 his heart was no longer in the game. As he got older injuries were taking longer to heal, and there was always the fear that the next bad one might be his last. The aftermath of his experience at the World Cup in England was beginning to bite. He played a total of fifty games that season, scoring a total of forty-two goals, the lowest of his career.

That year he went to the States for the first time when Santos played Benfica at Randall's Island in New York, a game they won 4–0, and then Inter Milan, beating them at the Yankee Stadium 4–1. The Inter match set an attendance record in America of 42,000 which stood until 1979. But not even this new experience could snap him out of his dejection, and his own showing was poor. There were better times ahead on the personal front. Back in Brazil, Rose was pregnant, and as he pondered the difficulties of bringing up a boy, he was presented with a girl, Kelly Cristina, born on Friday 13 January 1967. With the birth of his daughter his lust for life was restored and that year he played sixty-seven games for Santos and scored fifty-five times. After the usual South American tour, Santos went off to Africa and Europe for two months. The only cloud was having to leave his family for so long.

His first visit to Africa was an uplifting experience. 'Everywhere I went I was looked upon and treated as a god, almost certainly because I represented to the blacks in those countries what a black man could accomplish in a country where there was little racial prejudice, as well as providing physical evidence that a black man could become rich, even in a white man's country,' he said. 'To these people, who had little possibility of ever escaping the crushing poverty in which they found themselves, I somehow represented a ray of hope, however faint.'

The people massed at the airports and crowded on to the runways as his plane taxied in, even ducking still-turning propellers to keep their place in the queue to reach out and touch him. Fans arrived at the stadiums at dawn, some even camping there overnight, to make sure of seeing him play.

In one match in Dakar, Senegal, he was determined to put on a show for these people, and dribbled through the opposition defence and round the keeper twice in the first ten minutes. It did not have quite the effect he had imagined. The keeper burst into tears, held his hand up to the referee and had to be led away, weeping copiously. The game had to be halted while they found another keeper. Pelé went to the home dressing room after the game to apologise, but the original keeper refused to see him; Pelé had inadvertently shamed him in front of his own people.

The next year, 1968, was Santos's best ever. They won five major tournaments, and in eighty-one games Pelé scored fifty-nine goals. Santos made their second trip to the States, playing in Boston, Cleveland and Washington, among other cities. Even in this soccer outpost, he was still recognised, but at least he was able to walk down the street and go to restaurants without being mobbed.

At home, his business interests were increasing as in 1969 he finally fulfilled his obligations to Santos for the debts of the disastrous Sanitaria Santista adventure. Through the offices of a TV entrepreneur, Marby Ramundini, he was offered the leading part in a television *novela*, or soap opera. It meant getting up extremely early to tape an episode before training, or staying up late after a game to film. He was also an announcer on a radio sports programme. Ramundini also began acting as his agent for the endorsement of products, with a great deal of success since he was well aware of the value of the Pelé name and was not afraid to ask for large sums of money for its use. These fees were eagerly agreed to by companies who were similarly aware of the marketing value of the Pelé name, so Pelé found himself promoting a wide range of products, including bicycles, shoes, coffee and wristwatches. Nevertheless, he refused to be linked with any alcohol or tobacco companies and invested his considerable income in real estate. While Pelé prospered once more on the field, his earnings were soaring off it.

Finally persuaded to reconsider his decision to quit World Cup football, Pelé regained his pivotal role for Brazil during a highly successful and goal-filled qualifying stage completed by August 1969. Towards the middle of October, he was to reach a remarkable landmark in his career: his 1,000th goal.

The Brazilian press tracked down the number of goals he had officially scored since the beginning of his Santos career twelve years earlier. Suddenly there were articles in the newspapers about Celtic's Jimmy McGrory, whose 500 goals in the 1920s had made him a legend, and declarations that anyone capable of scoring 1,000 goals would be immortal. Coverage of his impending milestone was worldwide, and Pelé admitted that it made him nervous the closer it got.

Nervous or not, on 15 October, against Portuguesa de Desportos, he scored four in a 6–2 win to account for numbers 990, 991, 992, 993. A week later, against Coritiba, he got 994 and 995. He drew a blank against Fluminense when it seemed the entire world was watching, but in the next game, on 1 November, against Flamengo, number 996 went into the net. Then came a lull, a massive barren spell – well, two games – without a goal. Numbers 997 and 998 arrived with a double against Santa Cruz in Recife on 12 November, and number 999 in Paraíba, in north-east Brazil, two days later.

Santos arrived at Bahia to play Esporte Clube on 16 November. The anticipation was naturally immense for the entire country – except, it seems, for Pelé. 'When I came out on the field, I felt nervous. I had long wished the thousandth goal over and done with, but never so much as on this day. I had a sudden cold feeling that I was doomed to go for years and years without scoring another goal.' The locals had planned the most elaborate celebrations to show the rest of Brazil just how hospitable they could be; a special thanksgiving mass had even been arranged. Pelé got his chance right at the end, but after a dribble through the defence and around the keeper, his shot struck the bar and teammate Jair Bala scored from the rebound.

The next game was against Vasco da Gama on 19 November at the Maracana, where 80,000 braved a tropical downpour in the hope of witnessing a piece of history. Marked by the formidably built Rene, he was restrained for the opening half-hour, but finally caught his shadow off balance for a split-second. Evading the other defenders, he delivered what he thought was a goalbound shot, but Argentinian international keeper Andrade tipped it over. Buoyed up by this crack at goal, Pelé repeated the manoeuvre, but this time the ball struck the bar, and when he challenged to head in the rebound, Rene got there first for an own goal.

Then a great pass from Clodoaldo gave Pelé sight of the goal again, but as he attempted to dart between two defenders he was tripped by the sliding tackle of Fernando.

Was it a foul? The ball was probably Andrade's in any case,

but this was not time for debate. An excited hush came over the stadium as the referee pointed to the spot. Rildo, the Santos left-back, came up to take the kick, but the captain, Carlos Alberto, sent him away with a few choice words. This was Pelé's moment. His teammates retreated to the halfway line, leaving him to compose himself alone. He said later:

> A penalty kick certainly wasn't the way I had hoped to make my thousandth goal, but at this point I would have taken it any way I could, just to get the affair over with. I don't know how long I stood over the ball with Andrade watching me intently. I was trying to clear the cobwebs from my head, trying to forget the importance of this one goal to me, to my game, to my team. I was trying to relax and regain the calmness I had felt only moments before. For one split-second I remembered missing that penalty kick in that long-ago junior game at Santos, but I forced the thought away.

The giant stadium was silent. Pelé jogged forward and struck firmly with the side of his right foot. The shot was low, to the keeper's left. Andrade guessed correctly and went for it full length, but the ball was beyond his reach. It nestled in the back of the net.

Pelé chased the ball into the net and kissed it. The crowd roared, the media mobbed him on the pitch, joined by hundreds of fans. A thousand balloons took to the air bearing the news of his 1,000th goal. As the crush surrounded Pelé, his shirt was torn off and replaced by one with '1,000' emblazoned on it. He was carried around the field in tears and they let him down only so he could make a lap of honour. As he did so, Pelé dedicated his goal to Brazil's street kids, a new and growing problem at the time.

(Indeed, today he is entitled to point out that had more been done thirty years ago, Brazil would not currently be blighted by such desperate urban poverty.)

Was it disappointing that Pelé's 1,000th goal came from a penalty? No, says Armando Noguiera, Brazil's senior football writer. Pelé had already scored every type of goal imaginable, and this was one no one in the crowd could miss through ill fortune or a lapse in concentration. He added: 'If Pelé hadn't been born a man, he would have been born a ball.'

When I asked Pelé which of all his goals has given him the greatest pleasure, he unequivocally sites his 1,000th, the memory lingers on. He told me:

> I know I scored my 1,000th goal with a penalty kick, but you just have to look at the Euro 2000 semi-finals when Holland missed four during the course of the match and the shoot-out and all the penalties that have been missed in World Cup finals and important games, to understand that it is not a question of a simple penalty kick.
>
> Some people complained that I scored my 1,000th goal from a penalty. They wanted something special like a brilliant bicycle kick, or a beautiful header like the one against Italy in the World Cup final in 1970, or to watch as I dribbled through the entire opposition, or did something they had never seen before. They said, 'Why a penalty?'
>
> What they didn't understand or appreciate is that it was harder to have taken that penalty than to have tried to do something unusual in open play. I was a world player, I had performed for so many years for Brazil and for the world's top club at that time, Santos, yet when I

tried to take that penalty my legs started to shake because I was so nervous.

I didn't want to miss that penalty. Yet, I didn't strike it properly and the goalkeeper got a touch on the ball, but it still went in and I was so thankful. The goal in the World Cup final came to me naturally because it came as part of the game and I didn't have to think about it. But my 1,000th goal was so different. The pressure was unbearable. Imagine what it was like ... everybody stopped, there was a packed Maracana and they all stopped, they all wanted me to score. Yet later they said it was a penalty and they wanted more.

My answer to them all is that Pelé always does things differently. It was as if God wanted all the people to stop and look and take their time to see Pelé score that goal. God had said, 'Let's stop the game and watch Pelé's 1,000th goal.'

After his feat Pelé was substituted. In the dressing room, he sat, drained of all emotion. He took off his shirt and folded it neatly, ready to take home and treasure. Later, he was presented with an inscribed silver plaque. For once, the next day Pelé did not dominate the whole front page of every Brazilian newspaper. He had to share his own momentous achievement with another that had occurred on the same day: a moon landing by American astronauts Conrad and Bean.

But he was not yet finished. There were still 281 goals to score.

CHAPTER 6

THE GREATEST TEAM OF THEM ALL

Malcolm Allison: 'How do you spell "Pelé"?'
Paddy Crerand: 'Easy. G–O–D.'
ITV World Cup Panel, 1970

At the end of the sixties, Pelé was known in England as the Black Pearl. He preferred the nickname of Criola, or Negrao. The 1970 World Cup would rechristen him the Godfather of World Football. When, early in 1969, he was invited for the fourth time to play for Brazil in their build-up to the tournament in Mexico, his first reaction was to decline once again. He was eventually persuaded to change his mind because, 'I wanted to put to rest, once and for all, the idea that I couldn't enter a World Cup series without getting hurt.' João Havelange helped to sway his decision with promises of greatly improved preparation for the national side. He was also encouraged by the fact that the media had begun to analyse the real reasons behind the farce of 1966. And the venue was one that would suit the South Americans. Pelé's experience of playing at altitude and in heat would give him an edge, as would the warm welcome from the Mexican fans of which the Brazilians were assured. There was every chance, he felt, that they could win the World Cup for the third time. The balance was tipped for Pelé by a FIFA innovation: the introduction of yellow and red cards to deter the hatchet men. The 1970 tournament would be the first to be televised in colour, and it was fitting that the arrival of this bright new world should feature Pelé's kaleidoscope of talents.

Brazil's military junta had appointed Brigadier Jeronimo Bastos to oversee the preparations for the 1970 World Cup and to ensure that the shambles of 1966 was not repeated. It was decided that keeping the entire squad together for a protracted and costly three-month spell for intensive training and selected matches would be the best possible start. The new team coach was João Saldanha, a former member of the Communist Party, then outlawed in Brazil. He had the backing of Havelange, but by no means that of everyone else. A fifty-cigarette-a-day man, he had never played at a high standard and was earning his living as a broadcaster and columnist when he was abruptly called in to take charge of the national team. It was suggested in some quarters that the main reason for his recruitment to the CBD was to give them some respite from his merciless criticisms in print and on radio, but it would be rather glib to assume that this was the sole motive for bringing him into the CBD. He was an outstanding club coach with Botafogo but, as a narrow 2–1 win over England in the Maracana in 1969 suggested, he had a lot of work to do.

Saldanha, who died in 1990, had a reputation for being quick tempered and very opinionated. No one knew how the team would develop under him. He built his squad around Santos and wove together a team unit incorporating an enormous degree of flair which Brazil used to navigate their way through their qualifying group against Colombia, Paraguay and Venezuela. There was to be no repetition of the confusion over selection of 1966. Tostão became a regular goalscorer with nine to Pelé's six of Brazil's total of twenty-three in the six ties. They began on 6 August 1969 with a comfortable 2–0 win over Colombia in Bogota. Saldanha selected six players from Santos, two from Cruzeiro and one each from São Paulo, Fluminense and Botafogo, and his gamble of playing Tostão and Pelé together paid off.

Tostão scored both goals, pouncing first after keeper Lagarcha could only parry a thirty-yard Pelé free kick. Four days later, against Venezuela in Caracas, he put away a brilliant solo opener after seventy-seven minutes, and then in the final quarter of the game Pelé scored twice and Tostão completed a hat-trick for a 5–0 thrashing. On 17 August, in Asunción, Brazil saw off their only real challengers, Paraguay, by 3–0, taking their tally to ten goals in three matches in the process. Pelé, recalling the riots in Montevideo ten years earlier, was put at ease when he saw all the Brazilian flags among the crowd.

On 21 August they were back at the Maracana to take on Colombia in the first of three matches in ten days. Pelé set up Tostão for the first; Colombia equalised; Tostão restored the lead and Edu scored a third. Back came Colombia with a second goal, but Pelé extended Brazil's lead before being replaced by Paulo César of Flamengo. Saldanha also substituted Gerson with Rivelino, who scored four minutes from the end, leaving time for a sixth from Jairzinho. It was the first year in which two substitutes were permitted, but Saldanha used the substitution rule sparingly. Pelé felt the 6–2 win marked the point at which Brazil's confidence began to soar. 'What a difference from 1966, when nobody knew until the kick-off who was going to play, and when six or seven changes in the starting line-up were not unknown.'

Three days later Brazil booked their ticket to Mexico in front of 123,000 people, beating Venezuela 6–0. Tostão scored in the seventh, twenty-first and twenty-fourth minutes for one of the fastest hat-tricks in international football, Pelé's passing contributing to each of the goals. He was again the provider when Jairzinho got Brazil's fourth in the thirtieth minute. Pelé converted a penalty just before half-time and rounded off the victory with the best goal of the game, interchanging passes with Tostão and Jairzinho before whipping a stunning shot past Fazano.

A crowd of over 183,000, a record for a World Cup qualifier, packed the Maracana for the carnival against Paraguay on 31 August. With Paraguay out for revenge, and their defence on top form, it wasn't until near the end that a solo Pelé goal clinched victory for Brazil.

It was a formidable qualifying performance: a clean sweep of all six games, with twenty-three goals scored, only two conceded, and the team remaining virtually unchanged throughout. Yet after winning through to the finals in such spectacular style, Saldanha seemed to lose the plot, alienating a great deal of popular support by making wholesale changes. He engaged in major rows with the media. He had always been short-tempered, but now he resorted more and more often to using his fists to settle disputes.

No matter how relentless the media in England have been, it is rare that an England coach has responded with anything more than a verbal assault, although one or two have been tempted to go a touch further. But between Saldanha and the Brazilian newspaper journalists it was all-out war. As Pelé observed: 'He began to demonstrate a restlessness, an unsettled state of mind, which worried us all.'

Controversy was never far away. The new team doctor, Dr Toledo, sent Toninho and Scala home on medical grounds, yet their clubs' medical opinion was that they were fit to play. Then the full-strength team lost a match to Argentina, a side already eliminated from the World Cup by Peru, in Porto Alegre, and for the first time members of the squad openly criticised Saldanha's strategy. Indeed, there was an immediate inquest in the dressing room after the match. During the heated debate, even the great Pelé questioned Saldanha's tactics, to the applause of his teammates. Four days later, Saldanha created the biggest storm yet when he suggested it might be time to drop Pelé from the squad. General Emilio Garrastazu Medici, the dictator running Brazil at the time, sent word that he wanted to discuss team selection with the coach. In the meantime, Flamengo coach Yustrich added his voice to the general criticism. Saldanha, the master of unarmed combat, turned up at the Flamengo training ground in search of Yustrich – brandishing a revolver. Fortunately, Yustrich was not there, the gun was not fired, no harm was done and Saldanha was eventually disarmed by bystanders.

Instead Saldanha was the one to be fired, after he met General Medici and refused to bring Dario into the team on the general's suggestion. Antonio do Passo, head of the technical commission, told João Havelange that he had had enough of Saldanha's antics, and that he would have to go. First Dino Sani and then Otto Glória turned down the job before Havelange recalled Mário Lobo Zagallo, the World Cup-winner of 1958 and 1962. The position of national coach was the archetypal impossible job even then, and especially in Brazil. Managing a country with such high expectations as Brazil, England or Italy can be an enormous strain as well as an immense honour. Zagallo's return for the World Cup finals was universally welcomed in Brazil, and amazingly he would still be managing the national side in France in 1998, although he failed to survive the dismal showing in the final and the farce over Ronaldo.

But Saldanha was not going to go quietly. Knowing that his days were numbered, he set about shifting the blame – and in the most outrageous direction. 'Saldanha could not permit himself to leave with no glory, without some justification for being replaced, and he therefore decided to charge me with the responsibility for his fall,' says Pelé.

Saldanha claimed that Pelé was shortsighted, which was in fact technically true. When he had first arrived at Santos as a boy and been given a thorough medical, slight shortsightedness had been reported. But the condition had never affected his game. He certainly knew where the goalmouth was. In any case, if anything, Pelé's forte was having extra peripheral vision. When this excuse had been destroyed in the media, Saldanha changed tack and cited poor physical condition as the reason why Pelé should be axed. But all the players were below their peak as they had yet to begin their real preparation for the World Cup.

Saldanha's attacks on Pelé became increasingly wild in the weeks after his departure. The former coach went on television to say that Pelé was unfit and suffering from a 'very serious disease' which he was not at liberty to divulge. Pelé was so worried by this that he went to see Antonio do Passo to ask whether some medical evidence was being withheld from him. 'For a while he had me believing that I was suffering from cancer, or something equally frightening,' Pelé said later. Pelé never truly forgave Saldanha for his behaviour, and Saldanha never forgot what a formidable opponent Pelé could be, both on and off the pitch. Carlos Alberto, Pelé's skipper at Santos and for Brazil, was appalled by this treatment of a man who was not only his teammate but also a close friend. 'Pelé was the player in whom we trusted,' he said later. 'If Pelé is with us, we are with God.' But unfortunately there were many who believed there was no smoke without fire and who accepted Saldanha's insinuations that Pelé was burned out at the age of twenty-nine, and that he shouldn't be selected to go to the World Cup.

The Brazilians stuck with Saldanha's plans to arrive early in Mexico to allow the players an extended period to acclimatise to the heat and the altitude. Saldanha had originally decided that this should be two months; Zagallo felt twenty-one days would be adequate. As it turned out, the players adapted quickly, and were relieved not to have been encamped for as long as had first been anticipated with the risk of utter boredom creeping in. Even so, three weeks was a long period to spend in one spot before the tournament even began.

Zagallo was popular with the players, and in particular with the three most influential ones: Pelé, Gerson and Carlos Alberto. They formed a trio described by masseur Mario Americo as the 'Cobras', and would discuss at great length in Pelé's room the performance and morale of the younger and less experienced players, even approaching Zagallo and the technical committee when they felt strongly about something.

In the weeks leading up to the departure for Mexico, some of the players were in a confused state following a dismal 3–1 win over a local Mineiro selection in Belo Horizonte, Minas Gerais and a goalless draw at the Morumbi in São Paulo against World Cup finalists Bulgaria. Before their final friendly in Brazil, against Austria at the end of April, the Cobras held an hour-long meeting in Pelé's room at the Hotel Paineiras in Rio that effectively moulded the next couple of months.

As the players directly affected by the switch of tactics they had in mind, Tostão, Rivelino and Clodoaldo were later called to

Pelé's room. Dario's failure for Brazil had convinced the players that there was no place for an out-and-out centre-forward against tight European defences. Tostão agreed with the Cobras' idea that he should play at inside-left with Pelé taking a position slightly forward of him in the middle. Rivelino would adapt to a dual role as a covering midfielder while attacking on both wings. The young Clodoaldo would be used as a defensive midfielder.

Zagallo consented to let them try their formation against Austria. Gerson says: 'It was a friendly conversation. We didn't order him to do anything, but we tried to help Zagallo to solve the problems that he still had to select the best team, or the one that could become the best one.' Zagallo would observe from the stands, where he reserved the right to change tactics by communicating over the radio with Mario Americo. Felix was informed of his reinstatement in goal over Ado and Leao, but it wasn't until the team arrived in the dressing room that they were told of the changes – Piazza, brought in for Joel, did not know he would be playing as a fourth defender until just before he went out on to the pitch. Gerson delivered the final dressing-room talk.

That night in the Maracana the team known to be devised by player power mounted a confidence-engendering display with a Rivelino winner. The new formation now became Zagallo's favoured choice, too. Of the team that played Austria only Rogerio, substituted for his right-wing rival Jairzinho, did not make it all the way to the finals in Mexico.

Soon after the squad arrived in Mexico, the Cobras went to Antonio do Passo asking to be allowed to officially address the squad because they were not convinced that the younger players appreciated the magnitude of their mission. Do Passo gave a talk to the players before handing over to the self-appointed three-man players' committee.

But it was not all stern stuff. The players were already getting up to the usual pranks to lighten the mood and alleviate the boredom when they were not training or playing, and Rivelino, Felix and Brito were the principal jokers of the party. Rivelino recalls: 'Pelé was scared of two things, knives and snakes. If you hold a knife near him he jumps, he is like a cat.' When Rivelino came across a wooden snake, he slipped it in Pelé's bed. Returning to his own room, however, he was suddenly consumed with panic. He confessed to room-mate Edu. 'Can you imagine if something happens to him?' he fretted. 'I will not be able to go back to Brazil!'

But before he could go back to remove the snake, he heard the screams from Pelé's room. 'I heard him going "Aaaaaah!" He beat the snake with his guitar. The next day he came to me and said, "You son of a bitch."' Rivelino was just thankful that Pelé was still around to shout at him. 'I almost killed the *negrao*. Thank God nothing happened.' In fact Rivelino respected Pelé beyond belief. 'I learned a lot from Pelé. He was always an example. He knew that even the greatest player in the world had to be fit when he took the field. If he was not fit physically, he did not play; he did not do what his head imagined he was able to do.'

His Santos teammate, Clodoaldo, had already learned much from sharing a dressing room with Pelé. 'I would have been a fool if I hadn't profited by learning something from the greatest player of all time. I learned lessons every day. Pelé was always ahead of everyone in reasoning, speed and physical condition. One of his main virtues was that he observed everything, the supporters, the terraces, the goalkeeper, the work of the referee. If Pelé was without the ball, he was observing.' On the training pitch he noted Pelé's thoroughness, and how it helped him to embarrass even the classiest of world-class stars. 'When you were marking Pelé in training, he knew when he controlled the ball which was your worst side, and that that was the side which he should go to. He was always, always in front of everybody.'

Brazil were in Group 3 with England, Romania and Czechoslovakia. The Brazilians launched a highly successful PR exercise – distributing pennants and flags to the locals and praising all things Mexican – in a bid to gain a valuable advantage over rivals England and their taciturn leader, Alf Ramsey, who kept his upper lip stiff and his mouth tightly shut. The Brazilians knew how to win the charm offensive after seeing the big impression made by Santos in Mexico and indeed all over the world. 'Everywhere the club went, Pelé and Santos were welcomed in an extraordinary way,' said Carlos Alberto. 'Santos played in Mexico every season and the adoration they had there for the players like him and Clodoaldo was something to see.' When Brazil played Guadalajara in front of a 70,000 crowd, the whole city took the day off. On every street corner posters proclaimed 'Hoy no trabajamos porque vamos a ver Pelé' – No work today, we are off to see Pelé.

By contrast, Ramsey's abrupt style won England few friends. A year earlier, on a fact-finding tour to Mexico, after a goalless draw between England and the home nation at the Azteca, Ramsey had been asked if he had a message for the Mexican people. The manager who had taken elocution lessons for his speech impediment was not at a loss for words, but they certainly lacked tact and diplomacy. 'Yes,' he answered. 'There was a band playing outside our hotel till five o'clock this morning. We were promised a motorcycle escort to the stadium but it never arrived. When our players went out to inspect the pitch, they were abused and jeered by the crowd.' Unfortunately, by the time Ramsey arrived at the main point of his message – 'We are delighted to be in Mexico and the Mexican people are a wonderful people' – the damage had been done. When he returned to the country, it was as public enemy number one.

Ramsey's World Cup preparations were further sabotaged by the infamous Bobby Moore bracelet incident. After a visit to a jewellery store in the Bogota hotel where the team were staying for their game against Colombia, Moore was accused of having stolen a bracelet, arrested and detained in a police cell. The England captain was eventually released on bail in time to rejoin his teammates for the match before moving on to Ecuador. On his return to Bogota, he was rearrested en route to catch the plane to Mexico for the World Cup. He was placed under house arrest in the care of the president of a local football club. Following the intervention of the British Council, bail was granted and Moore was allowed to go to Mexico. As if all this was not enough, when England arrived in Mexico reserve striker Jeff Astle, who suffered from an acute fear of flying, was visibly the worse for wear. The two incidents were combined to produce a Mexican newspaper headline announcing the arrival of 'a team of drunks and thieves'.

Although Mexico as a venue suited Pelé and his samba team, it was nevertheless a politically volatile country, and the fact that it had pipped Argentina in the World Cup bidding back at the FIFA Congress of 1964 was something of a surprise. By 1970 strikes and terrorist bombings had pushed the country to the brink of anarchy. Two years after American athletes Tommy Smith and John Carlos had used the Mexico Olympics as a platform for the Black Panthers, there were fears that the World Cup might be hijacked for internal propaganda purposes.

Pelé had to be placed under guard after a group of Cuban trained guerrillas being held in custody tipped off Mexican police about a plot to kidnap him before the tournament. The Suites Caribes, the team's headquarters, a hacienda-style motel in the suburbs of Guadalajara, was transformed into a fortified camp. A former Brazilian swimming champion, Major Jeronimo Guarani, kept his Mexican troops at their posts around the clock. The front gates were guarded by two police cars and a handful of plain-clothed agents. Journalists were told that the official FIFA press accreditation was insufficient to gain entry to the hotel, and an additional card was issued to those vetted and cleared as reputable and safe.

Starved of access to the teams, some newspapers came up with wildly differing stories. Pelé was being moved to a different room every night to confuse potential kidnappers, said one; another suggested he was banned from even appearing on the hotel's popular verandas overlooking the Avenida Lopez Mateos. Even the stories of Pelé's myopia resurfaced. Apparently, America Club of Mexico had considered buying him from Santos, but didn't want to spend a vast sum on a player who could hardly see. It was not difficult to detect the hand of Saldanha in these reports, and indeed the axed coach was now in Mexico endlessly repeating his allegations. When Pelé did finally emerge from his refuge to train at the nearby Providentia Club, there was no escaping the seriousness with which the threats were being treated. Pelé was encircled by security guards as he climbed on and off the bus and had to pass autographs and even answers to journalists' questions back and forth via his minders. 'My job is thankless, but he is a patrimonio [a property],' Major Guarani explained. 'He is a symbol of Brazil.' Pelé joked that whenever he was fed up with persistent media attention he would warn journalists that Medici's SNI secret police were on their way, and they soon left.

Inside the camp, however, there was a deep concentration on the World Cup ahead, an inner calmness, a determination to cut out all these outside influences and to focus fully on the football.

'Pelé is always saying that we need to win, and that we shouldn't be scared about breaking a leg to do so,' said Mario Americo. 'It seems it is the last thing Pelé wants to do in his life as a player. He seems to be a child waiting for Santa Claus.'

It was an anxious wait, and in the meantime Pelé suffered more than most from homesickness. On the phone to his wife Rosemeri back at home, he had been told how his entire family, even his little daughter Kelly, all of whom he missed terribly on his long and varied footballing trips abroad, had been gathering before matches to pray for him and his teammates. 'Why don't you also pray, all of you?' she had asked him. The devout Pelé mentioned the idea to Carlos Alberto and Rogerio, both of whom approved, and Piazza was the next to join in. It wasn't long before twenty or so players were holding regular prayer meetings. 'There was nothing obligatory about the meetings. Not all the delegation were Catholic, and not all the Catholics felt like joining us, nor was there ever any pressure on them to do so,' explains Pelé. 'The idea was to unite us, not to separate us. Every evening we found a different motive as the basis for our prayers. We prayed for the poor, for the crippled, for the sick; we prayed for the victims of war in Vietnam, for the innocent victims of all wars, for the health of loved ones, and while we never prayed to win, we did pray that nobody would be hurt in any game, on either side.'

At first a small group would meet in one of the hotel rooms, but as it mushroomed, they gathered under a tree after dinner every evening. Each night a different player would offer a different prayer. 'Soon we had everybody from the cook to the president of the delegation,' says Piazza. 'There was a spiritual force, it made us feel united as a group and it gave us confidence when we came to the first games.'

Pelé felt it would have 'degraded the meaning of prayer' to pray

for victory, but believed that, by increasing the players' mutual
respect and understanding, the meetings nonetheless helped
them to achieve their goal.

CHAPTER 7

DATE WITH DESTINY

*'Brazil will only lose the Cup if they break the leg of Pelé,
the arm of Tostão, the knees of Gerson, the head of Rivelino
or if they kill all our team!'*
Gerson

Pelé knew this would be his last World Cup. He might even have been aware that he was about to achieve immortality. But if he was, there was certainly not to be any self-indulgence. He was never extravagant at the expense of the team effort or their quest for a result. And although the rest of the world was about to witness a wonderful event, it was not some cosmic happening, a spontaneous meeting of minds. It was put together by a master coach in Zagallo, and it had taken him a long time to acknowledge that Tostão and Pelé could function together.

The concern had centred on an injury to Tostão in the Brazil National Cup in 1968. He had been hit in the eye by the ball and needed surgery in Houston. Although he subsequently performed brilliantly and combined wonderfully with Pelé in the qualifiers under Saldanha, afterwards he had had to return to Texas for a further operation. As a consequence he had an understandable aversion to heading the ball for fear of permanent damage if he was hit in the same eye.

There was improvisation in abundance in this side, but it was underpinned by an organisational foundation, a framework, planning and discipline – a forerunner of total football. And Pelé was, at twenty-nine, in his best-ever condition entering his fourth World Cup. Such was his boundless energy, vigour and commitment that he was involved in virtually everything that occurred on the field.

Yet Brazil were not without their critics in the build-up to the tournament. Pundits pointed to a vulnerability in their defence. Before their first match, against Czechoslovakia, Pelé was fired up by comments made by the Czechs' outspoken coach, Joseph Marko, who dismissed him as a 'spent force'. The Brazilian press, meanwhile, seized on a Mexican computer prediction that Pelé would be injured in the first half and play no further part in the tournament.

As Pelé and Brazil lay in wait, England came to the World Cup with arguably the best team in their history, superior even to the one which had won the Jules Rimet Trophy in 1966. Bobby Moore's legendary composure remained intact throughout his extraordinary ordeal over the bracelet, which in no way affected his performance on the pitch. England beat Romania 1–0 in their opening match and prepared to take on Brazil, who began with a 4–1 unhinging of Czechoslovakia at the Jalisco Stadium in Guadalajara on 3 June.

In the wake of the draw in Mexico City, Pelé had ranked the Czechs alongside Brazil, England and Italy as the favourites. Captain Carlos Alberto recalled the moments before he led out the team for their first match of the World Cup. His last-minute prayers went out to his players. 'Brazilian players do have the habit of praying,' he said. 'We pray that He will be good with us even if he forgets the other team.' Other than that there were just a few words of encouragement. "Let's go, people – Pelé, take care of your back." Things like that.'

Brazil were a goal down in eleven minutes. Yet they were, from the very beginning, intent on reminding the world that their first round exit in England four years earlier had been an aberration. Nevertheless, when Petráš opened the scoring for Czechoslovakia, all the pre-match warnings of Brazil's weaknesses in defence prompted commentator David Coleman to utter the immortal words: 'All we have heard about them has come true.' Pelé was not worried. He had already come to the conclusion that the Czechs were not as good as their pre-tournament hype.

Rivelino equalised in the twenty-fourth minute with a swerving free-kick cannonball, after Pelé was fouled. Then, early in the second half, Gerson, from deep midfield, hit a fifty-yard pass to Pelé who, despite close defensive scrutiny, trapped the ball on his chest, turned and struck the volley all in one magical movement for a breathtaking goal. Clodoaldo dropped to his knees and cried in appreciation. Jairzinho scored the third and fourth. Pelé had been concerned that he had looked nervous before the tournament started, but there was nothing apprehensive about the way he took his two goals.

Pelé's influence on the match was mesmerising. Near the interval, for example, he took possession in his own half and moved forward, still inside the Brazilian sector of the centre circle, and shot with his right foot. The Czech keeper, Viktor, was yards off his line, and made a forlorn, embarrassing effort to scramble back as the ball looped beyond him but missed the upright by just a yard. 'Now I really have seen everything,' gasped the BBC's David Coleman.

It seemed an impromptu move, but in fact it had been carefully choreographed in advance by Pelé. He had intended using the long shot after seeing so many European goalkeepers stray off their lines. 'I wish I'd saved it for a more difficult adversary,' he chided himself. He would really have liked to have tried it against England, but once he had demonstrated it, no keeper ever left his line again, for fear that it might be brought into play. It was a shot that inspired generations of players after him, including David Beckham, who actually achieved it against Wimbledon.

Carlos Alberto had witnessed such wildly extravagant moves every week with Santos. 'Pelé was a player who, besides having a great technique – his acceleration, his heading – had great secret improvisation,' he says. 'Those things were done in one moment. He had an extraordinary perception of the game. Against Czechoslovakia he was the only player who realised the goalkeeper had advanced. Everybody was astonished. Some of the players shouted, "Are you crazy?" but when we saw the goalkeeper far from the goal and the ball almost going in...'

Those who thought that Pelé was past his best were proved horribly wrong. His performance also silenced the constant sniping of Saldanha. 'So much for myopia,' Pelé sniped back. But he was well aware of the dangers of complacency and over expectation of success. In the dressing room after the game, according to Piazza, Pelé clapped his hands and made a short speech. He said they had played well, but they must improve. Then he sat down beside Piazza. 'He knew what kind of person I was. He told me, "Piazza, if we don't say this there will be guys who will think that we are already champions."'

England were next up. 'We knew their defence was formidable;

it always had been and still was,' says Pelé. 'If they managed to score against us, I was afraid that Brazil might never reach the quarter-finals.' To counter this strength, Zagallo had a surprise for his players. People were looking forward to seeing how the Brazilian attacking game would fare against the primarily defensive style of England, but Zagallo decided that Brazil would play England at their own game. It would be like a game of chess. The first one to make a mistake would pay for it, probably with the championship of the world.

England's Bobby Charlton had played against Pelé only once before, when England lost to Brazil by five goals at the Maracana after the 1958 World Cup. He recalled an incident before the 1970 match that would be considered quite inappropriate these days, yet thirty years ago it passed by with hardly a mention. To fulfil a request for a photograph which had been agreed to, he and Bobby Moore went to Brazil's training session and ended up sitting around and having a social conversation with Pelé, who was keen to chat to them. Such evidence of sportsmanship and of the bonds between participants before the heat of battle would make the headlines now. Even then, nobody chancing to catch sight of the players chatting would have dreamed how much depended on the outcome of the game. Such a scene would very soon become a thing of the past, for a new age of cynicism was already dawning.

On the eve of the clash between the holders and previous winners, a combination good enough to grace any final, Brazilian fans swelled by Mexicans descended on the Guadalajara Hilton, the city-centre hotel where the England team were staying. The chants of 'Brazil! Brazil!' went on throughout the night, to the accompaniment of blaring car horns. The England players moved to rooms on the top floor at the back of the hotel and snatched what sleep they could, emerging the next day as if nothing had happened. That was the Ramsey way. The Brazilians travelled to the stadium in festive mood, the players beating out the *batucada*, the carnival rhythms, on anything at hand.

There was one piece of good news for England: Gerson was out with a thigh injury, though his replacement, Paulo César, was an unknown quantity to Ramsey's men. Their main concern, however, was how to stop Pelé. The idea was to prevent him from playing, the sort of tactic they would use at home against players of the calibre of Jimmy Greaves or George Best. Alan Mullery, now a high-profile radio and Sky TV analyst, was the player entrusted with the daunting task of marking Pelé. He saw it as the biggest challenge of his career. 'Alf saw me looking nervous and said to me, "If you were not good enough to play against this fella, you would be back home watching it on the telly." That helped me, and I went out and played one of the best games I have ever played. But I don't think we'll see one like him again.'

Mullery had already performed this function once before, when England had played Brazil the previous year in Rio. He explained:

> To be honest, I was a bit disappointed in the way Pelé played the first time I marked him. I know they beat us 2–1, but he didn't really put himself out too much and seemed a touch disinterested in the game. That certainly wasn't his attitude the second time I faced him. Then it was the World Cup, and he meant business, all right, so it turned out to be a vastly different kettle of fish. They were just superb, the best I've ever seen them, and Pelé was magnificent. It was an absolutely fantastic performance from him and the team.

Six years later, Mullery was in a shop at London Airport, queuing to pay for something, when he noticed that the man in front of him was buying a book with a photograph of himself and Pelé during their World Cup encounter on the front. It was Pelé's autobiography. 'The fellow, a foreign guy, looked at the cover, looked at me and nearly fainted. He asked me: "Is that you in the picture?" His legs began to wobble, he was so surprised. I was pretty pleased. That is most definitely my favourite picture of my career, because it evokes such great memories of such a great guy. It showed me chasing Pelé, and I think I am still trying to catch him up.'

Temperatures soared to ninety-eight degrees at the ridiculously timed noon kick-off, scheduled according to the demands of lucrative European broadcasting contracts. The heat obviously affected the England players far more than the Brazilians. During the game, every England player lost around ten pounds in weight, some even more. Pelé wasn't the only player who had to be stopped. The match was the classic contest between the samba rhythm of the Latins and a culture of football steeped in the traditions of team spirit, hard graft and organisation. This time, however, the reigning world champions were parading perhaps the nation's most gifted team as well. And they didn't come much more gifted than goalkeeper Gordon Banks. This clash in the Jalisco Stadium will always be remembered as the one in which Banks saved Pelé's majestic goal-bound header. As an eighteen-year-old I was glued to every kick of this World Cup tie on TV, like millions of fellow armchair fans, and it has been rerun an inexhaustible number of times since. But it is perhaps only now, with the new technology of digital freeze-frame slow motion, that the athleticism and sheer poetry of the movement can be properly appreciated.

In the tenth minute Jairzinho accelerated past left-back Cooper and raced to the line before delivering the worst possible cross, to English hearts: straight towards Pelé. Pelé hurtled over Alan Mullery, and leaped to place a perfect header towards the bottom corner of the goal. To Pelé's mind the header was spot-on as the keeper was in the opposite corner. He was already shouting 'Goal!' as Banks, distorting his body like a salmon leaping up a waterfall, threw himself into the air and managed to tip the ball so that it slid over the crossbar. 'He came from nowhere,' said an incredulous Pelé. 'One moment he was by the right-hand post as I headed down, the next moment, no, the same moment, he was by the left-hand post and he'd scooped the ball up and over the bar.'

Bobby Moore smiled and ruffled the hair of the Stoke City goalkeeper while Pelé swore under his breath at being denied a certain goal. Brazilian keeper Felix immediately recognised the magnitude of the Banks save. 'I clapped. It was the best save I have ever seen.' Rivelino was equally amazed. 'That save he made when the *criolo* headed the ball! Perfect!' Pelé concluded later: 'It was, in my opinion, the most spectacular save of the tournament, an impossible play, but Banks made it, and soon afterwards he made an equally impressive save on a free kick which, again, I was sure would be a goal. For me, Banks was the leading goalkeeper of the 1970 games, and quite possibly the leading defender in any position.'

In spite of the overpowering heat, it was a truly remarkable contest, and in spite of the Banks save, the inspired interventions of Bobby Moore and the fact that England were marginally more threatening and deserved a draw, the supernatural awareness of Pelé finally made the difference. The result was sealed for Brazil with a touch of genius when, fourteen minutes into the second half, Tostão embarrassed Moore with a nutmeg before searching out his striker partner, Pelé. With remarkable vision Pelé flicked the ball across to his right for Jairzinho to close in and score. Not even Banks could stop that close-range shot. In what seemed like a split-second Pelé had time to weigh up all the options. He first thought about taking a shot himself, then, spotting that Banks, Labone and Cooper had moved to cover him, he instantly reassessed the situation to feed Jairzinho instead.

Late on Manchester City's Colin Bell replaced teammate Lee, and Jeff Astle came on to replace an exhausted Charlton. Astle missed an easy chance from close range, badly scuffing his shot in front of goal and completely missing the target. Had he scored, perhaps Astle might not have ended up as a figure of fun on TV's *Fantasy Football*.

Despite their defeat, England could take much credit for an exhilarating game and did not suffer too much of a dent to their morale. Brazil, not surprisingly, were euphoric at having beaten the world champions. One of soccer's everlasting images is that of Pelé and Moore exchanging shirts after the game, smiling warmly at each other and embracing, each with a hand on the other's shoulder, conveying across the language barrier the mutual respect of the greatest defender and the greatest forward in the world. Pelé declared that players such as Banks, Moore, Cooper and the Charlton brothers would be good enough for the Brazilian team. Praise indeed.

In a 1976 authorised biography, Moore said: 'I used to love playing against Pelé, because there is no greater satisfaction than impressing against the best in the world. His mere presence on the pitch had to bring out the best in you, because only your best could ever be good enough. Pelé was the most complete player I've ever seen. He had everything.' When Pelé and Moore left the pitch that day, they felt that they would, in all likelihood, meet again in the final.

Overcoming England took its toll. Rivelino was left limping from a twisted ankle, so he was rested for the match against Romania three days later. Piazza and Paulo Cesar were picked in midfield with Fontana at the back. Romania proved awkward opponents. Pelé opened the scoring after just nineteen minutes, Jairzinho adding a second three minutes later, but then Brazil eased off, allowing Romania to narrow the gap.

Brazil needed to win to guarantee first position in their group, and with it the attractive opportunity of remaining in Guadalajara, which had by now turned into a miniature Brazil, for the quarter finals and perhaps a semi-final, too. But the Romanians, still in with a chance themselves, were in a ruthless mood. Romania had learned from England's tight marking game, and the tackling was the fiercest Brazil had encountered so far. According to Pelé, Romania 'confused tackling with street fighting', but this time he had no intention of being kicked out of the tournament. He scored again after the break, sliding in when the Romanians made a mess of a Carlos Alberto cross. Felix conceded a second to Romania late in the game, but Brazil were through by 3–2. Pelé and his team were left with plenty of admiration for the Eastern Europeans, and knew they had made the cardinal error of underestimating them.

The next day, 11 June, England beat Czechoslovakia 1–0 to claim the second quarter-final place from Group 3. They were to meet West Germany in León while Brazil entertained Peru on their 'home' patch. Peru, who had beaten Bulgaria and Morocco in Group 4 in León, were opponents to be feared and respected. Their coach was none other than Didi, Pelé's Brazilian teammate from the 1958 and 1962 World Cup sides. Didi was far from complimentary about Peru's opponents. 'Pelé, Vava, Amarildo, Zito, Zagallo, Djalmar and Gilmar just happened to get together by one of those lucky twists of fate that happen in football. I don't feel Brazil have those players today.' He damned Pelé with faint praise, predicting that he would once again be kicked out of the tournament. 'Pelé will again suffer from close tackling and rough play as he suffered in 1962 and 1966, and he is, although a more seasoned player, almost thirty years old.'

The fact that the players on both sides were used to playing each other, and the Didi connection, made the quarter-final very much a local affair. But for once the local Mexican crowd did not side with Brazil. Peru gained public sympathy because they had reached the finals for the first time in their history, and also because they had recently suffered from earthquakes which had killed thousands of their people.

Zagallo reverted to his first-choice midfield and attack to deal with the Peruvian threat. Rivelino returned, along with Gerson, while the youngest member of the squad, left-back Marco Antonio, came in for the injured Everaldo. It was not a happy experience for Marco Antonio, who was given a torrid time by Gallardo and Cubillas, and it would be his first and last start in the tournament. It was a typically open game between two South American sides intent on attack and showing off their skills, Rivelino opened the scoring in the eleventh minute, after a Pelé cross rebounded off Peruvian full-back Campos to Tostão. He fed Rivelino, who unleashed another of his specialist shots from outside the area. Gallardo pulled one back to make it 2–1 at half-time.

In the second half, Tostão stretched the lead with his first goal of the tournament when he latched on to a high, curved pass from Pelé, raised his foot and deflected the ball, rather than kicking it, past a confused Rubinos. Cubillas added another for Peru before Jairzinho finished matters at 4–2, keeping up his feat of scoring in every game, which he would succeed in maintaining right to the end.

Brazil looked formidable, their artistry and grace combining as a force that was now unstoppable. When the players returned to the dressing room, the battle between the Soviet Union and Uruguay to decide who would meet Brazil in the semi-final had gone into extra time. Instead of showering, the Brazilians sat by their radio to listen to the rest of the game. Espárrago's late goal ensured an all-South American tie. The players all smiled grimly at each other. This would be a different match entirely from Peru, not least for historical reasons. In 1950, when Brazil had hosted the World Cup and created the Maracana, the largest stadium ever built, as a suitable setting for what they assumed would be a Brazilian triumph, the Uruguayans had thwarted their dream. Ever since that nightmare in Rio, if there was ever a nation to induce paranoia in the masters of the world game, it was Uruguay. And the two countries had not played a World Cup tie since.

Meanwhile England's quarter-final tie against West Germany had ended in disaster. Gordon Banks, the hero of the hour against Brazil, had been ruled out by food poisoning, reputedly caused by a dubious bottle of beer. Into his place stepped Chelsea's Cat, Peter Bonetti, who has for ever carried the can for the heart-wrenching elimination of a side superior to the one that eventually won the World Cup. But there were other pertinent reasons, indeed, grave errors, that contributed to their downfall.

England had been 2–0 up twenty minutes from the end, and their semi-final place seemed assured. The Germans' substitutions had freshened up their side as the players began to wilt in the oppressive heat. Ramsey then made an error of judgement, replacing a tiring Bobby Charlton and Martin Peters with Colin Bell and Norman Hunter. At the time it seemed a logical move to save two key players for the next big match. Ramsey thought it was all over, but it wasn't this time. Yes, the first German goal was

Bonetti's fault – he went down too late for a Franz Beckenbauer shot and the ball skimmed embarrassingly under his body. Banks, of course, would have saved it. But there lies a problem, that Ron Greenwood tried to resolve by alternating Peter Shilton with Ray Clemence: that a reserve keeper often has little if any experience of such high-pressure World Cup ties. Banks would have been sharper to such play, whereas Bonetti, irrespective of his prowess at club level, just didn't have the experience.

Things went from bad to worse when Uwe Seeler stole unmarked into the England box for an equaliser to drag the game into extra time, where Gerd Muller claimed the winner to avenge West Germany's defeat in the final four years earlier. Bonetti never again played for England, while Sir Alf began his descent of the slippery slope leading to the sack when England failed to qualify for the 1974 World Cup.

Brazil were yet again embroiled in political infighting prior to their South American semi-final 'derby' with Uruguay. Uruguay opposed the Guadalajara venue, which they saw as virtually a home ground for Brazil, and demanded a switch to Mexico City. When their protests were ignored, they responded by deliberately arriving late for the game and refusing to attend the governor's reception. The night before the game against their bogey team was a tense one for the Brazilians. The universal entreaty from their countrymen was, in effect, lose the World Cup, fine, but don't lose this match. 'We could not afford to lose,' said Pelé, 'or we would have trouble facing a single soul when we got back to Brazil.'

At the Jalisco Stadium, Uruguay's tactics on the pitch were just as defensive as their political ones – and brutal to boot. They deployed a man-for-man marking regime with Pelé shadowed by Castillo, Gerson by Cortes. Brazil's nervousness in the form of an error by Bruto and a basic goalkeeping mistake from Felix, resulted in a grotesquely soft opening goal for Cubilla in the nineteenth minute. The Brazilians were on the very edge of despair, none more so than Gerson.

It was Pelé who rallied his troops. He darted through their stationary, demoralised ranks to collect the ball from the Brazilian net and carried it purposefully back to the centre circle, issuing words of encouragement as he went. It was a stirring message of defiance and determination, and it sent all the right signals to his teammates. The delightful seventeen-year-old adored in Sweden had come of age: now he was the father figure of the team, a true leader as well as a genius. As the Brazilian football writer Armando Nogueira commented: 'For the first time Pelé and Brazil shared the same destiny. In the past there had always been two entities. Their objectives may have been similar, but they moved towards them separately. In the past he had never been a leader, not even at Santos. Now Brazil and Pelé were integrated. He was leading this team to their destiny.'

Both Pelé and Gerson began to move to a variety of positions to shake off their markers. The intelligent and enterprising Gerson changed places with defender Clodoaldo to confuse the man-marking system, and the defender grabbed the equaliser in injury time at the end of the first half. From that moment the Brazilians were convinced that they would reach the final. But there were still pockets of self-doubt, as Tostão testified. 'Zagallo, who had a reputation for calmness, was behaving like a man possessed. He was calling everybody names, condemning the team for not fighting bravely enough, for having no soul. He did not say a word about football. All he talked about was the *camisa antarela*, the yellow shirt of Brazil, and what it meant to wear it.'

Twice Pelé came close to fulfilling his declared intention to score a unique goal. Before the match, watching film of the

Uruguayans in action, he had spotted how the keeper often kicked a short, punted pass to his midfield. Towards the end of the first half Pelé chose his moment. Turning suddenly as he trotted back to the halfway line, he slipped past a defender to run on to Mazurkiewicz's flat kick and volleyed a waist-high thunderbolt straight back at him from forty yards. The keeper reacted just in time, wrapping himself around the ball.

Zagallo regained his cool just long enough to make an adjustment during the interval, pushing Rivelino further to the right in midfield to allow Pelé and Tostão more space to exploit space on the left. More importantly, the yellow shirt was worn with pride in the second half. Fourteen minutes from the end, Jairzinho scored his sixth goal in five games from a Tostão pass, to put Brazil ahead. Finally, late in the game, Pelé dragged the defence out of position and stroked a pass into the stride of Rivelino, who cracked in the third with obvious glee.

Pelé had one last trick up his sleeve. With just a minute left, Tostão split the defence leaving Pelé one-to-one with Mazurkiewicz. It was only when Pelé veered off to his right that the keeper suddenly realised with shock that he had not taken the ball with him. Pelé had pulled off the mother of all dummies on the Uruguayan goalkeeper, allowing the ball to roll one way and going round him on the other side. Sadly, Pelé was once again denied his ultimate goal when his shot struck the post. But the old enemy had been put to the sword.

In the other semi-final, England's conquerors, West Germany, had gone down to Italy, the side responsible for dispatching Mexico in the quarter-finals. So now the entire host nation took Brazil to their hearts. The Italians had reached the final with an uncharacteristically entertaining and attacking 4–3 extra-time win over the Germans, who were minus the injured

Franz Beckenbauer. Otherwise they had progressed through the tournament with their customary efficiency. Their intentions had been clear from the moment coach Ferruccio Valcareggi announced his squad. The Azzurri arrived in Mexico with three goalkeepers, sixteen defenders and midfield players and only three recognised strikers, one of them the uncapped Gori of Cagliari. Their attack was built around Sardinian Luigi Riva and founded on their infamous *catenaccio* defence.

As the 600 million worldwide audience sat around their TV sets, one man was profoundly confused. Inside his private chambers at the Vatican, Pope Paul VI was torn between his allegiances to the nation of his birth and the world's largest Catholic country. According to the *Jornal do Brazil,* the pontiff would be spending the ninety minutes of the final fighting to suppress his desire to cheer for either side.

Two days before the final, as the Brazilians at last uprooted from the Suites Caribes in Guadalajara to head for Mexico City and even greater altitude, there was a calmness about the players, as if they were aware of their destiny. They might have felt short of breath on first arriving in the capital, but it was mainly a psychological reaction and quickly passed. The Italians had the advantage of having played their early games in Toluca, the highest city in Mexico, and their last game in the Azteca Stadium, the venue for the final.

Tactics were finalised at a series of meetings on the Saturday night and early on Sunday morning. Zagallo had already explained his plan to use Jairzinho to lure Facchetti out of position on the left-hand side. With the Cobras, Pelé, Gerson and Carlos Alberto, he had also stressed their best hope might lie in Italy's exhaustion after their efforts against West Germany only two full days before the final. Though Brazil had had no longer to recover from their semi against Uruguay, they had at least been spared the debilitating effects of extra time.

Both nations had previously won the Jules Rimet Trophy twice, Italy in 1934 and 1938, so there was even more at stake than this tournament alone. The victors, as three-times winners, would take permanent possession of the prize. *Catenaccio*, the famed, feared, and often loathed defensive system that often strangled opponents, was still lodged deep in the Italian psyche, but against Brazil they were meeting their match. Gerson had proclaimed that the Italians were petrified of playing Brazil; that they were terrified of Pelé. Nevertheless, as Pelé explained: 'The pressure one feels in the final is many times the pressure one feels in any of the games leading up to it. The final is everything; it is for the championship and the championship is all that counts. Second place may seem like a reasonable award to be proud of, but who remembers who was placed second to Italy in 1938? Or even to England in 1966? First place is all that counts.'

On 21 June, the temperature in the Azteca Stadium, much to the relief of the players and the 107,000 crowd, was pleasantly cool. From the start Mario Bertini spent much of his time impressing Pelé with his sly repertoire of dodgy defensive 'skills'. Pelé described him as 'an artist in fouling a man without getting caught'. Bertini's art even extended to complaints to the East German referee, Herr Rudi Glöckner, whenever Pelé went down under his challenges. He would run to Herr Glöckner screaming, 'Cinema! Cinema!' It was a classic attempt to provoke a potential match-winner into a reaction that would earn him a sending-off, or alternatively to take him out of the game without being caught by the referee. But Pelé, with his vast experience, was not going to fall for such an obvious trick.

Italy were a goal down after thirty minutes. Rivelino took the ball from a throw-in by Tostão and lofted a cross. His instincts told him that either Jairzinho or Pelé would be under it somewhere. Central defender Tarcisio Burgnich, attempting to assist with Bertini's thankless task, was completely wrong-footed, as Pelé literally hovered in the air. 'He was up there, waiting – it was an incredible thing,' says Rivelino. It was a wonderful goal – one of the headers of this or any tournament. 'We jumped together, then I came down, but he stayed up there,' said an astonished Burgnich. 'I thought Pelé was made of flesh and blood like me. I was wrong.'

Once he had opened the scoring, Pelé, ultra-confident before the game, thought only a gift would give the Italians an equaliser – and that was precisely what happened. A spectacular mistake put the Italians back into contention when Clodoaldo inexplicably back-heeled the ball towards his own goal. It was intercepted by Boninsegna, who rounded Felix.

Now Pelé feared that in that one isolated moment of Brazilian panic, the Italians might suddenly gain the upper hand. He felt that Brazil were more vulnerable at this point than at any other time in the entire tournament. Had the Italians seized the moment, a demoralised Brazil might have wilted. His rare attack of insecurity deepened when, with thirty seconds of the first half still left, Herr Glöckner blew for half-time – just as he was placing the ball once more in Albertosi's net. The suspicion swept over Pelé, leaving him in a cold sweat. 'Were we going to be victimised by a referee from Europe in favour of a European team, as had happened in the past?'

Half-time gave Pelé and his teammates the respite they needed to recover their equilibrium, and in the second half Pelé's fears that the referee might be biased, or had even been 'got at', proved unfounded. Indeed, he was full of praise for the fairness of the refereeing in the rest of the final. Gerson, supported by Pelé, took command, swinging the game back in Brazil's favour with an individualistic goal, collecting the ball deep, beating a defender, and cracking in a twenty-five-yarder after sixty-six minutes. From that moment on there were no more doubts in Pelé's mind about the outcome. Five minutes later, Gerson's free kick found him and, without looking up, he instinctively knew that Jairzinho would be on his outside as he directed Gerson's pass to the striker. Without breaking stride, Jairzinho put the ball away. The finale was a mouth-watering goal three minutes from the end. Tostão won possession ten yards from his own area, linking the first of nine passes. Rivelino, Jairzinho, a cameo dribble from Clodoaldo, Jairzinho to Pelé, then four touches from Pelé as he held up the play outside the Italian area, sensing Carlos Alberto roaring up on the outside.

Carlos Alberto has never stopped thanking Pelé for that goal. 'I never had a powerful shot, but Pelé made me take this one in my stride, and that's why the goalkeeper had no chance. I was lucky. It was the weight of his pass.'

At the end Pelé praised the Italians, if not for their methods during the game, for their sportsmanship and for the way they accepted defeat. 'You might have thought Bertini was my brother from the way he shook my hand enthusiastically and hugged me.' The expression of undiluted joy at the 4–1 victory was almost as flamboyant as the football itself. When the final whistle sounded, a sea of supporters ran on to the pitch, heading for Pelé. He hastily removed his shirt – 'I had no intention of being strangled by some delirious fan,' he explained – before they reached him and hoisted him aloft. Within seconds they had torn every piece of kit from his body and he was down to his underpants. Even his boots went.

Amid the lunacy of the dressing room Pelé eventually sought solitude in the shower, where he offered up a little prayer to thank God for all the many things He had done for him along the long road from Três Corações to three World Cup victories and the joy of scoring in a final. But if he thought the shower was the one place he would gain some privacy, he was wrong. 'I was immediately invaded by an army of newspapermen who came right into the shower, clothes and all.'

The players returned to the field to collect the Jules Rimet Trophy for the third time, now theirs to keep. Pelé thought of his family and friends amid all the mayhem, all the hugs and kisses. 'I thought of my wife and Kelly Cristina, of my mother and father, of my grandmother and Uncle Jorge, of Zoca and Maria Lucia, of my many friends back in Santos. I thought of so many things that in truth I don't remember exactly what I thought!'

Bobby Moore stayed to watch the final. In his authorised biography he said:

> Most people have their own special memory of him. In that match there was the first goal when he curled himself up around a difficult cross and made scoring look easy. Earlier in the tournament there had been the dummy to let the ball run one side of the goalkeeper while he went round the other. That was brilliant even though he screwed the final shot across the face of the goal. Against Uruguay, he picked up a loose clearance on the halfway line, turned and shot just over the bar with their goalkeeper stranded around the penalty spot. Even as a pro with a vantage point in the stand you wondered at first what he was doing. Then you were lost in admiration for the man's vision and appreciation of a situation.

Finally, back at the team hotel, Pelé sought the sanctuary of his room to finish his prayer of thanksgiving – which is why he does not feature in photographs of the festivities at the hotel before the official banquet. 'It was not that I didn't want to be there, or that I thought myself different from the others. It was that I felt a more important responsibility, and that was my duty towards God. I thanked him for our health, I thanked him for the health of our opponents, I asked for a safe journey home for all who had participated in the tournament, and then I had to stop because my room was being invaded.'

A call came through from Emilio Medici, the president of Brazil, who congratulated the players and spoke personally to Pelé and some of his senior teammates. Only the president could have got through. The lines were so jammed by journalists that Pelé couldn't get one to phone home.

The team bade farewell to Mexico and moved on to a presidential welcome in Brasilia, then Rio, and still it was impossible for Pelé to get a call through to Rosemeri, who was seven months pregnant with their second child. João Havelange told him that his wife was desperately trying to reach him. Eventually, after much arguing with operators and standing by the phone for ages, he finally got his call at three o'clock in the morning.

There was to be one final, unscheduled stop at São Paulo, but not for Pelé. He rented an air-taxi at dawn and flew home to his family, an early departure from the celebrations that was criticised by some sections of the media. Pelé, however, felt he would be judged more reasonably by the public.

In the wake of Brazil's triumph, the analysis of how they had pulled it off was everywhere. Would they have won the World Cup for a third time if they had not jettisoned their coach so close to the finals? Or was it simply down to the genius of Pelé and the players?

Gerson, the balding midfielder, believed that it would have been no different had Saldanha been left in charge. But Zagallo, who as a player had contributed vitally, if unspectacularly, to the winning of the tournament in 1958 and 1962, undoubtedly made a difference with his steadier approach, He had instigated the recall of Felix, discarded by Saldanha, though the keeper's erratic form hardly proved a point there. But it was Zagallo, too, who had tightened and clarified the tactics, emphasising the value of both defence and attack, the basis of his own effectiveness as a player. He it was who jettisoned the use of án orthodox left winger such as Edu and asked Rivelino to operate as a midfielder with the freedom to attack along that flank. Again, this was a throwback to his own game, where he had been nicknamed Formiginha, or Little Ant, for his tireless foraging up and down the left side of a 4–3–3 formation. Rivelino's interpretation of the role embraced more creativity.

It was the clinical assessment of Dr Eduardo Gonçalvez (Tostão until he took his medical degree) that Zagallo advanced the team tactically. 'He has not been given proper credit for his achievement. In our team there was a perfect integration of defence, midfield and attack. Under Saldanha we were entertaining, but the team did not have a sound structure.' Tostão was particularly impressed by the way Zagallo accommodated Gerson and Rivelino so that they complimented each other.

But there was no doubt, either, that Pelé had been the inspirational force. Tostão, a major influence himself, recognises this. 'I understood why Pelé was the best player in the world. He passed the ball well; he was intelligent, a warrior in the field, growing with each moment. There was no weakness, excess or pain in his football. It was simplicity itself. On the field I soon understood the movement of his eyes, his body, his thoughts, before the ball arrived.'

DATE WITH DESTINY

Pelé and his teammates enjoyed a $20,000 bonus, big bucks at the time, but the real pot of gold belonged to those who believed in Pelé and Brazil's vision of the beautiful game. A billion people witnessed Pelé's magic in the 1970 final. His performances in these six World Cup games were sublime, never to be repeated. And they never were, for he never again played in the World Cup.

CHAPTER 8

THE POLITICAL GAME: THE WORLD CUP 1974

'They moulded the best and most complete footballer when they made Pelé. That mould was broken up when he finished, and it has never been made again.'
Alan Mullery

The aftermath of the 1970 World Cup marked a new phase in Pelé's life. On 27 August, his first son – Edson Cholby do Nascimento – soon to be nicknamed Edinho by his family and by his godfather, Professor Julio Mazzei – was born. He now wanted to spend more time with his family and less travelling the world. He also wanted to concentrate on his business and to study for a university degree in physical education.

He made up his mind to finish his career with the national team at the end of the season after the World Cup victory. He would not accept any invitation to play in the 1974 World Cup finals. He explained that:

It was not a matter of age or physical condition – my

condition was excellent, as evidenced by my performances at the 1970 games, and, as for my age, in 1974 I would still be only thirty-three years old, and Djalmar Santos and Nilton Santos had both played World Cup football at the age of thirty-eight. I wanted to leave the national team while I was fit and in good enough condition to continue if I had wanted to. I didn't want to wait until the fans were booing me off the pitch.

He well remembered how this had happened to Gilmar less than a year after he had helped his country to win the 1962 World Cup. He argued that vacating his place as early as 1971 would give a young player plenty of time to get the experience he would need to be ready for 1974.

There was also a painful political reason. 'By 1971, I was beginning to learn some of the truth about what was going on in my country, the torture, the killings, the disappeared,' he said later. 'I didn't want to pull on a Brazilian shirt while the military were running the country.'

Pelé's farewell international was played at the Maracana – where else – against Yugoslavia, in front of 180,000 people. Naturally it was a highly charged occasion for him. At the end of the game he performed an emotional lap of honour, waving to the crowd, who responded, as they had throughout the game, with chants of 'Fica! Fica!' Stay. He held up his number 10 to the fans, the shirt he had worn with great pride for fourteen years, and dried his tears with it.

On the domestic front, his club contract ran until the end of 1972. He decided to renew it one more time for an additional two years. However, he made his plans for retirement public to give Santos plenty of time to find a replacement for him. Instead they scheduled as many matches as possible to make as much money as they could while he was still wearing their colours.

In the late 1990s, Manchester United were pilloried for taking £2 million in match fees and for promotional work by touring Australia, China and the Far East before a season in which they complained about fixture overload and opted out of the FA Cup. This was nothing compared to what Santos were doing nearly thirty years earlier in an era in which selling television rights for huge amounts of money was unknown. They were more like the Harlem Globetrotters. 'We played around a hundred games,' says Pelé. 'Yes, it got to a hundred games. Santos were a club who had to pay a lot of money for its players, so they played many games on top of their Brazilian League commitments. January and February in Latin America, June and July in Europe. Every year we would go on tours. At this time there was no concept of selling TV rights for large amounts of money.'

In every European country they visited they would buy up everything – jeans, shirts, every conceivable thing – to take home to their families. 'You'd come back loaded up like Santa Claus. Today you have everything here in São Paulo. You don't have to move out of the city for anything. Such a different time. What makes me feel sad as a human being is that today it's a much more commercial world than it used to be. People sell themselves much easier than they used to do.'

In the first six weeks of 1971, Santos toured South and Central America plus the Caribbean. It was in Jamaica that Pelé first met Clive Toye. The players were sitting around the pool relaxing prior to a game when three men introduced themselves: Clive Toye, head of the New York Cosmos; Phil Woosnam, a Welshman, who would become commissioner of the North American Soccer League; and Kurt Lamm, at that time connected with the American Football League.

Toye sat on the edge of one of the sun-loungers and started talking to Pelé. Professor Mazzei interpreted as the Brazilian did not understand too much English. Toye told him how the soccer league formed in the States in 1968, using mostly imported players, had failed, and that they were now forming. a new league, better financed with higher expectations of success. With improved public relations, and some big-name foreign stars, they felt they had the recipe for success.

Of course, there was no name bigger than Pelé's. Toye asked him whether he would consider joining them when his Santos contract expired. 'When the professor finished putting that into Portuguese, I stared at Clive Toye a moment,' says Pelé. 'The New York Cosmos? He had to be joking!' When Pelé declined Toye's offer, he suggested that Pelé discuss the proposition with his family. They were prepared to do just about anything to get him. The answer was still no. Pelé had been offered large sums to play for Barcelona, Real Madrid, or any of the top Italian clubs; he had been offered a blank cheque to play in Mexico. His answer was always the same. Having turned down these giants, why on earth would he want to play in New York? The executives took their leave assuring him that they wouldn't give up.

As Pelé contemplated a career when his playing days came to an end, there was no shortage of opportunities and offers. In 1971 Pelé was approached by Henry Stampleman, representing Pepsi Cola, who wanted him to teach football, planning their soccer schools around Santos's profusion of worldwide tours. Pelé liked their ideas, and after an initial one-year contract worked out well, a new five-year contract was signed. Professor Mazzei was also involved. They eventually made an instructional film, *Pelé – The Master and His Methods*, to educate children in the arts and skills of the game.

In addition Pelé finally opened his own offices on the fifth floor of a block at 121 Rua Riachuelo in Santos, where he established the Pelé Administration and Advertising Co. In came Jose Rodrigues to manage the offices, and Uncle Jorge handled the accounting. Business boomed, and he soon moved from the fifth floor to take over the entire third floor. By this time he felt confident he could stand on his own two feet in business. He had successfully negotiated the Pepsi contract on his own, so he decided to dispense with the services of his agent, Marby Ramundini, who remained a friend.

Changes were afoot at Santos, too. New directors replaced Antoninho, who had been the coach since 1967, when Lula retired, with Mauro. The new directors also wanted to dismiss Professor Mazzei, but Mauro refused. A year later Mauro was himself sacked, and replaced by Jair da Roas Pinto, who eventually got rid of the professor. It was a great personal blow to Pelé. The distressing dismissal of the professor took place in April 1972. Pelé's contract with Santos expired in the October of the same year, though he had, of course, extended it by another two years. Now he decided it was time for a contract on his terms, rather than along the lines of previous deals to which he had consented. If Santos were to earn money from Pelé's appearances, he should profit from them, too.

Pelé was criticised in sections of the media for making 'insane' demands, but he felt his negotiations were reasonable. By this time he had played over 1,100 games for Santos, half of them abroad, where the match fees of around $20,000 were reduced by half if Pelé did not appear. In previous contracts Santos had paid Pelé's income tax, but the law no longer permitted this, so his wages now looked much higher in comparison. He was accused by the press of delusions of grandeur because he wanted a hotel suite whenever the team played abroad. His argument was that he had to entertain heads of state and couldn't do this in a single room. He also felt that it was an illusion that he was the highest-paid player in the world. In fact he didn't think he was even the highest paid in Brazil. Pelé compromised with a final offer, which Santos accepted. He would play on for a final two years, one year on his terms, and one year for 'free'. Instead, the club would pay his salary to charity.

Brazilian players had even less protection under the law at that time than the rest of the country's workforce. There had been attempts to form a union, but these had fizzled out. Pelé felt it was time something was done about this. He approached other leading players and they formed a committee which went to Brasilia for an audience with the president. As a football fan, they felt he would be sympathetic to their cause. As a result, changes were made, but it would be five years before Pelé saw them come to fruition. This was the start of Pelé's move into the political arena of the sport, and it would not be the end by any means.

Difficulties over money were not confined to contractual matters. Pelé's match fees caused a more practical problem on one of his last tours for Santos, in 1973. It was a long and arduous tour that started in Australia and took in Saudi Arabia, Kuwait, Qatar, Bahrain, Egypt, the Sudan and various European venues. Having played their final match in England, Pelé, accompanied by his wife Rosemeri, and the rest of the team were on their way to Paris for a short break before returning home.

At the airport security check, the security officer opened Pelé's attaché case to reveal a mountain of cash. He immediately called over a customs officer, whose eyes widened at the sight of all this money. Looking up from the case, he considered Pelé carefully and, with typical British politeness, said: 'That's quite a bit of money you're carrying, sir.' It certainly was – over $90,000. Having played twelve games, Pelé had finally collected his earnings for the entire tour in London, and was carrying them with him as the safest means of getting them back to Brazil and into the bank.

By a supreme irony Pelé seems to have encountered one of the few people on the planet who didn't recognise him. By this time most of the Santos directors were already in the departure lounge preparing to board the plane. Despite Pelé's explanations, hampered by the language barrier, the customs officer was convinced that English taxes should be due on the money and was insisting that Pelé proved it was his. A group of reporters, some of whom had come to see them off, had gathered but, according to Pelé, none of them was inclined to ruin a potentially good story by identifying him and helping him out. Fortunately, one of the Santos management board had not yet passed customs, and he had to stay behind and locate the entrepreneur who had arranged the English game to confirm Pelé's innocence. The plane had long gone by the time they managed to convince customs, the security staff and the Metropolitan Police that the money was really his and Pelé and Rosemeri were permitted to leave. 'Since then I go in and out of England with an absolute minimum in cash,' says Pelé, 'I take credit cards instead.'

Although Pelé had retired from international football, his influence continued to be felt off the field. His patronage was a key factor in João Havelange's successful bid for the presidency of FIFA. The highest office in FIFA had always been held by Europeans, but Havelange had been plotting to take control, and after Brazil took possession of the coveted Jules Rimet Trophy he escalated his campaign.

Pelé's mere presence gave kudos to the Havelange campaign trail. He accompanied Havelange on his 1971–2 election tour of Africa, where Pelé's stature was immense. During the civil war between Nigeria and the breakaway state of Biafra in 1967, the wholesale slaughter was halted for twenty-four hours on both sides so that the people could watch Pelé take part in an exhibition game. Santos had toured all over Africa – Kinshasa, Brazzaville, Libreville, Abidjan, Cotonou, Lagos – and everywhere they went Pelé was treated less like a head of state than as a god. Havelange took full advantage of this. If there was a vote at stake, he called upon Pelé to be available for social events.

Having Pelé at his side did Havelange's cause immeasurable good. In spite of accusations – strenuously denied, and yet to be adequately proven – that Havelange offered inducements to secure votes, the Brazilian outmanoeuvred and finally defeated England's Sir Stanley Rous at the FIFA Congress in Frankfurt to become the new FIFA president.

Once Havelange had been elected, preparations for the 1974 World Cup in West Germany got underway. Pelé was invited to take part in the opening ceremony along with the former West German captain, the popular Uwe Seeler, an old friend as well as an opponent. It was a fitting and symbolic ritual in which Seeler presented Pelé with the Jules Rimet Trophy that Brazil had now won outright, while Pelé handed over the new FIFA World Cup Trophy.

For once Pelé was attacked by the foreign media. It was reported that he had demanded a $20,000 fee to take part in the opening ceremony. Pelé was shocked, and made a point of issuing a statement making it clear that he never asked for a fee, nor would have done. He had his problems with his own press, too. He was working at the World Cup as a commentator for a Brazilian television network, Banderantes Television, and as the figurehead of Pepsi Cola's public-relations network at the tournament. Many were nervous at the platform this gave him. The Brazilian media were critical of his TV work, suggesting that he was not equipped to comment and that he was depriving a professional journalist of a job. It was no more than the usual press sniping, but in those days, like most people in the public eye, he was extremely sensitive to it.

Yet this quietly spoken, mild-mannered man had another side to his character, which would emerge as he grew more outspoken in his views on the game. During the tournament he was to become a magnet for the media, who sought his opinions on every conceivable subject. But he refused to allow himself to be turned into a sideshow. He declined to put on his famous yellow number 10 shirt once again, despite an offer of £200,000 from sponsors Adidas to attract maximum press and public interest.

Brazil were playing in Group 2 with Scotland, Yugoslavia and Zaire. There were only three survivors from the 1970 team – Paulo César, Rivelino and Jairzinho. Tostão had been forced to quit on medical grounds. The night before their opening game against Yugoslavia, Pelé went to the Brazilian camp in Frankfurt to wish them luck. His conversation with Paulo César exemplified the new commercialism that was to become a hallmark of the Havelange years. Pelé thought that maybe Cesar would want to talk about possible tactics for the match, or how the training had been going for Brazil's opponents, but instead César asked him for his opinion on something that was obviously more important to him. 'Pelé, I've been offered a fantastic transfer to a French club once the World Cup is over. I'll be paid far more than I'm getting now. I'm going to accept, but I don't know if I should ask for more. It's a real problem. What do you think?'

Pelé couldn't believe his ears. This was what was preoccupying his former teammate just a few hours before a World Cup game? He advised César: 'Forget the offer and concentrate on the games you have to play, starting with the one against Yugoslavia tomorrow. When you've won the Cup, then think about the offer. But if that's all that's on your mind, I don't think you'll be seeing the final.'

Brazil were clear favourites to retain the World Cup, but Pelé detected that morale was not as high as everyone had been led to believe by the Brazilian press. Even so, the world champions would take some beating. Zagallo had altered tactics to adapt his side to the increasingly defensive leanings in world football, and there were no longer enough strong characters in the team to convince the coach to change his mind. The result was goalless draws against Yugoslavia and Scotland. In the second match Pelé was surprised and alarmed to see that there was more rough stuff from Brazil than from the Scots. Not even a 3–0 win over Zaire convinced him that Brazil were emerging from their defensive shell. He thought against such modest opposition they ought to have won by ten.

For the first time since 1950, the format of groups was extended to the later stages, with the last eight playing in two second-stage groups. There were no semi-finals; instead places in the final and the third-place play-off went to the winners and runners-up respectively of each group. Brazil qualified for Group A along with East Germany, Holland and Argentina. The first three had been Pelé's pre-tournament predictions: his fourth, Italy, had succumbed to Poland.

Brazil beat East Germany 1–0 in the first of these matches, but it was such an unconvincing win that the fans remained disgruntled. One bunch of them even stoned Zagallo's house. It was hardly likely to prompt a change of heart in the coach. Brazil's 2–1 victory over Argentina, notwithstanding their continuing defensive approach, convinced him that he had a winning formula.

Against a Dutch display of total football in Dortmund, the Brazilians turned into hatchet men. Luis Pereira was sent off six minutes from the end for hacking down Neeskens, and another five players were booked. Holland won 2–0 with two wonderful goals from Neeskens and Cruyff. Pelé had seen the warning signs when he watched the Dutch excel in beating Uruguay. He compared them with the Brazil sides of 1958 and 1962. He was particularly impressed with Johann Cruyff, dubbed the 'white Pelé', though Pelé never thought of him in those terms: 'He was a genius at the game of football in his own right.'

Although he was obviously upset by Brazil's exit from the tournament, Pelé did not go along with the popular verdict that his home country had resorted to foul play. He said:

> The press in England and indeed throughout Europe blamed Brazil for the violence. What I did not see in the papers was that the Dutch were just as bad. They were just more cunning about it. They knew how to foul and how to hurt without getting caught. After that game I went into the Brazilian dressing room. It was like a hospital. There was not a single member of that team who was injury-free. They had cuts, they had bruises, and Marinho had a gash in one leg from his knee to his ankle.

There was bitterness back in Brazil. Pelé of course took some of the backlash in the form of vitriolic accusations in the press that it was his fault for not participating. He himself felt that his presence would have made no difference, since the fault lay in the tactics rather than with any individual. Havelange, inevitably, found political undertones in the defeat by Holland. 'Because I had been elected president of FIFA and had beaten Sir Stanley Rous, they wanted to get revenge. They designated a referee, the German Kurt Tschenscher, to make sure that Brazil would not be world champions for the fourth time. The sending off of Luis Pereira was totally unjust. There was no way that we could win after that.'

Brazil were reduced to the sideshow play-off for third place in Munich. Poland beat them 1–0 as the crowd booed both teams in a meaningless contest. In the final, meanwhile, hosts West Germany beat Holland to take the new FIFA World Cup Trophy.

Back in Brazil, as the country mourned the demise of their national side, Pelé finally reached the end of his illustrious career with Santos. As might have been expected from the cash-conscious club, they seemed to be making his departure last as long as possible. For a whole month, sell-out crowds flocked to their games in the belief that each one might be Pelé's last, until the curtain really did fall, on 2 October 1974. Against Ponte Preta he was not in absolute top physical condition, but he was determined to go out in style. After twenty minutes he caught the ball and heard the gasps of astonishment from the spectators as he ran with it to the centre of the field, placed it on the centre spot, and knelt down with his knees on either side of the ball. He raised his arms in a cross to face the fans, turning from side to side so that they could all see him and he could see all of them, the fans who had supported him all those years. 'The tears were running down my cheeks without control.'

The fans rose to cheer him on as he did a lap of honour. It was such an emotional experience that he could not carry on. He ran down the tunnel and into the dressing room. There he thought he was alone with his thoughts, his prayers and his tears, but one wily photographer, Domicio Pinheiro from *O Estado,* a São Paulo newspaper, had hidden in the showers. He captured Pelé, as he wept, head bent.

When Pelé left the ground in his car he could still hear the noise of the crowd. He was certain that this would be the last time he would ever play.

CHAPTER 9

THE NEW YORK COSMOS

Pelé had two good feet. Magic in the air. Quick. Powerful.
Could beat people with skill. Could outrun people. Only five ft
eight inches tall yet he seemed a giant of an athlete on the pitch.
Perfect balance and impossible vision.'
Bobby Moore

As Brazil wept at the departure of their hero from one football field, Pelé tried to settle to the nine-to-five existence he craved so that he could see more of his family. As his business empire mushroomed, he hired an economist with business expertise, José Roberto Ribeiro Xisto, to rationalise his affairs. His investments had been made on a very ad hoc basis, often as favours to former teammates or old friends. He had properties all over the country, stores, apartments, land and houses. He had a dairy farm, a trucking company, an import-export business and an interest in a radio station. He had reached the stage where he had lost track of it all.

By 1973, Xisto's rationalisation helped him to shed many of

his poor investments, but there was one that was to prove rather problematical – Fiolax, a company that manufactured rubber components for the automotive industry. He had many partners in this enterprise, including his old teammate Zito; indeed, he was a very minor shareholder, owning only 6 per cent of the company. But as a result of poor legal advice, Pelé signed a note guaranteeing a bank loan for Fiolax. When the company was unable to repay the loan, the bank came to Pelé. Worse still, the government imposed a massive fine on Fiolax for a breach of government regulations relating to the importation of raw materials which had occurred, according to Pelé, through ignorance rather than corruption. Whatever the case, when he went through the papers he had signed on behalf of Fiolax he discovered that he was responsible for any liabilities.

The bank loan and the fine amounted to more than $1 million. Pelé felt the same as he had years earlier when Sanitaria Santista had gone bust: not only that he had been conned, but that he had been made a fool of. Once again, after all the warnings and all the bad experiences, he had signed documents he should not have signed. This time, however, Pelé had the resources to cover the bad debts, and like before, he was not prepared to allow his name to be tarnished by letting a company with which he was connected go bankrupt. It would have meant having to sell some highly profitable properties at cut price to raise the funds, but he could see no other way out.

However, his friends and colleagues had another suggestion to put to him. A delegation came to Pelé's house – Xisto, Professor Mazzei, Pelé's brother Zoca, and Edevar, a former Santos goalkeeper who was now a member of his office staff. Their solution was that he should move to the United States and take up the offer to play for the New York Cosmos made three years earlier and pursued constantly since by Phil Woosnam, who was now running the North American Soccer League. Before Pelé could respond, Xisto asked him to listen to the professor, who had a sheet of paper in his hand on which he had listed all the pros and cons of the plan.

The main negative point was the reaction of the fans and the media if he signed for a foreign club after refusing to play in the World Cup. He had announced the end of his career, and this would be seen as Pelé breaking his word. In addition, being black in the States was very different from being black in Brazil. He would also have to radically improve his grasp of English. In total there were twelve points against the move, but on the other side of the professor's list were eighteen reasons why he should go.

Chief among these was the fact that he would be able to clear all his debts and even come out with a tidy profit. He would be signing for a club with a strong power base, since it was owned by the giant Warner Communications. The opportunities for product endorsements would increase rather than dwindle. On the playing side, in the States there were far fewer games in a much shorter season than he was used to. It would be a good move for the family too: in America Kelly Cristina and Edinho would receive an excellent education.

These were all valid points, but the clinching factor his friends emphasised to Pelé was the enormous opportunity such a deal would give him to make a significant contribution to the game. There were, after all, plenty of other clubs who would pay him just as much money to return from retirement, but it was the chance to widen football's global family that finally lured him to the States.

He delegated the professor to open negotiations. There were meetings in Rome, Belgium, Brazil and the States, all conducted in the strictest secrecy to keep the media from finding out until they were ready to make an official announcement. Pelé hired

Brazil's top lawyer and drove a hard bargain in his negotiations with Warner Communications to earn a contract worth $4.5 million. He also insisted upon, and got, an exchange programme through which American and Brazilian sports coaches could share their expertise. Brazilian trainers would school young Americans in football, while US trainers would teach swimming, basketball and athletics in Brazil. He also persuaded Warner to sponsor a soccer school for the poor children of Santos. In return Pelé would play for the New York Cosmos for three years. During this time, and for a further three years after that, he would also be available to the Licensing Corporation of America, a Warner subsidiary, for promotional work. He would be on a 50 per cent cut of all endorsements. This, coupled with his playing contract, would earn him more in the States than he had made in his entire career with Santos.

At last, after one final all-night conference to hammer out the finer points, Pelé was ready to drop his bombshell on the world – just eight months after his retirement. On 11 June 1975, at the famous 21 Club, Cosmos held a news conference to unveil Pelé, their new thirty-four-year-old signing. The news was received, as anticipated, with a mixture of bewilderment, frustration and even anger in Brazil, where his adoring fans felt personally betrayed. He knew this would be the first serious test of his popularity. To enable Pelé to ride the storm, the package of benefits he had negotiated on behalf of his country had to be emphasised. A formal statement was made by a representative of the United States government declaring that Pelé's arrival would be conducive to relationships between the two nations. This was an idea from Warner Communications designed to appease the Brazilian government. If Pelé and other players of international stature came to the United States, it was argued, then football might finally conquer the one major nation in the world yet to take the game to its heart.

The tactic was, after initial misgivings in Brazil, successful. While the fanfares welcomed Pelé to the States, he was pilloried at first at home in Brazil and branded mercenary. But it wasn't long before the benefits to Brazil were acknowledged and his move to the States began to be hailed as the greatest export deal in the country's history.

New York Cosmos boss Clive Toye had been persuaded to hire Professor Mazzei to prepare the team and act as assistant coach to the Cosmos's Gordon Bradley. So the two families were able to keep each other company as they acclimatised to their new home. There were few problems, however. His relationship with his bosses and other teammates was excellent. Cosmos treated Pelé very well, and in return, Pelé played to the best of his abilities. There was no sense of just being along for the ride.

Pelé watched a couple of Cosmos games and was none too impressed. Then again, the general standard wasn't too high, and he was confident that he could make Cosmos shine 'like a jewel in a cabbage patch'. When he made his debut, against Dallas, 78,700 fans, many of whom had bought tickets six months earlier, came to see the game. It was also shown live on Brazilian TV, the cameras homing in on the banners bearing the grateful message 'Obrigado Brasil' – thank you Brazil.

Before Pelé joined Cosmos, they had lost six games and won three. With Pelé they won seven and lost six. But the season was a struggle. The most notable immediate effect of his arrival was the dramatic increase in the gate. Before Pelé, the average attendance had been 8,000 fans. Now it rose to 20,000, and to 27,000 for exhibition games. If Pelé was injured or out of the team, the attendances dropped back appreciably.

The team, strengthened on Pelé's recommendation by the recruitment of two Santos players, the Brazilian Nelsi Morais and Ramon Mifflin from Peru, set off on a tour of Europe and the Caribbean. Cosmos lost their first game 5–1 in Malmo but came back to win 3–1 against Gothenburg. Memories of the 1958 World Cup in Sweden were revived for Pelé with a big surprise in Gothenburg. At the airport he ran into an old friend: Lena – the girl with whom he had gone out walking, hand in hand, when they were both seventeen, and who had cried when Pelé left – by now married with two children.

On the pitch, another defeat in Stockholm, by a close margin of 3–2, was followed by a 4–2 win in Oslo. The final European game was a 3–1 loss to Roma in Rome. In the Caribbean there were two wins – including a 12–1 drubbing of Puerto Rico – two defeats, and a draw. Pelé's final tally was fifteen goals in twenty-three games. He missed the final match of the tour, in Haiti, to begin his close season travels with Professor Mazzei to teach and coach children at clinics in Mexico and Colombia on behalf of Pepsi Cola.

1975 also brought memories of home, as his sister, Maria Lucia, married a footballer she had known since their days in Bauru.

With his own family settled in the States, he then set off on a far more ambitious tour with Pepsi, a global adventure which turned out to be rather more of an adventure than he had bargained for. As well as taking in Japan, India and Uganda, an attempted coup in Nigeria resulted in Pelé and his entourage being ordered to stay in their hotel. Although the coup failed, there followed a week of mourning for its assassinated leader, during which time the airport remained closed. Finally, after six days of uncertainty, he was able to leave Nigeria, to the great relief of his family, who had feared for his safety.

A major overhaul at Cosmos for the start of Pelé's first full season saw Gordon Bradley made vice-president of player personnel and development, and replaced as coach by Ken Furphy, the ex-Everton, Darlington and Watford player who had managed Sheffield United. As a result in came defender Keith Eddy, midfielder Tony Garbett and striker Tony Field – all from Sheffield United. They were later joined by fellow Englishmen Brian Tinnion and Charlie Aitken. Pelé was not impressed by the appointment of Furphy who, he felt, lacked the ability to motivate. His regime was certainly far more rigid than Bradley's, which many thought was too easy on the players. Pelé also suspected that Furphy thought the Brazilian and South American players overrated. He was opposed to Furphy's defensive-minded strategy, which saw Pelé used in midfield instead of in the forward line, with Mifflin, in Pelé's view just the type of midfield player the team needed, languishing on the bench. He might have put up with Furphy's idiosyncrasies had they made any difference to the results, which they didn't.

After three wins and two defeats, Cosmos recruited Giorgio Chinaglia, an old friend of Pelé's, to strengthen the attack. On his debut he scored two goals, as did Pelé in a 6–0 win. But the defensive strategy was nonetheless maintained. They then won four and lost four, and in the final game of that sequence Furphy left and Bradley returned as coach. Morale lifted instantly and the team won seven of their last eight games, culminating in an 8–2 win over Miami with five goals from Chinaglia, two from Pelé and one from Mike Dillon. They ended the season only a few points behind Tampa Bay in the Eastern Division and with a chance to beat them in the play-offs.

The opposition couldn't have been tougher. Tampa had not lost at home all season and were arguably the strongest team in the league. Commentators felt this would have been a fitting final for the Superbowl in Seattle. In front of 40,000 fans, Pelé scored an equaliser at 1–1, but Tampa added two more without reply, Rodney Marsh scoring their third.

Nevertheless, Pelé's second season ended with sixteen wins and eight defeats, a big improvement on his first season, and he was presented with a 24-carat gold-encrusted football boot in commemoration of his 1,250th goal. Another award, the Pelé Award, sponsored by Pepsi, was set up in his honour, carrying prize money of $10,000 for the best player in the US or Canada.

Between 1974 and his second and final retirement in October 1977, Pelé did more positive good for the game in the States than anyone had before or has since. His successful four seasons were consistently played before crowds of 60,000 in New York. At the end of his US career President Jimmy Carter was moved to thank him on behalf of the American people 'for the smiles he put on children's faces, the thrills he gave the fans of this nation and the dimensions he added to American sports'. The president continued: 'Pelé has elevated the game of soccer to heights never before attained in America and only Pelé, with his status, incomparable talent and beloved compassion, could have accomplished such a mission.'

Despite such high accolades, 1978 was not such a great year, as his marriage to Rose failed. Pelé was the victim of the ambitious blonde glamour model, Xuxa. She became famous because of her affair with Pelé, but she repaid him by selling their sex secrets and informing the nation that Pelé liked his love-making accompanied by the sound of Marvin Gaye's 'Sexual Healing'. Xuxa switched her attentions to Pelé's successor as Brazil's No. 1 sporting god, Ayrton Senna. When she became pregnant, the Formula One star offensively said: 'If it is a girl I will send it to France, a boy I will send it to Switzerland, if it is black I will send it to Pelé.' Rose remained in New York until the beginning of 2000, when she moved back to Brazil.

Back on the pitch, Kevin Keegan, who won sixty-three caps for England, captained the national side and was twice named European Footballer of the Year while playing for Hamburg, treasures memories of an England appearance that never counted among his multitude of caps and two goals that were never recorded in his impressive tally. He played for England against Team America in Philadelphia in the seventies, when the North American league was buoyant and Cosmos were regularly filling their stadium. There were some really big names playing, but none bigger than Pelé. England won 3–1, and Keegan, one-time England coach, recalls the experience with enormous pleasure:

Pelé must have been around thirty-nine years of age at that time and I just couldn't believe how he played. I stood out there on the pitch just trying to imagine what it must have been like to have played against him when he was nineteen or twenty and in his prime. Here was this guy, nearly forty, but still very quick and agile, still full of movement, and of course that football brain never leaves you, no matter how old you get. I knew all about that phenomenal ability and all those tricks, but what surprised me was his level of fitness. I was out of the game for something like six or seven years before I went back to Newcastle, and when I trained with the players I thought to myself, 'I could still play at this level.' I knew I was as good as anybody, but also I knew that some days it would not be there. It isn't possible to turn back the clock, but Pelé seemed able to do it.

They didn't exchange shirts after the match, but they did have a brief chat. 'Well, I said "Well played" and "Good luck". But that was the only time I ever got really close to him in that game.'

Trevor Brooking was also in the England team that day. During the early noughties one of the main faces of BBC's *Match of the Day*, his key role in the game is with Sport England, formerly the Sports Council, of which he has been made chairman. As a player with West Ham, Brooking was part of the generation which followed the Hammers trio of World Cup winners, Bobby Moore, Geoff Hurst and Martin Peters. Brooking says:

> I met Pelé once or twice in the company of Bobby Moore. I feel Pelé was instrumental in the success of America's bid to stage the World Cup in 1994. When he played for Cosmos it was a star-studded franchise which made soccer centre stage in a country more used to a variety of other sports. Football in the States dipped to a certain extent once he left, but the World Cup finals there were a big success as a tournament, particularly from a marketing and business point of view.

It was through the Bobby Moore connection that Brooking pulled off a major coup: a World Cup interview with Pelé during the 1994 finals in the States. He explains:

> It's not easy getting hold of Pelé, as you could imagine, but I put in a request, and because of the West Ham connection and through his close friendship with Bobby, he agreed. In fact when we met up he clearly remembered me, did the interview, and he was great. The only trouble was that when he did meet me, he embraced me and called

me 'Trevor Brookling'. Of course Des Lynam and the rest of the BBC boys have never let me forget it. They've been calling me Trevor Brookling ever since.

Brooking confirms that he rates Pelé as the best of all time, but adds:

> I feel Johan Cruyff also comes into that category. I would select Cruyff in the top bracket of players of all time because I played against him on a few occasions and so was in a position to see his abilities at first hand. I started off, watching football, being in awe of the Real Madrid side of the fifties that contained Puskas and Di Stefano, and then moved on to Brazil with Pelé and co. and then the Dutch side of the 1980s. But Pelé edges ahead of them all, and in addition he has been a great ambassador. He always comes across as somebody trying to spread the message of football and its good points, off the pitch as well as on it.

Whether it's in the local bar, or in the highest footballing circles, whenever or wherever the debate gets round to the list of greatest ever footballers, Pelé inevitably comes out on top. The next five would have a familiar ring, the choice tends to revolve around Best, Cruyff, Diego Maradona, Alfredo Di Stefano and Ferenc Puskas – but the order varies according to personal preference.

'Whenever I am asked, I always name Pelé,' says Sir Bobby Charlton. 'Of course, you cannot compare players of different types, indeed of different eras. You cannot compare a goalkeeper with a striker. The reason why Pelé has come through the test of time is that he carried himself so well and lasted so long in the game; because he had this charisma, this aura, and used it on the field.' However, Sir Bobby's personal favourite is Di Stefano. 'He would be my choice only because he is a midfield player and I used to look for that type of player. But for all-round ability and as a prolific goalscorer, there is only one choice: Pelé.'

One of those top five to have played against Pelé in the States is George Best, who almost signed for Cosmos himself before Pelé. 'Warner Communications invited me over to New York to try to sign me for the club, but I wasn't that keen to live in New York, so I signed for Los Angeles instead. I suppose when I turned them down, they went out and signed Pelé.' Best, who also played for San Jose and Fort Lauderdale, recalls one classic encounter between Los Angeles and Cosmos: 'It was east versus west, black versus white. I was once given this action photograph taken of me during my time in the States with Pelé chasing after me and trying to trip me. If Pelé was out to trip you, well, that's some compliment! But somewhere on my travels that picture has gone missing.'

I was surprised to discover that Best's top player of all time was also Di Stefano. It is understandable that Sir Bobby Charlton should pick Di Stefano, given his affinity with his fellow midfield player, and even then he recognises Pelé as the greatest all-round player of all time. Best, though, names Di Stefano, because 'he is the most complete player I have ever seen'. It must be galling for Best to be so close to being the world's best-ever footballer, yet so often pipped to that honour by Pelé. I wondered whether he felt a touch frustrated by it, or maybe even resented being perpetually within touching distance of the summit only to find Pelé up there clutching his flag. Without hesitation he responds:

No, not really. The reason Pelé is the greatest of all time is because he played for Brazil. I played for Northern Ireland. Therefore it is a compliment to be mentioned in the same breath as someone who played for a nation that has now won the World Cup four times. The team I played for at international level never won anything. It never even had a chance of ever coming close to winning anything. What would it have been like had I played for Brazil?

As a twelve-year-old, Best first watched Pelé in the 1958 World Cup finals in Sweden on a black-and-white TV set at home in Northern Ireland, his imagination on fire with the exploits of a seventeen-year-old in the famous yellow of Brazil. Best recalls: 'It was obvious from the first moment I saw him at that age that he was going to be something special. For someone of that age to perform the way he did in the World Cup final, and to score such a goal you just knew he was a bit special. He developed into a player whose great strength was that he could not only score great goals, but was also unselfish and could create them for others.'

Even in the USA there was little chance of Best getting the better of Pete. 'Cosmos had all the top players – Beckenbauer, Chinaglia, Neeskens and Pelé.'

Yet there has been nothing less than deep affection between Pelé and Best, as George explained:

There are people in this sport you will bump into from time to time and it won't matter how long it is since you last saw them. Whenever I bump into Pelé, he will come over and give me a huge hug. He sort of pretends he doesn't speak English, but you can never be quite sure just how much he understands. He will say, 'Best! how are you?' and 'Best! what are you doing these days?' and you try to explain but you're not quite sure if he has taken it all in or not.

But there is always a sense of occasion wherever Pelé sets foot. 'He is one of these people who can walk into a room and suddenly the whole atmosphere changes,' added Best. 'It's the same with Sir Bobby. It's a feeling of respect.'

As the century drew to a close, loyalty became a scarce quality in football. The top Brazilian stars could not wait to quit their country. By the time of the 1990 World Cup, nine of them had deserted their homeland. In England, the likes of Steve Perryman and Alvin Martin were a dying breed, and once the Bosman ruling took a grip in Europe, not even four years left on a contract meant anything to Nicolas Anelka in his determination to make a financial killing by leaving Arsenal. Even the rules and regulations of the game were totally ignored. Anelka's brothers and agents were in touch with Real Madrid negotiating his £50,000-a-week-plus deal, net of tax, before the Spanish club had even agreed terms with Arsenal or had their permission to speak with the player. The power of soccer agents, whose growing influence FIFA is unable to curb, was easily able to circumvent the rules, and agents precipitated moves in search of even more money for themselves and their clients. Pelé, by contrast, played for just two clubs, Santos and Cosmos. And for his farewell match they met each other, with Pelé playing the first half for Cosmos and the second for Santos. In the dressing room after the game Muhammad Ali, at thirty-five just one year younger than Pelé and still fighting, cried with emotion. He hugged Pelé and said: 'My friend. My friend. Now there are two of the greatest.'

CHAPTER 10

SNAPSHOTS FROM THE 1980S

'I knew him as a nice, quiet, sincere man; a
gentleman and a sportsman.'
Bobby Moore

When he finished playing for New York Cosmos there were a multitude of offers, a variety of directions for Pelé to choose from. Indeed, the conclusion of Pelé's career on the pitch heralded the start of a brief film career and a new role as a global football ambassador. FIFA, UNICEF and Pepsi Cola instantly recognised Pelé's worldwide influence and appeal and all three organisations, in vastly contrasting ways, set about maximising Pelé's instinctive ability to galvanise both young and old. Firstly, FIFA recruited Pelé to their Fair Play Board. This was followed by his appointment as UNICEF's Goodwill Ambassador, where he was asked to take part in a multitude of fund-raising events. Pepsi offered Pelé a useful and lucrative contract to act as a globetrotting football guru, opening soccer clinics for children all over the world, mainly in underprivileged areas. Celso Grellet,

Pelé's business partner, says, 'Pepsi were deeply committed to the project and Pelé spent many years travelling the world setting up these soccer clinics. He loves children and thoroughly enjoyed the work. He is very comfortable in the company of children, and they adore him.'

It was perhaps inevitable that a celebrity of Pelé's stature would end up on the silver screen and he signed a contract with Time Warner to make a number of films, four in all. He also acted as spokesperson for the company. The best known of these films was John Huston's 1981 classic soccer film *Escape to Victory*, in which he starred with Sylvester Stallone and Michael Caine.

I use the word 'classic' only in the sense that it was at the time one of the few football-related films that had any substance and whose football action bore any resemblance to reality. That had a great deal to do with Pelé's presence. Several footballing 'extras' were attracted to the film because of Pelé's involvement, as well as that of Caine and Stallone. That said, *Escape to Victory* was essentially a film that had a cast of professional footballers who could not act, and a cast of professional actors who made less than convincing footballers. But no film before or since has boasted such a wealth of top-class players.

The film is about a team of Allied prisoners during the Second World War who play a football match against the German national team in France as the cover for an escape plan. The Allies are captained by Michael Caine, whose team includes Sylvester Stallone as the goalkeeper, plus several well-known footballers, including Pelé.

By pure chance the prisoners of war are able to round up a magical Brazilian, a world-class Argentinian, a dapper Englishman and a couple of Americans who have no idea about the game, though of course the goalkeeper turns out to be the hero. The

Germans go 4–0 up before Bobby Moore pulls one back a minute before half-time. Spurning the chance to escape during the interval, the Allies then score three more goals, the first through Ossie Ardiles after fifty-five minutes. The equaliser after seventy-six minutes is a spectacular overhead kick by Pelé, then Mike Summerbee has a goal disallowed before Stallone saves a penalty in the last minute. At 4–4, the referee is unable to blow the final whistle before the crowd invade the pitch, allowing Caine's team to escape in the rush.

The call for specialist extras had gone out to Bobby Robson at Ipswich Town, who asked for volunteers at a team meeting. Terry Butcher, one-time coach at Dundee United, and a leading Radio 5 Live pundit, was forced to turn down the opportunity of a part in the film, explaining that:

> I was under just a little bit of pressure to say no. I had got married in the January but only had time for a couple of days' break then, and I had promised the wife a proper honeymoon. I had booked a holiday in Cyprus before the offer to take part in the film came through, so it was a choice between meeting Pelé or going away with my wife. There was only one winner, even though Pelé is the greatest footballer in the world.

But Terry's central defensive partner at Portman Road, and indeed on occasions with England, and good mate Russell Osman was one of many who leaped at the chance. It proved to be the amazing experience Russell and the Ipswich players had hoped for.

Filming took place in Budapest. There were three World Cup winners on parade, in Ossie Ardiles of Argentina, Bobby Moore, captain of the English boys of '66, and of course three-times world champion Pelé, while a couple of the blond Ipswich extras made plausible German players. The players didn't really know precisely what would be involved. 'Bobby certainly didn't tell us about the haircuts,' says Russell Osman. 'As soon as we got to Budapest, we all had our hair cut to look like prisoners-of-war.' Osman played Doug Slure of the RAF alongside Bobby Moore and Mike Summerbee. Pelé had been retired a few years but was still pretty fit. It was a real pleasure and a privilege to be in his company on the same field,' Osman remembers, adding:

> All right, it wasn't a real game, but it was enjoyable nevertheless, and the only chance in my career I got to be on the same pitch as Pelé. It was simply a terrific thrill to be involved in a game with him, even though it was only for a film. His control of the ball was mesmerising. Before each take we would warm up and he was crossing the ball from the byline and performing a variety of tricks, back-heeling and so on, and all in those big army boots. I'm sure one of them was two sizes too big for him, but it didn't seem to matter, and certainly made no difference to his uncanny ball skills. He had the rest of us going all over the place. He is a one-off, so talented it is frightening, and I only got a glimpse of those talents years after he had retired.

The players spent five weeks in Budapest, on call all day ready for shooting. Whether or not it went ahead depended largely on the weather, but they had to be prepared to play at the drop of a hat without any time to warm up. The Americans involved, including the director, didn't appreciate the problems this entailed because they didn't understand football. It was down to Pelé and Roth, an American teammate from Cosmos, to try to explain that it wasn't always possible to do what they wanted. 'Pelé would take charge of much of the football-related action,' says Osman. 'He would say, "Give me the ball and try to kick me to make it as realistic as possible," and then he would take on everyone, and no one could get near enough to kick him. He made it look very easy.' The director allowed the games to run for as long as he could so that he could select the pieces of the action he required, and the footballers often played for ten to fifteen minutes at a time. Osman was pleased with the way the film turned out. 'You could see how they cut in situations that occurred in the action, but there was quite a bit manufactured.' Pelé's character was butchered on the field and had to be carried off, only to make a dramatic return late in the game to steal the late equaliser. In the first take, the overhead kick required for this was perfect. The ball was heading for the bottom corner of the net, but somehow little Laurie Sivell managed to tip it round the post. Bobby Moore crossed it to Pelé again, and again his overhead kick was perfect. Sivell went for it, but was unable to get anywhere near it. This time it screamed into the net.

Pelé was extremely approachable and socialised with the extras, who were dispersed among various hotels. Most of the English lads were together, and Pelé would join them when they went out for a drink, 'though you hardly saw him drink at all,' says Ossie Ardiles. 'But he would go around saying hello to everyone before disappearing into the night.'

'One evening he borrowed somebody's guitar and tried to play a bit,' Osman remembers. 'He was just an all-round nice guy. Stallone was not quite as friendly. He would clear off after a couple of drinks, saying he had had enough of Budapest, and the next thing we would hear was that he had gone off to Paris or somewhere and filming had to be held up until he got back.'

Ardiles recalls:

It was a very pleasurable month, playing football nearly every day. Of course, Pelé and Bobby Moore had been retired four or five years by then, while I was still at my prime, so I was much better than them. In fact I carried them. [he jokes]. When Pelé's character was deliberately hurt by one of the German team early in the match and came off with a bad injury, that left me and Bobby Moore to run the game. We were the real heroes of the side. Certainly not Michael Caine. He was awful – as good a player as he was an actor. He couldn't run twenty yards.

Ossie was thrilled to have the opportunity to work with actors like Stallone, even though he knew absolutely nothing about football. 'It was very difficult for him,' he says, 'but he did at least try.' As for Pelé, Ardiles had never met the Brazilian before the film and valued the chance to get to know him. As a South American himself, Ardiles was able to communicate with Pelé better than most. 'I would speak in Spanish and he would talk in Portuguese, but we understood each other.' He rates Pelé and Maradona as his favourite players of all time, saying:

And they are way above anyone else, in my view. Diego was even more talented than Pelé. He could do things with the ball that I didn't believe were possible. Of course, it is very difficult to make comparisons between such great players. Maybe if I was choosing a player for just one game I would go for Diego, but Pelé played for twenty

years at the very top, and if I was looking for a player for
a season, or indeed for four or five years or even for a
decade, then it would have to be Pelé.

In 1983 members of the Football Writers' Association, a mixture
of elderly veterans and up-and-coming journalists, and their
guests, all in black tie, ambled into the Cafe Royal in London.
A relic of a bygone age, the Cafe Royal, with its impressive high
ceilings, large chandeliers and echoes of the time when Britain
ruled an empire, was then the venue for the FWA annual dinners,
at which the Footballer of the Year award was presented.

Nobody expected this night to be anything out of the
ordinary, but Jeff Powell, the *Daily Mail*'s chief soccer writer, in
his first year as chairman of the FWA, had planned something
special: the presence of Pelé as guest of honour. Dennis Signy,
then the secretary of the FWA, recalls: 'Only three people knew
– Jeff, myself and my wife Pat, who organised the dinner. We
didn't even tell the committee.' Keeping this quiet from a club
comprising about 1,000 journalists must rank it as one of the
best-kept secrets ever.

Their problem was ensuring that nobody spotted Pelé as they
smuggled him in. Fortunately, they knew the habits of the vast
majority of their members – namely to assemble before dinner
in the upstairs bar and then make a late dash for the dining
room on the floor below with seconds to spare – but the slight
headache was the stragglers waiting around the lobby for the lift.
They timed Pelé's arrival to take place just before the dinner and
entertained him in a private room downstairs. 'When everyone
was seated for dinner, I went down to bring Pelé up to the dining
room,' says Dennis. 'But there were still a few people milling
around and when we ushered him into the lift, we found Dave

Underwood, the former Liverpool, Watford and Luton goalkeeper, in there with one of his mates. As we got in, Dave said, "Well, who is that with Dennis Signy?"'

Jeff Powell led the 1983 Footballer of the Year, Kenny Dalglish, to the top table. Kenny noticed there was an empty seat right at the centre. 'Who is that for?' he asked. 'Hang on, you'll see,' replied Jeff. He stood to say grace and then announced: 'Somebody has just arrived who has come a great deal further than most of you. I have great pleasure in welcoming Pelé, the Footballer of the Century.'

'The whole room erupted,' says Dennis. 'There was tumultuous applause. I have never heard any welcome like it at any of our dinners before it or after it. It was just sensational.' Mike Ingham, who at the time was chief soccer commentator for Radio 5 Live, will never forget that moment. 'It was one hell of a surprise, all right, When Pelé walked into the room everybody stood up. As he passed, he recognised one of the guests sitting at our table, Peter Lorenzo, who had interviewed him at the 1970 World Cup. Pelé acknowledged him, and Peter was so overcome with emotion that he was almost in tears.'

Traditionally, the incumbent chairman of the FWA makes the presentation to the Footballer of the Year, but on this special occasion Jeff handed over the honour to Pelé, who presented Dalglish with his coveted trophy. Dennis recalls: 'Kenny was suitably touched.' The evening was a massive success, made so by the appearance of one man. But he couldn't stay too long – he had to get to Luton Airport to catch the last remaining flight before midnight. When it was time for him to leave, he walked the length of the top table, embracing everyone and shaking hands. His entourage was getting very agitated because they had a tight schedule, but he was clearly enjoying himself and not in any particular rush.

Before he boarded his flight, he said, 'I must phone my radio station in Brazil.' Jeff, who accompanied him to Luton, says that he used a public telephone to make his call. 'And the first thing he said was: "You'll never guess who I have just been having dinner with. Bobby Charlton and the players from the 1966 World Cup team." He was enthralled to have sat with so many of English football's greats.'

It was not only in England that the great man created excitement, but north of the border, too. In 1989 he went to Scotland as a FIFA ambassador to promote the Under-17 World Youth Championships.

The one-time Scotland coach, Craig Brown, remembers: 'He was excellent. He went to every venue and made a huge impression. He stayed on to watch a few games, including the opener, Scotland against Ghana, at Hampden Park.'

FIFA's head of communications at the time, Keith Cooper, agrees.

> I was astounded by his sheer professionalism when he came to promote the event to a typically sceptical Scottish press. He flew in to Glasgow and came straight to Hampden Park, fresh off the plane, right in front of the TV cameras to reel off a couple of promotional spots in English without a moment's rehearsal, the beaming smile unaffected by fifteen hours on an aeroplane. We then sent him off on a promotional tour around Scotland to meet the media and dozens of schoolkids who had won the privilege. His patience was endless. In Dundee, after countless photos and autographs, he persistently sought out one father who had earlier taken a snap of his son with Pelé to say he thought the camera had not worked

properly and maybe he would like to do it again because he didn't want the boy to be disappointed. Would any other star ever care that much?

When we came out of the ground in Dundee we were almost an hour down on our schedule on the way to Aberdeen. We were heading for our car down the road when Pelé noticed a young father walking up the other side of the street with a small child. Having just done his duty with 500 youngsters in the stadium, he still insisted on going out of his way to hold the baby and chat to its stupefied father. Pelé genuinely finds babies irresistible.

Cooper was even more thrilled to have the opportunity to actually play with Pelé. On the long June evenings in the park gardens of their hotel in Dunblane, the hobby footballers of the FIFA staff realised the ultimate football fantasy with the help of an energetic little guy in a white tracksuit with nifty ball control. 'We could call to him for a pass (and get it) or say, "Great ball, Pelé" (frequently), or "Good try, Pelé" (hardly at all), and on the only occasion when he did try to beat one man too many, somebody whispered, "Who the hell does he think he is, bloody Pelé or something?"'

A couple of years later the Under-17s were in Italy, and once again, so was Pelé. They were in Montecatini, a Tuscany spa town normally inhabited by elderly ladies who go there to take the waters. Not a classic football crowd by any means, so Pelé thought he could take an undisturbed walk for ten minutes. Within less than two minutes, the traffic in the main street of the genteel resort was jammed solid. 'Everyone wanted him,' says Keith Cooper. 'It was staggering how the man's appeal went right across the whole range of ages, gender and nationalities.'

On Pelé's visit to Scotland, a friendship was forged with

Andy Roxburgh, the former Scottish coach now on the technical committee with UEFA on a full-time basis. 'I would describe him as more of an acquaintance than a friend,' says Andy modestly, but after showing an initial reticence he recounted some detailed chats and personal recollections which would suggest that he qualifies as a close associate of Pelé's. Certainly they have served together on FIFA and UEFA technical committees. In any case, to count yourself among Pelé's 'acquaintances' is rare indeed. In spite of his outward affection for the ordinary man in the street, whom he treats in the same way as the highest and most powerful people he meets, deep down Pelé is an extremely private man and very few can claim to be a part of his small inner circle, let alone an 'acquaintance'.

'I don't really know what to say about Pelé that people haven't already said about him,' comments Andy apologetically.

> He is just so incredible with people. It is not only about having remarkable ability and charisma, but how he comes across to the public. If a superstar is arrogant or ignorant it diminishes that image. The few times I have been in his company he has always set a fantastic example. Even if he has a pressing and important appointment he will not rush off or run away from the last autograph. Instead he will say: 'I will deal with this first.' He is very focused on his view that the people come first, and you don't come across many like that in football. For someone of such magnitude, he is so sensitive to the fans and the people around him. That makes him a great sportsman.

Andy's memories of Pelé are full of small personal insights, such as his passion for the local salmon in Scotland and his tendency to seasickness, revealed in Cincinnati. Andy and Pelé were due at a dinner at a local floating restaurant.

'I hear we are having dinner tonight on a ship,' Pelé remarked to Andy.

'Yes, that's right.'

'I get seasick.'

'Don't worry,' Andy told him. 'The ship's tied to the dock. It won't be moving out to sea.'

Pelé had panicked at the thought that they would be dining as the ship sailed down the Ohio River, bobbing up and down in the waves.

As a one-time member of UEFA's technical department, Roxburgh has been compiling a survey of the experts' favourite players of all time, so has his own views on the perennial debate.

I have never seen Pelé live, only on TV, so his image to me is built more on reputation. It is apparent that people will vote for a player of their own generation, particularly someone from their formative, impressionable years. For example, Platini named Cruyff, and so did Rummenigge. Rinus Michels went for a player from the sixties, Di Stefano or Pelé, so it doesn't surprise me when you tell me that Bobby Charlton chooses Di Stefano.

My favourite player is Puskas, which underlines how old I am! He would be my choice because I saw him play when I was growing up and became fascinated by him when I saw him twice in Glasgow playing for Real Madrid. But whatever era you come from, football people from the last fifty years would have Pelé either at the top or certainly within their all-time top ten.

The 1990 World Cup is remembered in England for Paul Gascoigne's tears in Turin as England went out agonisingly on penalties to West Germany in the semi-finals. England had come so close, yet again. For Brazil, 1990 marked the nadir. They did not progress beyond the second round. Pelé had predicted ominously after they won their first group game against Sweden by 2–1: 'As soon as we play a good team, we'll lose.' One of the fundamental problems was that nine of the Brazilians' top stars were playing abroad, and a team assembled to deal with the European style found itself dispatched from the tournament by Diego Maradona's decidedly non-European Argentina. It was Brazil's first defeat in four matches at the hands of their South American rivals.

The tournament was also notable for the emergence of Cameroon, a side which gave Pelé immense pleasure during the competition. He has always predicted that one day an African team will win the World Cup.

The following year, in Munich, Pelé gave me an exclusive interview during which he delivered his verdict on the England side that had so nearly made the final. It is interesting to look back and see how accurate his assessments were of John Barnes and Paul Gascoigne.

Pelé remembered the great goal he had seen Barnes score at the Maracana seven years earlier. 'But now he's become a completely different player,' he said. 'When I saw him dribble past all those defenders he was quick, sharp and in great condition. Now he looks slow by comparison. He is still technically an outstanding player – one of the best in the world – but he looks a little fat, slow and lazy in his style. Maybe he is out of condition, and that is the problem.' No one in English football had dared to criticise Barnes in such a manner, but coming from such an eminent source, it was a difficult point to ignore. Barnes had problems reproducing the dazzling skills he showed with Liverpool for the England team. It always appeared that while playing for his club he had ample time and space with the ball delivered to his feet and the chance to step up a gear. In an England shirt, it was never the same. He often found a defender assigned to close-mark him throughout the game and a second defender in close proximity to cut out the space if he did beat his marker.

Graham Taylor, Bobby Robson's successor as England manager, tried to release the Barnes talent with a free role behind the front two strikers, but the tactic again failed to produce the anticipated results. Pelé thought Barnes ought to have played abroad, where the regime would have been much tougher than in England. Glenn Hoddle lost around a stone in weight after joining Monaco from Spurs. 'In Italy it is very hard, because they have the sort of mentality you have in international football. They play a man-to-man marking game, and you have to be fit to combat that,' reasoned Pelé. Barnes had opportunities to move to a foreign club, but never took them up. Instead he became the highest-paid player in British football when he signed an extended contract with Liverpool, which made him the first £10,000-a-week footballer.

Pelé's assessment of Barnes was spot-on, and proved to be prophetic, for he never really made the grade as a consistently outstanding international. Pelé's advice to Paul Gascoigne, on the other hand, might have seemed sensible at the time, but as it turned out it was misplaced. 'Gazza reminds me of the trouble we had with Rivelino when he was young,' said Pelé. 'Even at the age of seventeen Rivelino was a strong character. He had already broken into the national side, but he could not settle down and he was always causing problems – a strong-willed character, difficult to control. Then he got married, and he changed. I don't know whether this is the answer for Paul Gascoigne, but it might be. Once Rivelino was married the best of his football was allied to a new influence on and off the field.' Pelé also felt that Gazza needed better players around him, strong characters in particular.

It is worse when you are a strong personality, a gifted player and the best in the team, because everyone expects so much from you. Gascoigne needs to be in a side where there are two or three other big names in the team, and then it will be easier for him to gain control of himself. Gascoigne ranks among the great players I have seen in English football. It is always a problem of style for a highly talented player in English football to integrate into a system. Usually there are only one or two skilful players in the England team, and how well Paul Gascoigne can fit in will depend on the England coach finding a way of integrating him. I don't know too much about Paul Gascoigne's character, but I know enough about him from what I have seen on the field. He did well enough in Italy in the World Cup, and players do change when they are on the big stage. The important competitions bring the best out of them. We shall have to wait a little longer before making a realistic assessment of this player's true worth in world terms. We'll be in a better position to judge him in another three years, when he plays in the World Cup in America. I've heard about his bad knee injury – and thank God, over the twenty-five years I played I never had such a serious ligament injury. He must learn from the experience of Ruud Gullit, who has suffered the same sort of problem, and also needed an operation. The mistake that Gullit made, which should be an example to Gascoigne, is that he came back too quickly. He was not truly fit, and he had problems again. Gullit has recovered, but only after much hard work and many operations. The temptations will be great for Paul Gascoigne to play as quickly as possible. He must resist them and take his time.

Of Gazza's impending move to Lazio, he said: 'Every good player will succeed in Italy if he doesn't have injuries. The best players are in Italy, and that will suit him.'

Gazza was then twenty-four, and as we all now know, a combination of that career-threatening injury and personal problems, notably a stormy marriage, eventually conspired to turn him into a shadow of his former self. Regrettably, despite a few moments of magic in Rome and some ever rarer ones with Glasgow Rangers, his best was already behind him, and the future was paved with a succession of downers both on and off the field. A wonderful goal against Scotland at Wembley was the closest he came to being a winner with his country, and he was never to play in another World Cup.

Pelé was very much in favour of the new FIFA directives on red cards, and in fact called for even more stringent refereeing to curtail the activities of the hatchet men. He had no sympathy for players who whinged about the deluge of red cards and suspensions. 'I do not like the foul from behind, and the punishment available has always been insufficient in my view – maybe a yellow card, sometimes nothing or just a free kick. I like to see the defensive side punished a little bit harder. If that means sending a player off if a genuine goal chance is ruined, then so be it. Personally, I'd make the defensive wall illegal. The free kick should be just against the goalkeeper.'

Four years before the advent of the Bosman ruling that allows free transfers at the end of a contract, Pelé was already pinpointing the diminishing loyalty in the game. At the time David Platt, Trevor Steven and Chris Waddle were playing abroad, a combined transfer value of £20.75 million even in those days. Pelé commented:

> I don't blame players for following the money – they have to think about their futures, We footballers are not like doctors, we don't have such stability. We have short careers. But I have to look on the other side, the effect that these fees are having on the players and on the game. It saddens me to say it, but players are losing their love for the sport, their commitment to the team. It has reached a point where you could even argue that they don't care, because they play for one team one year and another team the next.

Pelé moved on to the subject of the comparisons and contrasts between English football's two greatest ambassadors, Bobby Charlton and Gary Lineker.

Pelé has a great admiration for Charlton, so it came as a surprise that it was Lineker, in this capacity, who edged ahead in Pelé's eyes – because of his extraordinary record as soccer's Mr Clean, having never received a single booking in his entire career. At the time Lineker was about to take on world champions Germany at Wembley. He was just four short of Charlton's all-time record of forty-nine England goals, but it was one he was doomed not to overhaul. A missed penalty prior to the European Championships in Sweden was to deprive him of even equalling it after having come so close.

Pelé said:

> Wherever I go around the world I hear the name of Gary
> Lineker mentioned in the same breath as the words 'fair
> play'. I was at a tournament very recently where the FIFA
> president João Havelange made a speech before the game.
> He told everybody what a great example Gary Lineker is
> to football. Gary Lineker has never got the yellow card in
> his career: that is absolutely fantastic. He is the perfect
> example, not only to his fellow professionals, but also as a
> model to all the kids around the world on how to behave.

Pelé also expressed his unflinching affection for Charlton, soon
to become Sir Bobby: 'Bobby Charlton is loved in your country,
and off the field he is a gentleman. But not always on the field.
In fact, he was not that good a character on the field. Whenever
I was playing against him he was always shouting at the players,
always fighting with the other English players.' No doubt Pelé
meant arguing rather than actually physically fighting; Lineker,
however, was rarely seen losing his cool with anyone. He was by
then thirty-one, and Pelé thought he could continue to the age
of thirty-five, but after reaching forty-eight England goals he
semi-retired, quitting English football for a couple of years in
Japan with Grampus 8, where a lingering toe injury curtailed his
appearances to a mere handful.

Lineker and Pelé met at a Football League versus the Rest of the
World game at Wembley in the late 1980s, when Gary was still
playing for Barcelona. Pelé was the guest of honour. 'It seemed to
me as if Pelé made a big fuss of Gary as he went down the line of
players, being introduced to each one,' remembers Lineker's agent
Jon Holmes, who has guided both his football and television

careers. He definitely went out of his way to talk to Gary. Lineker confirms modestly: 'Oh yes, he did have a little chat with me before the game. I do recall that, even though it was a few years ago now.'

That was a game for which Diego Maradona threatened not to turn out unless he was assured of a massive personal-appearance fee. 'Maradona did play, but he created such a kerfuffle beforehand,' says Lineker. 'It was the sort of thing that would never happen with Pelé – they are totally different characters.' Pelé has asked for personal-appearance fees for overseas games, but only for those in which he was contracted to appear with Santos. He would insist upon what was contractually his by right, but never caused the kind of ill-feeling Maradona did on that night at Wembley.

It was while Lineker was in Japan that he received one of the surprise telephone calls of his life. 'I was sitting at home when the phone rang one night and I thought, "Christ, I know that voice." It suddenly struck me that it was the great man himself. I must admit that as soon as the realisation hit me, I went to jelly.' It turned out that Pelé and Lineker had a mutual Japanese adviser at the time who was looking after their affairs in Japan. 'We had a chat on the phone, and ended up having a drink together at a little party.'

Many illustrious British players have named their all-time greats in this book. So what of Pelé's most-rated footballers from Britain? It was no surprise that he named a fellow goalscoring legend, Jimmy Greaves, as the striker he most admired, along with Charlton. Gascoigne was included in his list of all-time greats then, but since he failed to fulfil that enormous potential, in 2000, nine years later, Pelé would probably review his opinion. Otherwise he picked the names one would expect – Gordon Banks, Peter Shilton, George Best, Bobby Moore, of course, and Sir Stanley

Matthews. 'How can you forget Stanley Matthews? He played on until he was fifty. It makes me think that perhaps I retired too early. George Best was a fantastic player with enormous skills and dribbling ability. Bobby Moore was hard but skilful.' While acknowledging that he had not personally seen enough of Kenny Dalglish and many others who might feature in such a list to give a competent assessment, he mourned the fact that there have been precious few really world-class players emerging from the home of football. He explains:

> The base of the game in England will not change until the coaches from youth teams start to change their mentality. Only then will the emphasis be transferred to the very top. It has been very hard to change the pattern of English football over the years, although I must say the reliance on strength, power and running was worse before. Now the English game has become more skilful, and more skilful players are emerging. There is now more of a balance in world football; even the world champions, Germany, are looking for more quality players to tip that balance in their favour.

Pelé endorsed the elitist philosophy then sweeping across Europe on its way to England, the movement towards a Premier League and then a European Super League. He advocated anything designed to improve quality and dispense with quantity, to reduce the workload on top players. 'The same thing has happened in Brazil, where we have had too many teams and the quality was diminishing.'

On all sides the pressure was multiplying on superstar players. 'In my country they're forever saying, here is the new Pelé, or the new Zico. Players such as Paul Gascoigne and John Barnes must live under the same pressure. So much attention is paid to this type of player, right from an early age, and it gets to the stage where they cannot develop.' And indeed it transpired that neither Barnes nor later Gascoigne would truly fulfil all their immense potential to make an impact on the world scene.

CHAPTER 11

FROM FOOTBALL STAR TO GLOBAL AMBASSADOR

*'Pelé is like Muhammad Ali, the most famous person on the
planet, and not just in football terms but in every sense.'*
Tony Banks MP

Celso Grellet has been the major influence on Pelé's professional
life for a decade. Like every Brazilian boy, he played beach
football for fun, but although he didn't advance beyond that as
a player, he made a massive impact on the game behind the
scenes. An academic with a degree in business administration
and law and a flair for marketing, he became managing director
of São Paulo, his home-town club, in 1978, and made his mark
in the twelve years he spent there before leaving to join forces
with Pelé. He was responsible for maximising the marketing
potential of Brazil's big clubs and inspired a breakaway of the
elite teams in 1987, when he helped organise the Clube de Trese
League, in which São Paulo joined forces with Flamenco and the
other top clubs. Grellet sat on the board of directors of the new
league and took control of their marketing activities. He had

also brought innovative marketing techniques to the national team, which, in the early 1980s, was a big novelty in Brazilian football.

Grellet met Pelé after Pelé had finished his 'second' footballing career in New York with the Cosmos at a dinner party given by mutual friends. It was inevitable that the two would gravitate towards each other given that they were both so full of ideas about the future of the game.

They set up Pelé Sports and Marketing in 1990 and it was officially launched in grand style a year later. He designed for Pelé the same sort of marketing plan that he first formulated for São Paulo and then for the Clube de Trese. The game plan was to maximise Pelé's global popularity with a small group of multinational companies rather than the previous scattergun approach of small deals which filled every available moment of Pelé's time without enhancing his reputation. It was a simple but highly effective strategy.

The company was started with the purpose of dealing with the multitude of marketing and sports activities surrounding Pelé and his image worldwide. There were really two objectives in the conception of the company: to deal with the variety of activities and approaches to Pelé and also to develop football teams within Brazil as well as the management of stadia. Celso recalled: 'We began with many diverse activities, including buying and selling television rights, organising tournaments and working on the development of the game in Brazil as a consequence of the so-called Pelé Law, which opened the way for foreign investment in Brazilian football. Pelé was instrumental in opening the way for much-needed funding in the same way that football has been developing in England with big investment and the move towards clubs becoming well-financed enterprises and plc's.' Pelé and his

Sports and Marketing company acted as consultants on how this new finance could be best used.

The major foreign investment was coming from Switzerland in the shape of companies like ISL, who have been involved in selling television rights for World Cup tournaments and were one of the first major investors to put a great deal of funds into big clubs like Flamenco. The foreign investors were entering into long contracts with the marketing arms of the clubs and Pelé Sports and Marketing were involved with the development of that process.

As well as the work his company was taking on, the reinvention of Pelé in the 1990s as a global ambassador was brought about by his commercial links with MasterCard and Umbro. These lucrative contracts did more than boost Pelé's bank balance: they helped to reawaken Pelé's worldwide connections and provided him with a platform from which to address the international media.

Tony Signore, an agent for MasterCard, recalls his experience of negotiating with Pelé's friend and advisor, Hélio Viana, for Pelé's first personal appearance for the credit card in 1990. With great fondness for Hélio's negotiating powers, Tony says: 'For me it was a great moment when MasterCard initiated a vote among journalists and coaches to define the greatest World Cup team. The Brazil team of 1970 won that vote. It was essential to get Pelé along to Rome, where the presentation was being held. We only wanted Pelé for thirty minutes for the press conference, but even if Pelé turned up for only a minute, it would have been worthwhile.'

Pelé himself was delighted to attend, he felt it was an honour, but he would leave all discussions about appearance fees to Hélio, who passed Tony a blank piece of paper and asked him to write down a number which he felt would be appropriate for Pelé's appearance at such a significant event for MasterCard. Tony wrote down a figure and passed the piece of paper back. Without reply, Hélio passed back the number with an extra nought on the end of it. MasterCard discovered very quickly that Pelé does not come cheaply.

A year later, MasterCard, already delighted with the response from that first Pelé involvement, entered into meaningful discussions about a contract and nine years later Pelé is still the main spokesperson for MasterCard International.

As spokesman for the two giant conglomerates, Umbro and MasterCard, Pelé became a focal point for World Cup tournaments in particular. The two ventures worked well. There was never any clash: the companies operated in two different industries and had two vastly different aims. Umbro's involvement with Pelé was tied around the sport, and they used him to endorse their branded sportswear and boots. They also developed a boot range with Pelé's technical advice in that area. MasterCard, meanwhile, used him for big events, to spearhead their World Cup and European Championship launches as one of the main sponsors of those events.

Peter Draper, now the group marketing director of Manchester United, was the marketing director of Umbro when Pelé was taken on board. He analyses the significance of the Pelé contract, not merely from Umbro's point of view, but to the development of Pelé as a global ambassador.

> When we first came into contact with Pelé, it was through his solicitor, whom Pelé called 'Mr Manion', who had handled his contract with Cosmos. Pelé had a place in New York and was commuting back and forth to Brazil. Umbro started in the UK in 1924 but formed a joint venture with a company in South Carolina, and

Before a match, in the black and white stripes of his beloved Santos.

Right: Swapping shirts with Bobby Moore after Brazil defeat England in the 1970 World Cup.

(© Allsport)

Below: *That* save – thwarted by Gordon Banks in the 1970 World Cup.

(© Allsport)

Left: Left: Jubilation for Brazil as they win, and keep, the Jules Rimet Trophy, 1970. *(© Allsport)*

Below: Another one for Brazil, against Italy in the 1970 World Cup final.

(© Allsport)

Right: Santos wins again,
as two royal admirers,
Queen Elizabeth and
Prince Phillip, look on.
(© *Allsport*)

Below left: Relaxing with
old friend and business
partner Celso Grellett.
(© *Pelé Sports & Marketing*)

Below right: Signing
autographs with Aston
Villa chairman Doug Ellis,
and Villa player Lionel
Martin, 1972.   (© *Terry Weir*)

Nelson Mandela and Pelé, heroes to millions, meet in South Africa, 1996. *(© Popperfoto)*

Below left: Tackling Bill Clinton at the opening of a sports school in Rio for deprived children, 1997. *(© Popperfoto)*

Below right: Celebrating Ronaldo's World Player of the Year Award, with Roberto Carlos, 1988. *(© Popperfoto)*

Above: Showing off new-born twins, Celeste and Joshua, with wife Arissa.

(© *Popperfoto*)

Right: Pelé and his two younger children from his first marriage, Edinho and Jennifer, 1981.

(© *Luiz Alberto*)

Left: Dancing with Sean Connery and Sepp Blatter before a charity match in Rome, 2000.

(© Popperfoto)

Right: Those famous feet leave their mark in Vienna before the World Sports Award of the Century, 1999.

(© Popperfoto)

Above: With Diego Maradona at the Match of Friendship at the Palais Royal, Paris, in June 2016, before the opening of Euro 2016. (*© Domine Jerome/ABACA/PA Images*)

Below: As a New York Cosmos legend, Pelé lights the Empire State Building 'Cosmos green' to launch and celebrate the team's 2015 spring season, New York, April 2015. (*© Dennis Van Tine/Geisler-Fotopres/DPA/PA Images*)

that organisation eventually bought the business. So for six to seven years Umbro were controlled from the US, and there was dramatic growth. Pelé had made a huge impact in the US and the company felt that he was the right choice to further that growth. Even though he had retired, he was still a star figure in the US, even with those people not involved in soccer or interested in the sport. They still knew Pelé, and he was of course known to a knowledgeable football audience in the UK. Pelé still had some arrangement with Time Warner in the States from his days with Cosmos, but his involvement with Umbro and MasterCard widened his global contacts.

Umbro was looking for someone who would give them a fashion element and also to root itself in football. Who better than the greatest player of all time to represent the company as a spokesperson?

Pelé was, of course, still worshipped in Brazil and famed throughout South America. But irrespective of a player's status within the game, once he finishes playing there is always the danger that he will go off the boil in terms of the public's awareness. He still had a lot of big commercial deals, but they were mainly in South America. The contracts with MasterCard and Umbro provided him with a vehicle to get back into public recognition in another field.

Pelé still retained his down-to-earth sense of humour, though. Marisa D'Amico, who has worked alongside Pelé for many years on the MasterCard account, recalls the 'p-p' story:

Pelé told this story while launching a credit card. It really took everyone by surprise. He was holding up a giant picture of the card with Sepp Blatter, and then he performed his usual media duties. Before the launch we discussed what he might say and we all felt it would be entertaining if he was to tell some of the things that had happened to him over the years. He told one that had us all taken aback, if highly amused. Someone like Pelé is accompanied wherever he goes, but he explained to all the assembled media and dignitaries that there is one occasion at least, where he has to go alone – the toilet. There was this guy standing next to him using the toilet who looked up to see who had come in to stand next to him and looked again as he made a double take. He turned around the second time too quickly because he was so shocked to think he was there next to Pelé that his whole body turned as well. And kind of got Pelé! When he told this story to all the gathered journalists at this press conference, I thought it was really funny, but I couldn't believe that he told it.

Marisa also recalls celebrating her birthday with Pelé. She explained: 'Around a dozen of us went to a restaurant. The dessert arrived with a candle in it, and Pelé started to sing. How flattering to have Pelé spending your birthday with you and singing to you as well!'

She reveals the side of him his public hasn't seen. 'He plays the guitar, he loves to sing and dance, but he cannot do it very often because he is such a public figure and so easily recognised. Most of the time he has to put up with standing in VIP areas with bodyguards surrounding him. It is not what he would want to do, but he puts up with it with a smile and good nature.'

At that time, though, Pelé signed a two-year contract with

Umbro worth a modest $100,000, but for that he was only obliged to make two appearances a year. The managing director of Umbro USA, Warren Mersereau, who moved on after the 1994 World Cup to head up the Adidas football operations, successfully conducted the negotiations. Peter Draper says: 'It was a fantastic deal for us. We signed Pelé relatively cheaply at first, but we got as much as we could out of those two sessions, which consisted of one guest appearance and one photographic session a year. From our photographic session we were also able to shoot a TV commercial which ran in the States on regional channels around specialist games.' Umbro widened their involvement with Pelé and brought him to Europe to spearhead their participation in trade fairs, while MasterCard used Pelé as their figurehead and spokesperson to launch their credit cards and advertising promotions around World Cups and European Championships.

The idea of having a spokesperson to front your operation is all very well, provided that such a figurehead behaves in a way that reflects his status in the game, reflects well on your brand name and is appropriate to your business. Pelé achieved precisely that for Umbro, but ten times more effectively than they had anticipated. 'He has never been a Muhammad Ali in the sense of all that bravado, but you would put him alongside Ali as far as status goes,' says Draper. 'He was the ideal spokesperson because he held himself in the right manner, he was strong in what he had to say and he commanded attention wherever he went. When Pelé spoke, his audience listened. You have high expectations of your heroes. I certainly do. So does the public. But invariably it is one huge let down. Pelé lives up to his reputation and then a little more.'

So successful was the deal for Umbro that they eagerly extended Pelé's contract once the two-year deal expired, signing him up for a further four years. This time, however, his fee was $1.2 million. But Umbro were delighted with the impact he was making on their behalf, as Draper explained:

Over the years we would roll him in and roll him out, and whichever country we were in, whatever the language, the differences in the audiences, he was a model of how these things ought to be done. I first came into contact with Pelé around 1991, when he was involved with a personal appearance for Umbro at the Chicago Sports Trade Show. I knew Pelé was popular, but I was shocked to discover fans queuing for four hours to get his autograph. It was just unbelievable, because I was so pleasantly surprised by the way he dealt with all of those fans. I've seen it so often in the past, and more so nowadays, that there are people in the game who feel they are being imposed upon if they give you two minutes of their time, and then they are away as soon as that commitment is fulfilled. They don't look you in the eye when they sign an autograph, and feel such things are a chore. In contrast, Pelé wanted to sign those autographs, took his time and had to be pulled away when his time was running out. He came across to me as a very humble man, very appreciative of people who had helped him along the way; a man who doesn't take anyone for granted, and that includes his fans. He also came across as genuine. The sincerity of the guy shone through.

The first photo session with Pelé is one that Peter won't forget. Umbro hired the photographer Walter Yoos, the most celebrated sports photographer in the US. According to Peter, he made Pelé work really hard. He wanted a Pelé special – one of his bicycle kicks – and set up a mattress on the floor of the New York studio to cushion his fall. 'He must have shot Pelé's bicycle kick more than forty times when he finally said, "Just one more should do it." Pelé responded: "I think you've got it, Walter!"'

Pelé was absolutely mobbed wherever he went with Umbro, but he took it all in his stride. He met and greeted their guests at dinners, where a specially compiled video of Pelé the player in action would be shown, and then he would say a few words to break the ice. He went to South Africa in 1996, where he met Nelson Mandela. Celso Grellet was privy to the meeting and recalls:

From the moment Pelé walked into the Government Palace all the employees, some 500, besieged him for autographs and pictures. When Pelé finally got the chance to meet Mandela, both men clearly had a visible mutual respect for one another. They spoke for some time and obviously enjoyed each other's company. Pelé admired Mandela for his personal fight against apartheid and was well aware of how he had spent a large part of his life in prison. Pelé respected his fight for freedom and peace.

Mandela was very impressed with Pelé. He knew a lot about the Pelé history, about his career in Brazil and America, and his charity work for children for UNESCO. He was very informed about Pelé's career and his life. They established a very good relationship. Pelé had said to me that it was one of his dreams to meet Mandela because of the circumstances of his life. And the feelings were the same on Mandela's side.

He also went to Australia, Germany and London, where a dinner was organised in celebration of his classic World Cup header that brought the great save from Gordon Banks. On that occasion Banks and Pelé were reunited at the Dorchester to promote the Umbro Cup tournament at Wembley, at which Brazil played England in 1995.

Pelé himself never played at Wembley, but the day after the Dorchester dinner he was out on the Wembley pitch in the pouring rain with a huge umbrella to launch the tournament. Peter Draper remembers:

> We could hardly get him into the stadium. We organised a car to collect him from outside the Conference Centre to take him the short distance to the stadium. People were running down the side of the car all the way just to get a glimpse of him. He must have taken ten minutes to complete a journey that would normally take a minute, and then we had to get him out of the car and up the steps. It just illustrates the magnitude of the interest in Pelé, even now.

Umbro knew he had always wanted to play at Wembley, so they invited him to come and play there for them, as part of their deal with the FA was that they have Wembley at their disposal for one day a year.

Pelé's contract with Umbro lasted for the best part of the decade, during which time the company also had a four-year commercial link with Brazil. 'We couldn't have asked for more from Pelé,' says sports marketing manager Simon Marsh. 'Everyone wants a piece of him, and even though his time is precious we always had access to him whenever it was possible.' The relationship was terminated amicably owing to changes within the company, but Pelé's MasterCard contract is still going strong.

In 1993, however, Pelé found himself in conflict with the all-powerful João Havelange, whose election as president of FIFA he had done so much to promote. They had clashed on two occasions before, starting with a mysterious cooling of relations between the two men. Hélio Viana, Pelé's friend and advisor, says: 'We met Havelange in a restaurant in Rio in 1987, as he happened to be dining in the same place. I told him that Pelé would like to talk with him.

'A more formal meeting was arranged for the next day. Pelé was curious and mystified as to why a rift had occurred with someone he had always looked up to and admired. Havelange then surprised us when he said, "I invited you three years ago to be part of FIFA's seventieth anniversary, but you didn't appear."

'Clearly Havelange was upset by this and had held it against Pelé, but we told him that an invitation had never been received.' No more than a misunderstanding, there was no reason not to resume normal relations, and Pelé even agreed to help Havelange promote Ricardo Teixeira, Havelange's son-in-law, to become president of the Confederação Brazileira de Futebol (CBF), the CBD's successor as Brazilian football's ruling body. Teixeira had been a mediocre law student with a history of unsuccessful business ventures when he married Havelange's daughter Lucia. But under Havelange's guidance his fortunes prospered. Pelé was told Teixeira would bring big changes to football in Brazil with new ideas and new rules, in line with changes Pelé himself felt needed to be made.

'We did help Ricardo. The Brazilian team were sponsored by a small company within the country but we brought Umbro to the CBF, and Umbro were a big company at that time,' says Helio.

However, the accord between the CBF and Pelé did not help Pelé when it came to a match to commemorate his fiftieth birthday in 1990. There were organisational snags because of a decree from the Federation run by Teixeira. Helio says: 'Teixeira would only give permission for those internationals still playing in Brazil to participate, although all the top players were abroad by this time. Pelé accepted the situation without comment.' However, it was clear that Pelé himself was far from pleased.

Breaking point came in 1993, when Pelé, through his own company, had bid for television rights for the 1994 Brazilian Championship. According to Pelé, a member of the CBF had demanded a $1 million bribe to ensure that his application was successful. Pelé refused to pay up and the contract went to a rival competitor, Traffic, who acquired the rights for $1 million less than Pelé's company had offered and took 20 per cent of the gross.

Traffic was part-owned by Kléber Leite, who happened to be president of Flamengo, a leading Brazilian club. When running for office, he had taken a page in the *O Globo* newspaper to reproduce a letter of support from Havelange. Allegations were made that before the election Leite was recorded discussing ways to discredit Pelé, though none of these were ever implemented.

Pelé nevertheless aired his suspicions and went public with his claim that a bribe had been solicited in the television negotiations. Teixeira decided that the allegation referred directly to him, even though Pelé had not identified an individual, and brought an action for slander against ME.

Havelange was unrepentant about siding with his son-in-law, as Pelé was banished from the 1994 World Cup ceremony, explaining:

> I have given every attention and kindness to this lad, but playing soccer is one thing, being a businessman

is another. This lad shouldn't have done what he did. Ricardo is married to my only daughter. He's the father of my grandchildren. Whatever he needs, I will do for him. When I was a boy my father used to slap me if I was disrespectful. That is what I have done metaphorically to Pelé. He must learn to show respect. I launched him in the national team when he was only seventeen.

Pelé responded: 'Havelange has been my idol since the 1958 World Cup, and because he's the boss of FIFA, he can say who comes in and who stays out. But his son-in-law is president of the Brazilian federation, and I will not serve corruption.' It was a feud that was to fester on for the remainder of Havelange's term of office.

Before the 1994 World Cup got underway, Pelé had more important personal matters to attend to in the form of his second marriage. Pelé tied the knot with Assiria Seixa Lemos that June. Assiria had a five-year-old girl, Jemima, named after her mother, from her first marriage to an American, which had ended in the late 1980s. Pelé first met her when she was studying in America, but it was not until a year after they were first introduced that they started dating. By the beginning of 1993 the romance was becoming serious. Celso takes up the story: 'Now Assiria has completed her doctrine in theology and, like Pelé, is a very religious person. She has just launched a CD on which she sings and plays gospel music. It has been a great success in Brazil – Assiria has perhaps surprised everyone.

'It isn't easy being Pelé's wife. Both are invited to so many functions, and she naturally attracts much media attention because she is with him.'

That may be so in Brazil, perhaps throughout South America. But really little is known about her or, indeed, about Pelé's private life outside of South America, which he protects with as much passion as he devotes to his marriage. Again Celso opens the door:

> They live in São Paulo where they have a farm around two hours' drive from town, a place where they can get away. They also have an apartment in New York and a house in East Hampton, Long Island. They stay in the house in the United States every December for Christmas and during the summer in July and August. They are very happy indeed. Yes, they are very happy even though it is not easy to be married to a guy like Pelé who travels so much and is away from home so often with so many commitments all over the world. But Assiria is very supportive, and often travels with him, even though she knows she will have to share him with so many other people during the time they are away.

The next big trip abroad came later in the year – time for the next World Cup. Pelé had always dreamed of a World Cup hosted by the United States with England there to take on Brazil. Many years before the event he had told Rodney Marsh and Dennis Tueart that the World Cup would come to the USA. They laughed and told him he was crazy.

Although an earlier bid to stage the tournament in 1986 had fallen on stony ground owing to the fact that at the time, the NASL having collapsed, the USA did not have a professional football league, they were chosen to host the finals in 1994 ahead of rivals Brazil, Chile and Morocco because of their superior stadia, organisational ability and communication technology.

Yet football was clearly still a mystery to the average American. Before the World Cup draw, with the tournament just over two years away, an awareness survey in the States revealed that few people knew that the draw was taking place, less still what all the fuss was about. It attracted little media attention, certainly nothing that would detract from the saturation coverage of baseball, basketball and American football. England manager Graham Taylor posing with a New York policeman for the US tabloid photographers back home raised a few smiles from the locals, but no one had the first idea who he was. In the US, soccer was synonymous with only one figure: Pelé.

Nonetheless Pelé's dream had been realised. But after the qualifiers had been decided there was one part of his vision missing. 'I have fought for the World Cup to be staged in America, and now history will be made – but without England. For me that is a big loss. People who love the game wanted to see England taking part, and the sad truth is that they will have lost respect by failing to qualify.'

He was right. England were now regarded by the rest of the football world – even the tiny soccer nations of Africa and Europe – as a second-rate power. At home, without the national side in the World Cup draw, there was an insular disinterest in the greatest show on earth taking place across the Atlantic in the summer of 1994. Before the tournament I flew to Rio to spend a day with Pelé finding out what he thought was wrong with the English game, and how we could put it right.

Pelé was at his most expressive and expansive, and his verdict was a damning indictment of the fall from grace of the England that had won the World Cup in 1966, the 1970 team of tremendous vitality and stature and the valiant side that reached the semi-finals in 1990. 'England don't have the big stars, the big names, the influential players any more,' Pelé grimaced. 'Unfortunately, that has also been a problem for Brazil.'

But now Brazil had Romario, Careca, Dunga and a thriving new wave of talent on view when Brazil beat England in the States in the summer of 1993. Where was the English talent? Pelé struggled to name only Paul Gascoigne as a world-class performer. 'One big name in the national team is terrible, not good enough. Gascoigne is a tough player, and he is important to the team, but he cannot be expected to do it alone. When English league football was in its prime there were great players around like Bobby Charlton, his brother Jack, Bobby Moore, and Gordon Banks. You cannot compare Paul Gascoigne with any of them. In the best England teams there were four or five outstanding world-class talents besides the names I've mentioned. Where are they now?'

It didn't matter whether the FA appointed Kevin Keegan, Glenn Hoddle, Bryan Robson or Ray Wilkins to replace Graham Taylor. 'England need good players more than they need a good coach. The players are the base. The coach can be a father figure, someone who has the respect of the team; he can co-ordinate, organise, but the team needs quality players.' He accepted that the Third World nations had to some extent caught up, but there was no doubt that at the same time England had declined. 'They see so many games from around the world on TV, probably every country in the world. It's easy to learn.'

So were English kids spoiled for choice, with video games and alternative sports providing better incentives? Were youngsters in other parts of the world more hungry? There was a time, after all, when kids from London's East End and the north-east had few options other than games that cost little to play, such as football and cricket. 'We have lost a lot of youngsters to video games and other sports here in Brazil, but worse than that, we have lost a lot of open spaces around or inside our cities where the boys can play football, and that is the same in England.' He recommended a complete overhaul of the structure of the game in England, starting with a change in our philosophy, to develop our home-grown talent into the highly skilled international stars of the future. It was a widely held view even then, but still the FA and the Premiership are not listening.

Pelé wanted to spread the gospel of 'beautiful football' just at a time when our own game was crying out for help and guidance, pointing out:

> I want to work with the kids; the amateurs, not the professionals. Preparing and coaching the youngsters is the way forward. The big problem in countries like England is who prepares the player. I have had soccer schools in the United States and in Japan, and I did it once with Bobby Charlton, touring countries in the Far East. After the World Cup I would like to come to England to hold seminars.
>
> The coaches in England rely too much on strategy and who you should mark. That's not how to teach the youth. Let the kids play, let them develop their own personalities. Then give them strategy.

The English public might have mourned the absence of England in the States, but no tears were shed over the absence of their hooligans; indeed, it was one of the most relaxed tournaments of modern times. English support was instead transferred to Ireland, playing in only their second World Cup finals – especially after they succeeded in beating Italy and Mexico in their group and went on to the second round.

When the tournament hit the States, it was still not broadcast coast-to-coast on the main networks, but mainly on the Hispanic stations. Except, of course, when Pelé hit town: then it was a different matter. He had never been in greater demand with the media. The MasterCard Pelé column was syndicated worldwide throughout the tournament and he was inundated with requests for interviews, comments, predictions, anything.

It was only during the tournament that Pelé began to believe that Brazil could win. He had initially tipped Colombia as outsiders, but they were blasted out of the competition, losing all their group matches. He switched his prediction to a fourth win for the favourites after Brazil roared into the semi-finals for the first time since 1970 by finally beating Holland 3–2 in their quarter-final in Dallas, having established a 2–0 lead in the second half. 'We can take on anybody now,' said Pelé. 'Our confidence has grown in each match. Things are looking good.' Their beaming boss, Carlos Alberto Perreira, commented afterwards: 'I said it would be an open game – and it was one of the most spectacular.'

In the semi-finals, Brazil left it until the eightieth minute to take the lead with a goal from Romario against an exhausted Swedish side, by that stage down to ten men. It was on to the final, where they beat Italy to take the World Cup for a record fourth time. It was, however, an unsatisfactory finish: the championship of the world had to be settled on penalties after the score remained at 0–0 at full-time.

Italy's Roberto Baggio couldn't bear to see Brazilian captain Dunga raising the game's most precious and prestigious prize. The world's number-one player turned away, head bowed, condemned to relive the most cruel moment in soccer history for the rest of his days, for ever remembered as the man who missed the penalty that made Brazil world champions. The tears of joy after his two-goal semi-final triumph against Bulgaria had turned to tears of torment.

FROM FOOTBALL STAR TO GLOBAL AMBASSADOR

Pelé leaped up and down with an uninhibited joy during the tense penalty decider in front of a crowd of 94,000. But this time it wasn't the beautiful game that triumphed, it was the beast of the shoot-out. And Baggio was not the only Italian to loft his penalty kick over Taffarel's crossbar. Captain Franco Baresi, who had made a remarkable comeback after microsurgery on his knee during this tournament, missed the opening shot, crashing to the ground in disbelief and disgust with himself. At the end Baresi and Baggio flung their arms around each other, united in their desolation, after collecting their losers' medals and waiting for the glittering prize to go to Brazil. The South Americans may have been the people's choice for the title but this was far from a classic Brazilian team.

At least one spectator was harking back to Pelé's glory days. Bobby Charlton: 'From what Romario was saying before the tournament, he was obviously hoping this would be his World Cup. He did score some important goals, and Brazil are always looking for a hero to hang their hat on. But he didn't come good. You can't compare him with Pelé. I wouldn't hesitate to give Pete ten out of ten. Romario gets five.'

CHAPTER 12

LAI PELÉ: PELÉ'S LAW

'There is only one Beethoven. There is only one Sinatra.
There is only one Pelé!'
Pelé

After Brazil regained the World Cup in 1994, President Fernando Henrique Cardoso announced that the country's national hero was to be appointed minister of sport, declaring that he was 'a symbol of Brazil that has come up from the roots, that has triumphed'. It was those roots which gave Pelé the inspiration to try his hand at politics in his quest to change life for the better for future generations.

The world of politics was as far removed from the beautiful game as you could get. He moved into the pale green buildings in the capital, Brasilia. His full name, Edson Arantes do Nascimento, was engraved on the brass plate on his office door, and was used to identify him whenever he addressed the Brazilian Congress. During his term of office he attempted the seemingly unattainable: to revolutionise the football structure of his country.

'I don't belong to a political party, I am independent,' he said. 'That way I will be able to achieve something. My work is to help the children. I am not here to play politics – that way I can get out of here quickly.' As it turned out, that is precisely what he did.

In his quest to root out corruption in football and to bring in new regulations, he again found himself in renewed conflict with the CBF president, Ricardo Teixeira, and the latter's father-in-law João Havelange, president of FIFA.

Pelé became a mover and shaker in his own right, presenting his proposed reforms personally to Cardoso at the presidential palace, but in parliament he complained constantly about the lack of money coming into his ministry. 'There is just one thing that makes me upset in the ministry: our funds are very small and sometimes I need to beg.' When he criticised other ministers for failing to collect the 4.5 per cent of the sporting lottery that was theirs by rights, one replied condescendingly: 'Pelé, you are very new to this, you will not be able to understand.'

As a player Pelé might have been sent off more times than one would think, mostly for dissent, but politics was a far dirtier business than coping with the hatchet men on the pitch. 'I'm learning a lot about Brazil and politics. Sometimes it is very difficult but it is important for my life. Football cannot carry on the way it is, something has got to change. Everything I have and everything I am, I owe to football. The only thing I want as a minister is to repay a little bit of what I received. This is what I am most passionate about.'

Pelé's master plan was to provide players in Brazil with the same freedom their European counterparts now enjoy as a result of the Bosman ruling. Bosman, a Belgian player, successfully took his club to the European Court claiming restraint of trade. Every player in Europe has benefited from the resulting ruling which allowed players at the end of their contracts to switch to any club of their choice within the EC without a transfer fee prohibiting their move. He also wanted to allow clubs to form leagues that would not be under the control of Teixeira's CBF. In August 1997 Pelé announced his intention of bringing before the Brazilian Congress a bill restructuring the professional leagues for the benefit of the players and the game at large. Havelange was infuriated.

Havelange and Teixeira were adamant that Brazilian football was well organised and didn't need Pelé's interference. Havelange patronisingly advised Pelé to stick to organising schools sports and campaigning for new gymnasia around the country. His bill, declared the FIFA president, contravened FIFA regulations, and if the so-called Pelé Law was passed Brazil would be banned from the 1998 World Cup in France.

Pelé wasn't intimidated by this threat, dismissing it as farcical. 'Brazil won its place at the World Cup finals on the field, not through a decision by FIFA,' he said. 'Some years ago Maradona told me that Havelange was going gaga. I defended him and fought with Maradona, but now I think he really is becoming gaga.' Indeed, Havelange's latest action served only to diminish his standing in world football and to reinforce the view that he had become a dictator.

Another of Pelé's visions was multipurpose sports stadia for major cities, or *Pelézinhos*, as they became known. He also wanted to convert Brazilian clubs into commercial enterprises which could go public and offer shares on the stock market. Many of the clubs in Brazil are run as private trusts and, apart from pensions and personal taxes, are exempt from income tax for overseas transfers. Consequently it is a lucrative business to sell the best players abroad. Pelé wanted to change that, and to make it compulsory for clubs to publish annual accounts and to be run in accordance with company law. He was, too, an outspoken critic of the corruption that had infested the Brazilian game. 'If the CBF had to explain the contracts it made with Pepsi, Umbro and now Nike,' he declared, 'lots of people would be in prison.'

In early 1998, as the Brazilian Congress prepared to debate Pelé's bill, he said:

> The biggest problem with both FIFA and the CBF – with both Havelange and Teixeira – is that they forget to put something back into the game. They talk a great deal about how much money they had made, but for who? What do they give back to the game as its base? I have never denied that he looked after me when I was young. I have frequently expressed my gratitude for that. Yes, he did indeed look after me as if I was his son, and that is what puzzles me so much now. His anger, his rage. Yes, he gave me values, just as my own father has always done. Lessons about honesty, being decent, never dishonest. All I am trying to do with this bill is enshrine some of those values on the statute book. He should surely be pleased with what I am trying to do.

Yet even though Teixeira and Havelange's daughter Lucia were by now divorced, the ties that bound Havelange and Teixeira remained.

During his three-year tenure as minister of sport, Pelé made a real contribution to the furtherance of Brazil's national game. He was also, as a member of the government, entertained by royalty and world leaders, accompanying the Brazilian president on a state visit to England, where the Queen decided to bestow upon him an honorary knighthood. After the ceremony at Buckingham Palace, he turned up at Stamford Bridge, home to Chelsea FC, with the entire presidential entourage.

Shaun Gore, head of community affairs at Chelsea Village, had been surprised to get a call from the Foreign Office asking what sort of arrangements the club could lay on for VIP guests from abroad, and what sort of community services it provided. Gore supplied them with this information and was then summoned to a meeting at the Foreign Office.

It was arranged that the Brazilian visitors would call at Stamford Bridge to help launch a schools initiative. Gore explains that: 'The chairman, Ken Bates, gave me the go-ahead to attend the Foreign Office meeting. I expected to find myself in an office with a secretary going through what had been discussed on the phone. Instead I was shown into this huge room and there must have been thirty people there, from the head of protocol to the head of the Special Branch. I was told that the president of Brazil and his wife would be on a state visit along with the minister of sport – Pelé.'

When the presidential party arrived, Pelé was sporting a red ribbon round his neck with a medal on the end of it. The honorary knighthood, which Gore had not known about in advance, was big news that day and there was a massive media attendance at Chelsea's ground. Gianfranco Zola and Graeme Le Saux were present, along with the Duke of Kent, our sports minister Tony Banks and secretary of state for education David Blunkett. The children involved had been given Brazilian football kit to wear in honour of their guest, and they were overjoyed to be allowed to keep them.

Tony Banks recalls with affection the time Pelé inspected his beloved Stamford Bridge. He says:

He came down there with the president of Brazil, along with myself, David Blunkett and the Duke of Kent to launch a schools initiative. I remember congratulating him on his honorary knighthood and felt overawed as much as anyone else present on that day. Those type of feelings are an acknowledgement of how much he is revered. I must say this was one of the few times that whoever was advising the Palace were spot on. It was great that the Queen had made him Sir Pelé, and I didn't feel it got very much publicity at all on the day.

There cannot be many people in the world who are too busy to accept an invitation to dinner at the White House with an American president, but on a visit to the States Pelé was already committed to an official engagement and had to turn down President Bill Clinton. Celso Grellet was responsible for Pelé's global image and knew it was not an event to be rejected lightly. 'But Pelé is not the sort of person to let other people down and once he had accepted the other engagement he stuck by his agreement,' says Grellet. 'He told me not to worry, he would make sure he was available to meet the president another time.'

As luck would have it, just two days later Bill Clinton visited Rio, and Pelé, in his capacity as a minister, was invited to welcome him. 'I was standing beside Pelé,' relates Grellet, 'and he said to me with a little smile, "Look out for what I'm going to do." And he picked up a ball, threw it to Bill Clinton and showed him how to control it. It seemed such a ridiculous thing to do because clearly Clinton had never kicked a football before, but with so many photographers present, that picture of Clinton and Pelé playing football was an image that went right around the world. It even appeared on the front cover of *Time* magazine.'

That impromptu kickabout with the president of the United States was a trick of marketing brilliance which demonstrated Pelé's natural instinct for a photo opportunity that would best reflect his image. Had he gone to a formal dinner with the president, there would have been no press or photographers invited – it would have been strictly private. 'He joked with me that I might understand marketing, but he understood it better. But it was instinctive, from someone without a marketing background who pulled off a marketing coup.'

For the 1998 World Cup, João Havelange and Sepp Blatter planned a spectacular draw featuring some of the greatest players of the past. But not Pelé. It was a glaring omission that was bound to attract controversy, and it was obvious that Havelange's row with Pelé was behind his exclusion. It was to have far-reaching consequences, not least that, for the first time, the undisputed rule of Havelange was questioned. The circumstances surrounding the dispute convinced many FIFA delegates that the time had arrived to think seriously about an alternative to the autocratic leader.

At a press conference prior to the big event at the refurbished Stade Vélodrome in Marseilles the Pelé issue was high on the media's agenda.

'Why hasn't Pelé been invited to take part in the draw? We do not have a problem with Mr Pelé,' replied Blatter. So why had he not been invited to take part in the draw along with the other great footballers? 'We have no problem with Mr Pelé,' Blatter repeated. Sensing that the questioning would continue, Blatter made his comment a third time before he was asked. His tone made it plain this was all he was prepared to say on the matter.

Pelé was among the 1,500 special guests, but his presence

would be confined to the background, not featured in the main stage event in front of the 38,000 gathered for the draw followed by a special exhibition match between Europe and the Rest of the World.

The then British minister of sport, Tony Banks, was among them. As he took his prestigiously positioned front-row seat at the Stade Vélodrome, 'I was looking down at this seat next to me with a name on it I didn't recognise, thinking, "Who is this?"' The popular Chelsea-supporting minister was baffled by the FIFA name on the seat beside him labelled 'Edson Arantes do Nascimento'.

'This guy comes along and sits down next to me, and I was completely flabbergasted. It was Pelé. I had forgotten his full name.' They talked about football generally, but Banks was shocked that the rift with Havelange had gone so far. 'It was an odd situation to see just how far apart these two powerful men were. Pelé should have been on the platform pulling out the balls; instead he was banned from the ceremony by Havelange. Even when it came to the seating, Pelé was positioned at one end of the front row, with Havelange at the opposite end so that the pair would not have to meet on the way in or the way out. It was incredible.'

Pelé's period of office as sports minister ended in 1998, before the World Cup finals. The reasons for this are, like so many aspects of Brazilian politics, unclear. Stories did the rounds that he wanted to take time off for France 98; that there was a feeling in the government that he was not able to devote enough time to the job. But when it was suggested that he should step down there were howls of protest from the public, until finally he decided to resign on his own terms.

A motion was put forward in Congress to make him an

honorary citizen of Brasilia, which was vociferously opposed by a Workers' Party activist, Lucia Carvalho. She accused Pelé of, among other things, racism, citing as evidence his unwillingness to admit that he was the father of the child of a white woman who had brought a high-profile paternity suit against him. The proposal was vetoed. This slur so outraged the rest of Brazil that just about every other major city in the country immediately offered him honorary citizenship.

Pelé left an important legacy in the Pelé Law. This legislation is designed to make Brazilian clubs more business-orientated, although Pelé concedes that there are some concerns over the revolutionary changes. 'There are a lot of companies now trying to acquire teams. In one way this is good, but on the other side is the worry about creating a monopoly. If organisation was better, then maybe we could protect young players in Brazil. Brazilian football is now really a supermarket for foreign clubs.'

Meanwhile, France 98 was about to get underway. The sixteenth World Cup finals in France featured thirty-two countries, the highest number ever. And this time it featured both Brazil and England. One of the main criticisms of the tournament was the fiasco of the distribution of tickets. Who can forget the farce of thousands of England fans jamming the phone lines when a paltry few thousand more tickets suddenly became available after so many complaints and so much lobbying? In other major footballing nations, too, the ticketing policy generated much the same confusion and anger.

Pelé Sports and Marketing had successfully been involved in the 1994 World Cup, despite the logistical problems of the long distances between games in the States, so when the CBF asked for tenders to handle the commercial side of part of the Brazilian ticket allocation in 1998, Pelé's company put in a bid.

According to David Yallop, in his book *How They Stole the Game*:

> When Ricardo Teixeira realised that the Pelé bid was the highest received, he telephoned one of the rival under-bidders and advised them of how much they would need to increase their bid by to ensure that they won the contract. The rival duly got the business and proceeded to sell thousands of air travel, accommodation and ticket packages. The result was at least 4,000 customers who, having arrived in France, discovered that there were no tickets for them. Legal actions are currently in progress.

In the early stages Pelé named Alan Shearer as England's only hope of winning the World Cup, and voiced grave misgivings about the composition of Glenn Hoddle's midfield. As David Beckham and Steve McManaman awaited their big chance, he was damning about the lack of domination in England's midfield. Unless Paul Ince and David Batty could reassure Hoddle that this most vital of departments could function without more creativity, then the England coach had to consider a change. As it turned out, France 98 was the launching pad for Beckham and marked the beginning of Shearer's decline.

Meanwhile, the world looked to holders Brazil in anticipation of the emergence of a new Pelé in the twenty-one-year-old Ronaldo. Current European Footballer of the Year and twice voted FIFA World Player of the Year, the young man with the gorgeous girlfriend and dazzling talents certainly had all the potential and credentials. Pace, dribbling prowess, spectacular goals and big money transfers to PSV Eindhoven, Barcelona and Inter Milan made him one of the most recognisable figures world football had offered since Pelé. Pelé himself merely remarked: 'There is only one Beethoven. There is only one Sinatra. There is only one Pelé!' but he was nevertheless full of admiration for the young Brazilian. 'He is a terrific player, a great talent and no doubt the key man in the Brazil team, but he has a lot of pressure on him and a lot of responsibilities.'

Pelé was impressed, too, by England's young hope, David Beckham. 'From my point of view, he is a very important player for the team, he works very hard, he has good vision, good movement and good delivery.'

There are many cynics in journalism, it is a natural trait, and one English reporter observed that he thought Pelé was all things to all men, and had a happy way of giving you what you want. In other words, a good story about an English player for the pallet of the English media, and no doubt something similar for the Germans and Brazilians, too. That has never struck me about Pelé, in the numerous interviews in which I have been present. Normally he is prepared to be honest, perhaps not brutally so, but will give a real assessment none the less.

One of Pelé's laments is that the modern player is in danger of losing his identity, his personality, in the crazy pace of the modern game where winning carries so much reward. No longer do players perform with smiles on their faces, and so lose that rapport between performer and audience. Footballers are paid such vast amounts that the ordinary working man has long ago lost any sense of identifying with them, even more so when contracts are blatantly disregarded and broken. But Pelé perceived in Beckham that endearing quality of still being in love with the game, as well as with the Spice Girl he was to marry, Victoria Adams. 'But you must give him freedom. Some coaches might try to put him in one position, I would not. I would organise the team and let him free. He knows what to do, where to go to make things happen. He reminds me of Gerson, my teammate in the 1970 World Cup finals. He is one of those rare players who can always get in perfect crosses with deadly effect.'

Nothing stirs Pelé more than a goalscorer of genuine quality, and he had high praise, too, for a young Englishman, Michael Owen, first unleashed by Hoddle late on in England's group match against Romania. Pelé saw similarities between the eighteen-year old Owen, whose transfer value subsequently soared to £25 million, and the samba-rhythmed kids on the conveyor belt from the Copacabana. He goes on to say:

> The way he moves, the way he dribbles, the way he controls the ball, his technical abilities remind me of a lot of young Brazilian players. He has that Latin style which is certainly not typical of English players, and that is what has surprised me most about him. In fact for me Owen is one of the best surprises of this tournament. He showed the form everyone has been talking about, and he showed it in a grand fashion before a world audience. He has a very bright future and I am personally looking forward to seeing him mature into one of the sport's top stars. England should be proud to have a player of this calibre with such tremendous talent.

Pelé also had some advice for twenty-year-old French striker Nicolas Anelka, whose sulky behaviour had not endeared him to the English fans. 'Anelka has ability, he knows where the goal is and he is very cunning. But he now ought to go to Italy or Spain to see how he can escape their tight marking.' Anelka, of course, subsequently signed for Madrid and Paris St-Germain. Another

French player he rated was Patrick Vieira. 'I regard him as highly as I did Johan Cruyff.'

Pelé was anxious about the standard of refereeing at this World Cup from the start. 'It is so erratic. There is some sort of misunderstanding by all the referees. Some are calling certain fouls that others are not. There is no consistency. When there were five red cards in one day, it was strange, because some players who had been playing in a certain way and had not been carded were suddenly carded. There has to be a balance. Too many red cards spoil the game, but only two red cards in the first twenty games is not a good balance either.'

England progressed to a second-round meeting with Argentina, beating Tunisia and Colombia but going down 2–1 to Romania in their group matches. England lost Beckham in the second half when he was sent off after retaliating to a tackle by Simeone and yet again their fate was decided on penalties, with the scores level at 2–2 at the end of normal time. Yet again, their number failed to come up in this lottery and they were out of the tournament.

Pelé cited Michael Owen's brilliant solo goal as one of the best, if not the best, of France 98. Of the attacking, inventive players in the World Cup, Pelé named Owen alongside Zinedine Zidane and Ronaldo.

At last we have a World Cup of goals. It's been an exciting tournament, especially the second round, which was fantastic. The number of goals and chances and the fact that teams came here with more intention to move forward than before has made for a more wide-open game. The fans love it. The new FIFA rules outlawing the tackle from behind and getting rid of the grabbing has allowed the creative players such as France's Zidane, Brazil's Ronaldo and England's Michael Owen to attack. Unfortunately, in the middle of the first round, the refereeing changed because FIFA told the referees to get tougher, and it confused everyone. Each referee seemed to have his own rules. But it got much better and eight very strong teams – Italy, France, Denmark, Holland, Argentina, Germany, Croatia and Brazil – advanced to the quarter-finals.

Brazil steamed into the quarter-finals, with a decisive 4–1 victory over Chile, but their place in the final was another prize that had to be decided on penalties. This time the unlucky losers were Holland. France disposed of Croatia by 2–1 to set up a battle for the FIFA World Cup trophy between the holders and the host country.

But the tournament was to come to a dismal end for the 1994 champions and their new star, Ronaldo. Although he was carrying an injury he had scored four goals en route to the final and had been outstanding in the semi-final with Holland. He knew he would need surgery once the World Cup was over but in the meantime he was just one more game and one more painkilling injection away from glory.

It was not to be. Unknown to the rest of the world, on the eve of the match he suffered a seizure and had to be rushed to hospital. Coach Zagallo deemed him unfit to play and his name was absent from the first team sheet submitted to FIFA. Instead Edmundo was listed. As the world's press speculated on the reason for Ronaldo's exclusion it was obvious that something was amiss in the Brazilian camp. The team failed to appear for the warm-up; then, when a new team sheet was hastily distributed less than half an hour before the kick-off, this time including Ronaldo, it was clear that the Brazilians were panicking.

While questions were being raised as to what kind of effects the medication absorbed into Ronaldo's system to ease the pain of his injured knee could have had, and whether these might have caused the seizure, theories about his late inclusion were circulating. The shadow of Nike was the most prominent. Ronaldo was the fulcrum of the company's massive global advertising campaign and they had virtually 'bought' the Brazilian team with a formidable sponsorship deal. It was suggested that one of the many clauses in their contract specified that, if he was fit, Ronaldo had to be selected. There were dark mutterings that Nike had been consulted about Ronaldo's hospital examination and much debate as to whether the player should have been allowed to start the final.

How far was Zagallo's decision influenced by outside forces? How reliable was the evidence of team doctor Lidio Toledo and his assistant, Dr Joaquim da Mata, who took Ronaldo by car to the Lilas clinic for his pre-final tests? Meanwhile, involved in the argument that was raging on in the Brazilian dressing room as to whether Ronaldo should play was none other than Ricardo Teixeira. Clearly, suspicions that the Brazilian federation was far from purged of its manipulative core could not be discounted.

The Brazilian team were shaken by this incident, but even if Ronaldo had been on top form it is unlikely that the defending champions would have been any match for France. The hosts powered to a 3–0 victory with two goals from Zidane and one from Petit, despite having Desailly sent off in the second half. The whole of France had been united by the success of their team, and the country which had staged the third World Cup in 1938 was at last able to celebrate winning it.

Yet 1998 was a mixed year for Pelé. The inspiration for his footballing career, his father, died, but the year also saw the birth of his twins, Joshua and Celeste – so important to Pelé that his daughter should be named after his mother. She had then turned seventy-six, and was and remained a major influence on his life, living only an hour's drive from São Paulo.

The following year saw the *Daily Mail* publish a salacious article on their sports pages with the incredible claim that Pelé had somehow confessed to a homosexual affair with one of the coaches who cared for the young players of Santos.

Celso Grellet explained why Pelé thought long and hard about a response and decided the most dignified way to deal with the situation was to ignore it. The central character behind the insinuation was Diego Maradona. Pelé did not want a confrontation between the two. Yet Pelé's advisors were tempted to issue some sort of retraction statement on his behalf. While the slur on Pelé's sexuality received no publicity in England apart from the one-page lead article in the *Daily Mail,* the story was published with large headlines throughout South America.

Celso explained:

Pelé is heavily involved in the anti-drugs campaign, particularly the abuse of drugs in sport, and Maradona was clearly an ill man. Pelé felt it was best not to respond because no one could possibly take Maradona seriously. There is no doubt from my point of view that Maradona has made some ludicrous accusations, the one about Pelé's sexuality being just one of many, as a result of pure envy. Maradona was very jealous of Pelé and has been ever since Carlos Menem, the former Argentine president, invited Pelé to the country as his special guest because Pelé was his favourite player. It angered Maradona that the Argentinian people might place Pelé above him.

Maradona's drug problem increased and his health deteriorated. Celso added:

> There were a lot of statements from Maradona regarding Pelé, silly things. Then one day I was very surprised to receive a number of calls from journalists to ask for my comment because Maradona had said that Pelé had had a homosexual experience. It was never true, but Pelé is a big man and he decided that he would not respond and create a big battle between himself and Maradona.
>
> Pelé has a lot of respect for Maradona as a player but felt that the media should not give any credence to the comments of an ill man. It would have been too easy to have said bad things about Maradona in return, but Pelé would not do it. In fact, Maradona was making a lot of statements about a lot of people. Pelé felt that the best way to protect Maradona from himself was not to create a conflict between two such high-profile figures. For me it was a very sad episode because I have always thought that Maradona was the best footballer in the world after Pelé.

CHAPTER 13

WORLD CUP POLITICS

*'Pelé is to Brazilian football what Shakespeare is
to English literature.'*
João Saldanha

As MasterCard's official world championship soccer spokesman through to 2002, Pelé was in Tokyo, where the sponsoring company launched their Asia Pacific FIFA World Cup 2002 campaign, for the World Cup draw. As part of his contract, he appeared in company advertisements and promotions in support of world championship soccer events around the world, including the World Cup.

Football's future is an issue close to Pelé's heart, and in Tokyo it was clear that he was deeply concerned about the growing influence on coaches of fat pay cheques, which are leading them to become more interested in protecting their lucrative jobs at the expense of allowing individuals to express their natural talents. The stifling of such freedom of expression in players depresses a former footballer who himself symbolised ultimate freedom of expression. He says:

> The speed of the game is much faster now. It is much more difficult to find space. When I played you were used to getting some tough games; now they are all tough. Coaches today try not to give space to the opponent. In my day, we used that tactic in some hard games, but not all games were defensive. Today you see even Latin teams, even the likes of Brazil and Argentina, playing like some of the European sides, with very tough marking, which ensures that the speed is very fast.

The most worrying problem to him is that coaches have too much influence and power over the team and the players. The coach has a lot of responsibility and he doesn't want to lose, so he will instruct his players to play defensively. It then becomes more difficult for them to change that approach because of all the outside factors that are making the game more competitive: the merchandising in the game, the prices on the players' heads and pay TV, cable TV and terrestrial TV all investing in football. 'You feel that it doesn't matter what kind of game it is, people still want to see it. If there are no good players no one worries, because that's normal,' Pelé said. 'But I feel that is wrong, that it is important to try to give them more freedom to show the public their qualities.' Stifling players' natural instincts can make for robotic football. 'But if you have good players, you will see a good match, as has always been the case.' He was particularly concerned about current and future generations. 'Even at under-15 level you hear coaches saying, "You have to mark", or "Work hard", "Run here", or "Stay close". The kids are treated like machines, and they don't change as they develop.

They should not be treated like that.'

Pelé was impressed by the leap in standard shown in Japan in 1993 by the professional J League, which began with the signing of Gary Lineker for Grampus 8 in Nagoya. He felt that the Japanese would improve still further as more players moved abroad and gained experience with foreign clubs, such as happened to Hidetoshi Nakata in Perugia in Italy. Pelé adds: 'I had a farewell game here twenty years ago and the level of the Japanese players was very good at that time, but they did not play with too much spirit because they were not used to playing in the same league as they do now, and did not have too many foreign players, which they now have. Today I think the quality is fantastic.' He considered the J League 'very competitive' and said that any team visiting Japan would now expect a tough game.

He also felt that Japanese players were developing their own style of soccer which incorporates qualities from both Latin America and Europe. 'Most of the Japanese players have talent, quality and finesse on the ball like the Brazilians, yet they also have the same running power as the Europeans.' Steve Perryman was a coach in Japan, and Ossie Ardiles was on his way back, while Arsène Wenger became highly respected after his spell of coaching with Grampus 8. Manchester United and Arsenal had been linked the week of the World Cup draw with Shinji Ono of recently relegated Urawa Red Diamonds. Ono, the David Beckham of Japanese football, was one of the personalities involved in the draw. At long last Japanese players were beginning to make a mark in Europe and South America. Pelé laughed: 'Nakata may be my colleague with MasterCard in the future. He's a big name now.'

Even though Sepp Blatter had by now replaced João Havelange as FIFA president, Pelé would not be involved in the draw procedure, explaining that 'Now Mr Blatter and I work together, but he didn't invite any former players to be involved in the draw.' Indeed, FIFA were not parading the usual suspects such as himself, Michel Platini, Sir Bobby Charlton or Franz Beckenbauer, to avoid any suggestions of favouritism as Brazil, England and Germany were involved in the bidding for the 2006 World Cup. Instead, the retired sumo wrestling star Konishiki, better known as Dump Truck, tennis player Kimiko Date, bright young Japanese footballer Shinji Ono, Korea's Ahn Jung-hwan, French World Cup-winning coach Aimé Jacquet, now technical director of the FFF, Mexican World Cup sensation and ex-Real Madrid striker Hugo Sánchez, and Dutch coach Frank Rijkaard were among those who pulled out the bright red balls.

England's chances of qualifying were dealt a massive blow by their exclusion from the nine European seeded nations in the draw. For the second World Cup running, they faced the ignominy of not even being among the top nations in Europe, let alone the world. The last time England enjoyed the protection and prestige of a seed was back in Italia 90, and even then there was a suspicion that the decision was manipulated in order to maroon English hooligans on the island of Cagliari. England's dearth of competitive games in the run-up to Euro 96 was blamed for their failure to amass sufficient points to merit a top seeding in 1998. For 2002 they have no such excuse.

FIFA's seeding committee decided to take into account performances in the Euro 2000 qualifiers and the qualifiers and finals of the World Cup in France. England stumbled through to Euro 2000 but, after drawing in Rome and topping their World Cup group, sending Italy into the play-offs in the process, they made no significant progress in France, where they went out on penalties to Argentina in the second round. Even their current FIFA world rankings would not have helped Kevin Keegan's cause.

England were ranked just ninth in Europe before their Euro 2000 campaign culminated in a defeat by the Scots at Wembley, and the new list was sure to relegate the country to eleventh place.

The downgrading of England and Italy from world champions to also-rans was hard for some to accept. While the English contingent at the draw shrugged this off as inevitable, the Italians were taking it personally. One journalist in particular was livid, having been reassured on the flight to Tokyo by the Italian FA president on the FIFA committee that his country was assured of a prestigious seeding. 'How is it possible that Italy are in the second pot? They are three times world champions. Croatia were fifteen months ago bronze medallists in the World Cup, and they, too, are in the second pot, as are England, an historic country. Yet Norway, Sweden, the Czech Republic are seeded. The history of football is not being respected.'

Pelé smiled politely, and said that it was difficult to analyse. 'I respect any team that is now on a different level, but there are some countries, big former champions like Uruguay, who today do not play well. Yugoslavia was rated not so long ago as one of the best teams in Europe, but today they are not. Any sport must treat everyone equally. No nations of past glories and power should be given special treatment. The balance of power has shifted around the globe and current form does not respect tradition.' Pelé obviously felt that discretion was called for to avoid offending either England or Italy, but the reality was that on current assessment, irrespective of the anomalies, neither country had a good cause for complaint.

According to Pelé, Franz Beckenbauer worries about the future of German football, too. 'He says to me, "I don't know, Pelé, where we will be in four years' time when our best player is still Matthaus and he is nearly forty years old." We all worry about the future.'

At around the turn of the century, Pelé believed that, because the world shrinks, football from all of its corners is becoming much more even in standard. The Africans were then hard to beat, even the United States were no pushovers, and Japan, as hosts, were competitive in the 2002 World Cup.

The 2002 World Cup was the first ever to be held in two countries: Japan and South Korea. Pelé's view was that it was a positive development. 'The first time a World Cup is changed in some way you don't know exactly how it will go, but the Japanese people are very well organised, and they have a sense for administration. The stadia I have seen have not been selected just for the World Cup but for the future of the game here, and I think they will be very nicely prepared.'

Potential problems had been discussed in FIFA committees between Sir Bobby Charlton, Franz Beckenbauer and Pelé, among others. One concern was that June rains might make the pitches heavier and more difficult. The kick-off times were not ideal for television in many countries, including Brazil.

Although Pelé himself was under considerable pressure to perform for Brazil and keep them on top of the world rankings, he recognises that the pace of the game has intensified, and so many games at the highest level cannot be sustained by the top players. Yet the pressures have changed, and the salaries have been magnified out of all proportion to the days when he evolved into the world's richest footballer, earning six times as much as the president of Brazil in a decade. The pressures then were more political in nature. At the time of the World Cup in Mexico, Brazil was suffering a lot of political strife. 'We simply had to win, or good political people would have been removed. Four years later, the army took over, and that offended my philosophy. I didn't want to play, so I didn't. That is real pressure

– fighting for something you believe in, not just playing football for a lot of money.'

The Maracana, as famous a name in world football as Wembley, is still easily the most evocative of football's great cathedrals, and any player would be privileged to play there. Deep in the bowels of this spine-tingling amphitheatre are huge, well-appointed dressing rooms – the home one named after Pelé, the away one in honour of Garrincha. There is an indoor synthetic pitch where the teams can warm up, the baths are luxurious and the players' individual benches are equipped with oxygen at half-time and after the game. However, the players can find themselves waist-high in water if anyone is crazy enough to stage a match during the rainy season.

The crescendo of noise created by a capacity crowd makes the walls shake. For many players, it is literally a moving experience: a long, narrow grate on the left-hand side of the tunnel is designed for the use of those whose bladders are affected by the overwhelming atmosphere.

The Maracana is where Pelé scored his 1,000th goal and where the great Brazilian teams have performed in front of nearly 200,000 hypnotised fans. Built in 1950 for the World Cup, which the host nation lost to Uruguay in the final, it was for many years the largest and most spectacular stadium in the world, at one time regularly accommodating 170,000 supporters.

When I arrived there a few days ahead of the inaugural World Club Championship in January 2000, the stadium was a broken-down, crumbling ruin. There were pneumatic drills and pots of paint all over the place as workmen struggled to polish up the old stadium in time for the tournament. The Maracana's deterioration had been well documented, but it was still a massive shock to see at first-hand the scale of decay. You had to steer carefully through the rubble, jagged concrete and the stench of urine to view the pitch which, by contrast, was in immaculate condition.

The Maracana was being transformed into an all-seater stadium for the first time in its glorious history. As a result its 110,000 capacity was reduced to 75,000 for this tournament. There were plans to undertake more work in time for its fiftieth anniversary later in the year. But in terms of facilities and modernity, not even a revamped Maracana is a patch on existing European grounds. Yet although it is clear that they have neither the stadia nor the infrastructure to stage the world's biggest sporting event, Brazil, along with England, Germany, South Africa and outsiders Morocco, were in contention to host the 2006 World Cup. And the country with the largest income disparity in the world could hardly justify spending the hundreds of millions of pounds it would take to get the facilities up to scratch.

Pelé was strongly opposed to Brazil's candidacy for 2006, and once again his arch-enemy Ricardo Teixeira was a focal point of his objections. 'The president of the CBF can't keep on talking nonsense. Brazil has not got any stadium which is fit to stage a World Cup match or meet the conditions set down by FIFA. I worry that Brazil is bidding. Their intention is to make money but not to do a great deal of work for it.' Brazil, he says, are the best team in the world on the pitch, but their administration is terrible. To bid for the World Cup was simply a waste of money, and if asked to help the bid he would refuse. He was not the only one: Tostão, his colleague in the 1970 World Cup-winning side, had already publicly declared his opposition.

It was a tough line for Pelé to take, because it is open to misunderstanding within Brazil. But he is not against his home country ever hosting the tournament, just not until they sort out their administration, organisation and funding. 'I don't want to participate on the committee that has been set up because I don't have confidence in them and I do not trust those people.' In England the FA's 2006 campaign director, Alec McGivan, commented: 'The biggest problem Brazil had was that Pelé was not supporting them. If you were running the Brazil bid you would be distraught that the nation's most famous son was not backing his country. Imagine if Bobby Charlton was not supporting England.'

Instead Pelé spoke out unreservedly in favour of South Africa, arguing that the last tournament was in Europe, and that every continent except Africa has hosted the finals. He favours rotating the World Cup between continents. He saw 2006 as a good time to support an African bid in the hope that perhaps they would in turn give their backing to Brazil for 2010. In doing so he risked incurring the displeasure of two of his contemporaries in the world game, now FIFA committee colleagues, who found themselves in opposite corners of this particular struggle: Sir Bobby Charlton, who led England's vigorous £10-million campaign, and Franz Beckenbauer, who played a prominent role in Germany's claims for the tournament. 'For England, it won't change anything in the game globally, whether they have the World Cup or not,' he said. 'For Africa it would be a great achievement and good for the future of football.'

The FA were in a weak position from the start, having struck a cosy arrangement in the committee rooms in the days of Sir Bert Millichip's chairmanship. In return for German backing for their bid to host Euro 96, Millichip promised to support Germany for the 2006 World Cup. The subsequent amnesia on the part of Millichip clearly annoyed the Germans, who intensified their campaign to beat England.

Pelé's quick-fire solution for England and Germany was that they should stop bickering over who should stage the competition and join forces to unite the European vote. It was a suggestion that had been mooted but rejected by the FA, who had their own agenda on the matter. After years of sneering at the way João Havelange ran FIFA, cajoling votes to acquire power and keep it, the FA appeared to have adopted some of his methods themselves.

Favours were granted to countries which had votes on FIFA for the 2006 bids in a wide variety of ways. Peter Withe, for example, was on the FA payroll while coaching a rival national team in Thailand. FA chief executive Graham Kelly and chairman Keith Wiseman were kicked out of Lancaster Gate in a cash-for-votes scandal after promising the Welsh FA £3.2 million in grants in return for their vote for Wiseman to be elected to the FIFA executive where, although he wouldn't have been able to vote on the final outcome of 2006, he would have had an influential voice. Kelly admitted that there had been a private internal FA strategy to tour the world offering what he felt were acceptable inducements in return for votes.

While England and Germany went head to head, the clear favourites were South Africa, whose bid Havelange and then his successor, Sepp Blatter, had endorsed. In England, Tony Banks, before his elevation to minister of sport, had also been an outspoken proposer of the South African bid. How ironic, then, that Banks should have to resign as sports minister to take on the position of special envoy for England's 2006 bid, which he had been pushing relentlessly from the moment he swore his oath of allegiance in the House of Commons on his appointment, and that Germany should have been chosen as the host nation.

One of the world's biggest clubs opted to participate in the first World Club Championship. Manchester United's Champions' League triumph in 1999 qualified them for the tournament and both the FA and the government felt it would assist England's

World Cup bid for the side to be there, even if it disrupted the English season, and especially for United, to such an extent that they were obliged to withdraw from the FA Cup, of which they were holders, for one season. It subsequently transpired that back in March 1999, when United had been in the semi-finals of the FA Cup, the FA had been approached by FIFA to host the World Club Championship tournament. They had declined, a refusal that surely would not have endeared the FA to FIFA. Instead Brazil accepted an invitation, and immediately the ramifications of the South American venue began to impact on the FA and the Old Trafford club.

As well as to the Maracana, Rio is home to Brazil's most famous landmarks, Sugar Loaf mountain and the Christ statue on Corcovado Mountain, and, of course, the Copacabana and Ipanema beaches, where they still play beach football. There are numerous laid-out beach football pitches with goalposts. These are sacrosanct: no one puts down their towel and little umbrella here. The three-mile Copacabana is a human zoo, unbelievably densely populated, particularly at weekends. Even the mosaic pavements are bustling with cyclists or joggers. On New Year's Eve three million locals, all dressed in white, bathe in the waters of Copacabana to purify their souls on the one night of the year when the lady of the sea is there to be worshipped.

It was the perfect backdrop for the new tournament. The games generated pure excitement amid the ubiquitous samba rhythms. Sir Alex Ferguson has experienced some special moments in the great stadia of the world, and it takes something special to make him starstruck. Nothing topped leading his team out at the most famous venue of them all. The spiritual home of football in Rio was a place the Manchester United boss had always wanted to visit.

Dwight Yorke, too, relished being in a land of uncounted legends and of the unsurpassable legacy of Pelé. The spiritual connection that drove him, inspired him and ultimately made him a footballer was at last fulfilled. Ever since he booted his first ball along the beach or dodged those exuberant, boyhood tackles in Tobago's dusty streets, Yorke's sporting instincts have urged him to think Brazilian, play like a Brazilian and laugh and win like a Brazilian. He confirmed with all the emotion of a long hooked fan:

Brazil is my football country. It always has been. They are the team I have supported all my life. In the Caribbean, the Brazilians have forever been the footballers the people really loved. I wasn't any different. They are so brilliant to watch, to admire, and I followed them in the World Cups and marvelled at their skill and ability to entertain. Pelé was always in your mind. Maybe we were a bit too young to have seen him play, but that didn't stop us wanting to be him.

Pelé wrote off Manchester United's chances of winning the tournament because of the heat in Rio and the skill of local favourites Vasco da Gama. 'Do not underestimate how vulnerable the temperature change will make them. They have come from an English winter into a Brazilian summer. I know all about their quality and the fact they are European champions, but they must adapt to the heat, even at night. It will be decisive. The winner of Vasco v United will go on to be champions, and, for me, it will be Vasco.'

It was during the half-time break, as Manchester United trailed 3–0 to Vasco da Gama, that I found Mario Zagallo trying to eat a sandwich in the one and only, and extremely cramped, cafeteria on the top level of the Maracana. But he was more than delighted to stop and chat away merrily about Pelé. The superstars of Brazil are highly approachable, and the coaches nothing like the insular, standoffish, suspicious football folk of England. While the English champions were being pilloried for closing their doors to the locals and just about everyone else in their first two days in Rio, it was open house for the media among all of their rivals.

Zagallo told me:

> My happiness was not only to have been privileged to have played with him in one World Cup, but also to have a major part as the manager in the other two. But of course, the best of them all was the 1970 World Cup finals, especially the game against England. Pelé came up to me, gave me a hug, and told me that we had to be together again for Brazil to win the World Cup for the third time. And we were.'

Pre-tournament favourites United ultimately suffered the embarrassment of coming third in their group and spent the last three days of their stay in Brazil topping up their tans, while Vasco da Gama took on Corinthians in the final, decided in the dying moments by a missed penalty from Edmundo of Vasco.

CHAPTER 14

LIFE BEYOND SIXTY

'Pelé still retains great status within his own country,
and throughout the rest of the world, for that matter.'
Gordon Taylor; PFA Chairman

As his sixtieth birthday was celebrated, Pelé's mission to ensure that the game thrived in the new millennium continued. He remains determined to tackle what he regards as the evils of commercialism and has a clear idea of the way ahead. He still insists that a position within the game is not for him. Coaching and management jobs are for 'crazy people', he says. 'I never want to be the president of FIFA, or of the Brazil football federation.'

In the light of the suspicion that Ronaldo's 1998 World Cup appearance just hours after the youngster's traumatic seizure was a symptom of the mushrooming influence of sponsors, Pelé is adamant that the integrity of the game must be preserved. The main fear is that accountants, sponsors, and the national backers are forcing the modern footballer to play far too many games at the current frenetic pace, thereby threatening to shorten their careers. France's 1998 World Cup star Emmanuel Petit warned that some players are already taking drugs and many more will be tempted to take them just to get them through so many high-stress matches.

In October 1999, Pelé teamed up with another master of the game, Johan Cruyff, to announce his intention to fight rampant commercialism in the sport. 'If the commercial side wins this battle, then players and fans will be the big losers,' he declared.

> My motto is the same as Johan's. People only turn up to see good football played by good players. Rivaldo is the best player in the world. But he will not play for as long as other great players if he has to carry on at this tempo and with so many games for Barcelona and Brazil. Johan and I entertained millions all over the world. Neither of us was built, coached or trained to be physically the best. We had the best skill in the world, and that's why people remember us. There will never be another Pelé. I can't see a seventeen-year-old winning the World Cup. I can't see a player of great skill scoring hundreds of goals in his career. Now players are physically abused and suffer when they've played a few seasons in the modern game. 'Kill' is the foundation of the modern game, and the skill level is much lower.

Cruyff concurred, saying:

> We've reached decision day. The leaders of all the competitions, from the domestic championships, the Champions' League, FIFA and UEFA, have to face up to the harsh truth and act urgently. They must all cut back on their games to save professional football and ensure that it can be entertaining. If they don't make these cuts they will collectively kill the game. I'm appalled by the

techniques and skills of the players. I only see robots out on the pitch now. Footballers now are trained only to be fit and strong enough to deal with the number of games they're expected to play. There are no more than one or two coaches who are taking the time to teach their players skills and tactics. The players now compete in games, rest for a day then have to play again. It's a crazy circus, It grieves me as a sincere lover of football.

Yet the powers that control the game were still expanding, showing little or no interest in cutting back on the fixture log-jam in order to protect the players. Undeterred, Pelé has called for a world football calendar to unify the fixtures and prevent exhaustion and injuries to players, and has joined Sir Bobby Charlton, Michel Platini, Franz Beckenbauer and Cruyff on FIFA's think-tank with a mandate to guide the future of the game. Although Sir Bobby doesn't agree with all of his colleague's ideas, he says, 'Pelé wants to do something for the game and I am always quite prepared to help him. But I feel at times that he is pushed by other people into a position where he has to deliberate on all sorts of subjects and it's a touch out of his control. He is expected to have an opinion on just about everything.'

On the modifications he would like to see made to the modern game, he still advocates giving players the choice between throwing and kicking the ball back into play after it has gone out, but he does not believe that goals should be made bigger. 'If you want to score more goals, practise more,' he says.

Pelé spoke out against the foreign mercenaries who plunder English soccer as the national game was engulfed in debate over a lack of home-grown talent. Pelé blames the influx of highly priced foreigners for squeezing promising English youngsters out of Premiership football, and even the First Division, thereby depleting the resources available to successive national team managers. He expressed his disgust with the worldwide trend towards jumping between clubs and countries. 'I see Italians and other nationalities going to England and playing for clubs there. They turn up and they kiss the badge on the shirt, pretending to the fans that they really love the club. Then, one year later, they go to another team somewhere else and do the same thing. That is not good. These players don't have the heart. They just play for money.'

The growing influence of foreign players in key positions throughout Premiership sides has already been raised at FA level, but legal concerns prevent the imposition of quotas on imports from other European Union countries.

In Brazil, the 'Pelé Law', his legacy as minister of sport, has come into force to clean up the game there, long dogged by corruption and financial and political exploitation of clubs by egocentric, ambitious club presidents. Both Brazilian finalists in the World Club Championships, Corinthians and Vasco da Gama, made bargains with Mammon, selling their 'brands' to American finance houses which took over their merchandising, commercial activities and stadium development. The size of Vasco's deal is unknown, but Corinthians', according to accountants Deloitte & Touche, is worth $70 million, or £43 million, over twenty-five years.

Meanwhile, Pelé contested all the accolades for the new millennium, along with Muhammad Ali. The World Sports Awards of the Century took place in the opulent surroundings of Vienna's State Opera House, where Pelé received the ultimate award as the footballer of the millennium in a vote overseen by IOC president Juan Antonio Samaranch. Carl Lewis and Nadia Comaneci were winners in their categories, and Mark Spitz pipped Britain's Steve

Redgrave for the title of Watersports Athlete, and Alain Prost, Michael Jordan, Jean-Claude Killy and Steffi Graf were among the other winners. Ali received the award in the contact sports category in a fitting finale to the event. 'I have had many victories in life, won many medals and championships, a lot of fights,' he said later. 'Nothing, not even the Olympic Gold or the world title, means as much to me as this.' For Pelé, it was the same. As he collected his huge crystal trophy he confessed that his legs were shaking for only the second time in his life. The first was before the penalty that became his 1,000th career goal.

In England Ali was named the BBC's Sports Personality of the Century; in France Pelé was *L'Equipe*'s Sportsman of the Century, ahead of Ali, with Carl Lewis coming third.

Ali's global recognition is enhanced by his high profile in the States, where boxing is one of the most popular professional sports, whereas soccer is enthusiastically followed only in schools. Yet Pelé was one of the few non-Americans honoured in *Sports Illustrated*'s millennium gala awards at Madison Square Garden. He was nominated in the Athletes Who Changed The Game category. Nobody from outside the States was very familiar to the organisers. Baseball, American football, basketball and ice hockey were among the main category winners and Peggy Fleming, the ice skater, beat Pelé in the Athletes Who Changed The Game section, while America's victory over the USSR at ice hockey was adjudged to be the century's greatest sporting moment. In this context, the mere fact that Pelé was honoured at all demonstrates his appeal even in a country where football hardly merits a mention in the national newspapers. Similar polls conducted on the other side of the Atlantic provided a very different picture. For example, *The Daily Telegraph* readers' poll voted Donald Bradman – an Australian batsman Americans have probably never heard of –

runner-up to Ali. Sebastian Coe was third, Jack Nicklaus fourth and Pelé fifth, while Carl Lewis languished in twenty-fourth place. Fifty-one per cent of *Mirror* readers chose Ali as their sportsman of the millennium. Pelé (13 per cent) came second, ahead of Bobby Moore, with Lester Piggott fourth and George Best fifth. However, Reuters, the worldwide sports and news agency service, put Pelé above Ali in their awards.

Whatever the variations, it is clear that Pelé and Ali are the world's best-known and best-loved sportsmen of the century. Like Ali, Pelé feels he has set the right example to the youth of the world, notably underprivileged black children who might have otherwise never believed it possible for them to emerge from poverty and inequality to succeed. Sport has always been an escape for many such kids. Pelé might have had a hard streak on the field, but he kept himself clean off it, and his good name and status meant as much to him as all his spectacular goals.

He puts it like this:

> I think we can say that, together, certain sportsmen have done a lot for society over the past one hundred years. Today you see black people all over the world, in football, boxing, tennis, golf. That was something important people like Muhammad Ali and myself have given to humanity. Throughout history there have been sportsmen who have achieved great things and broken down barriers. To me, winning trophies or awards has never been important for my own personal pride. What is important is what you give to people. When you get these awards, when you are a face in the world, you have an opportunity to give a message to young people. Drugs are a worldwide problem and I try to show the poor kids that I am here and I am

clean, and they can be clean too. I come from the same background as these children. We were very poor indeed. In our neighbourhood the struggle was to have enough money for food, not to buy football boots, so I understand the problems of the children living in poverty.

The two titans of sport first met in New York twenty years ago. Pelé admires Ali not only for what he achieved as an athlete, but because he worked so hard to show the world that we are all, as people, equal. 'Everyone remembers that he was a funny guy with a great sense of irony. We first met when I was at the Cosmos. When someone asked Ali what he thought of me, he said, "I don't know if he's a good player, but I'm definitely prettier than him."' After that, they discussed their philosophies of life in private. Ali wanted to know about Brazil and its problems, while Pelé gained a greater understanding of the racial problems Ali had faced in the United States. 'Since then, I think we have learned that sport brings people in the world together, black and white, rich and poor, they can all be part of sport.'

Within Pelé's private inner sanctum, there have been long and exhaustive discussions about what his magic formula is. They are not quite sure it can be put down to any one aspect of Pelé, but cumulative aspects of his life, his football and his personality. Celso Grellet says: 'There are a lot of explanations, but not any one single reason.'

There is no doubt that a big advantage he has over other sportsmen is that football is such a universal sport – by far the biggest single sport in the world in terms of popular appeal. The difference between Pelé and Muhammad Ali is that boxing is not as popular and does not have such a worldwide base as football, not to mention the fact that it has many detractors owing to its inherent violence. So arguably Pelé is a more important figure than Ali. Another significant factor is that Pelé has never jeopardised his image, which cannot be said of players such as Diego Maradona or George Best. Off the pitch his behaviour has been exemplary and has maintained credibility.

This is not to say, of course, that he has not suffered problems, trials and tribulations, the most recent of which was the conviction of his son Edson for murder after appeals for the charge to be reduced to involuntary manslaughter were finally defeated. In 1992 Edson and a friend allegedly had been taking part in a *pega*, an unofficial car race involving high speeds and reckless stunts, when a man was knocked off his motorcycle and fatally injured. Pelé's son denied responsibility, claiming that he had stopped to try to save the dying man. But he and his friend received the minimum sentence for the offence, six years' imprisonment under a work-release programme, which means they were locked up in jail at night and allowed out during the day. Even this incident, however, did not tarnish Pelé's reputation.

There is a special magic to Pelé's personality which lies in the way he treats people who want to have part of him, an autograph or a picture. There is a magic, too, in the pleasure he derives from giving something back to his fans, particularly children. It is not false – it comes naturally, and has its roots in his upbringing. Many famous people do not like this aspect of fame, and it shows. Some don't like fame itself. But Pelé loves it, and that the people respond to his enjoyment.

He has cut across boundaries of race and religion, uniting generations of children in their desire for a real icon. Even the current generation, who of course have never seen him play, regard him as their big hero, and he is still a role model all over the world for youngsters. He is one of the few human beings who have become more influential, more popular, more famous and more legendary after their glory days than during them.

In his public appearances Pelé has sometimes overshadowed prime ministers and royalty. When he was appointed a global ambassador for UNESCO, the occasion was marked by the gathering heads of state from around the world. As soon as Pelé's car arrived at UNESCO's headquarters, he was mobbed. They didn't even wait for him to leave the car park. Everybody, including all the heads of state, asked him for a picture or an autograph.

Yet in spite of this, or perhaps because of it, he remains an intensely private person. Even Sir Bobby Charlton doesn't profess to know the real Pelé, saying: 'Of course, we are always friendly when we meet, but you never see him on his own. There is always an agent, sponsor or some member of his entourage present.'

Pelé has done more than anyone to communicate the beauty, athleticism and power of football to the world. In doing so, he has touched just about everyone, from those who love the sport, through those with a fleeting armchair interest, to those who never saw him play but know of him for his ambassadorial role.

FIFA's director of communications, Keith Cooper, likens Pelé to Elvis, a figure who transcends even death. 'It was only on a visit to Graceland in Memphis, Tennessee that I have ever sensed a phenomenon of comparable dimensions. Elvis and Pelé: nothing in common, it seems, except their boundless recognisability and appeal.'

One of my favourite lines about the great man was overheard from Franz Beckenbauer. Beckenbauer, himself no stranger to fame and its attendant pressures, was sitting next to Pelé in the VIP box at the European Championships in Sweden in 1992. Children were literally climbing over the Kaiser to get at his neighbour, who was visibly embarrassed at his friend's discomfort. 'No problem,' Beckenbauer reassured him. 'I love sitting next to you. It's the only way I can get people to leave me in peace!'

Clearly Pelé had no ambition to move into management when he finished playing, but his affections naturally always gravitate back towards Santos. Celso explains Pelé's links with his former club:

> He has acted as a consultant to the last administration, but cannot devote as much time to the club as he would wish. In fact he really has very little time at all because he spends most of it running his own businesses. But he remains an honorary member of the board and sometimes, when he can, attends their board meetings which usually take place every three months. In the last year he has tried to create a school for young players, been a scout and even helped train the kids at Santos.

But Pelé's time is at a premium. The passing years do not fade the memories of the generations that loved him as a footballer, and admired him as a world ambassador. Pelé needs a full-time staff to deal with his diary, his travel, his multitude of businesses. Celso added: 'The menu of activities has grown and grown, it is now very extensive. Naturally it started in South America but it quickly developed on a worldwide basis as well.'

Expansion has not tailed off. Far from it. Pelé is still a big name in world sport, and his influence and stature has not waned anywhere in the world. Just prior to Euro 2000, graced by Pelé with his usual incomparable presence, Celso was preparing for the next stage of Pelé's worldwide dominance, a personal internet site. Celso said: 'We launched the Pelé website in Brazil in the middle of July 2000 and a European one in October when Pelé was sixty.' Indeed, Pelé's sixtieth birthday saw him become a grandfather for the first time, as his eldest daughter Kelly Cristina and her American husband had their first child.

The name Pelé transcends so many generations. New technology as well as existing genuine worldwide love for the man will propel him into the minds of the latest generations of football followers from an early age. It will ensure that Pelé's stature and image and incredible footballing abilities are never forgotten.

So, Pelé can, with pride and justification, have little to regret. As he reflected on his life and times, he told me: 'Sometimes you think, that in your life, you might want to change things, or you could have done something differently. But this is my life, and I don't want to change it because that is how it is. I would do everything again. I thank God for my life.'

Pelé selected two defining moments in his career:

One is my first goal for Brazil against Sweden in the World Cup final in 1958 because I was the youngest player in the World Cup, just seventeen years old and I had just come into the national team. I had also played against Wales, and I had scored the goal for Brazil to qualify for the finals, but it was very important for me to have scored a goal in the final.

Equally important to me was to score my 1,000th goal because it was a world record and because it was in front of a full house at the Maracana. Everybody respected such a milestone, such an achievement.

Completely fulfilled in his life within the sport, content and happy with his private life embracing his entire family and his second marriage, there was still a massive void. Pelé felt there was one major issue still to be resolved and it was in the political arena. Pelé might have been more than a touch unimpressed by the complex world of Brazilian politics after three years as minister of sport, but looking at the broader spectrum, he was ill at ease with the levels of corruption within his own country that helped maintain the huge divide between the Brazilian classes.

'Pelé is one of the big names in the world, everybody knows Pelé,' he says. 'Pelé has enormous respect, yet even the power of Pelé in Brazil cannot stop corruption and the death of children in my country. This makes me feel very, very bad.'

It pushes Pelé into thinking that he owes it to those children, just like he was, to re-enter the political arena.

> One question I have to ask God one day is, why? I have worked in the government, I have been minister of sport, and I have done a lot to try and help, but unfortunately power is in the hands of bad people. I would like to do something more, but I am afraid that there are a lot of politicians who don't want to change things, they don't want to help people and this cannot be changed just by one person, it can only be changed by a team of people with the will to make those changes.

He does not rule out a future move into the political arena to aid his social conscience and come to the aid of his own people.

His mood was earnest and he says that, 'Since I am young enough to look ahead and still do things in the future. I take a lot of different paths, but really the only thing that bothers me is the social differences that exist in Brazil. This is bad. I don't know why this problem cannot be resolved. Perhaps I will have to find out.'

CHAPTER 15

THOUGHTS ON THE BEAUTIFUL GAME

*'The modern game is all about now and no one has
the patience to wait.'*
Pelé

Just when most people are contemplating retirement, Pelé reached his sixtieth birthday with a new landmark in mind: 'I want to be able to kick off at the Maracana when I am one hundred years old. Sixty? I feel twenty-five. I've talked to my friends about it and they are right, it doesn't hurt to be sixty.' Perhaps this is because there is a history of long life in Pelé's family. His grandmother on his father's side lived to be a hundred, his own father died aged almost ninety and one of his aunts, his father's sister, died aged ninety-two. Pelé's life has always been stable and healthy. When he stopped playing for Brazil he weighed 77 kilos. Even now he is still only 82 kilos, only three more than when he played for Cosmos, and that was some twenty years ago. So what was his recipe for longevity? 'I do a normal amount of exercise, but I also help select Santos's young players and train them twice a week, which keeps me close to football. Besides that I go to the beach, there's also a gym in the house and I like to play tennis – hard.' Pelé showed no sign of slowing down: 'Every time I see Bobby (Charlton) or (Franz) Beckenbauer all they talk about is their golf. Everybody plays golf. I feel too young to play golf. It's a nice walk, but I don't feel there is any emotion in it.'

With all his youthful energy and the enormous amount of respect he receives everywhere he goes, as well as his footballing expertise, it is still a surprise to many people that he hasn't tried his hand at coaching. Despite a number of offers, Pelé, with his customary forthrightness, was clear on the subject: 'I don't want to be a coach. For thirty years, I've been loved and respected by everybody and the door has been open for me all over the world. If I had become a coach they might have wanted to kill me after a couple of months.'

Nevertheless, coaching, both from a football politics and a youth development perspective, is a subject Pelé, who still coaches at Santos, has strong views on. Against the backdrop of the appointment of Swede Sven-Göran Eriksson – England's first overseas coach – he discussed the subject. At the time of Eriksson's appointment, the FA Technical Director, Howard Wilkinson, suggested that the new manager might contemplate disregarding qualification for the 2002 Finals in Japan and Korea to concentrate on a more long-term, visionary development programme aimed at building a team capable of making a challenge at the 2006 Finals in Germany. Pelé disagreed with this thinking. He argued: 'It is not good to say you don't need to qualify for a tournament. It is necessary for the players and the country to have the incentive of the chance of winning. It is not good for the young players to be deprived of that. Any coach must not take that incentive away.'

Ever the internationalist, Pelé had no problem with the FA's radical decision to appoint a foreign coach to the England job. 'Modern football involves a big exchange of players from all over the world and I don't see any problem with coaches coming from outside either. The problem is if they don't succeed. I know that Eriksson is one of the first of the modern coaches, and one of the best.'

Certainly Pelé applauded the FA for handing Eriksson a five-year contract, believing that one year, even two, is too little to change anything. Any coach needs at least three years to prepare a team. He continued: 'In the end, the crowd is the same for everyone and that's why I would never accept a coaching position, even if there was a lot of money on offer. I know that if I was given the job of preparing a team in Brazil I would instinctively understand which players to pick, but I don't know whether they would be capable of doing what I wanted. Often it's not the players' fault, but if the team doesn't do well the public don't care, the coach is the first one they blame.'

In an age when coaches are only one bad result away from the sack, Pelé lamented the lack of stability this causes and believes that continuity in the coaching staff is one of the key factors in engendering confidence in the players. 'But the modern game is all about now and no one has the patience to wait.' Because of this, the pressure for instant success can make stresses of the job unbearable, tensions that force managers out of their jobs. It is a trend that Pelé deplored and found upsetting. Indeed, in three instances in Brazil around fifteen years ago, successful club coaches received an invitation to work with the national team, but turned the chance down. This hardly boded well for the future.

Against this, Pelé felt modern coaches have excessive influence over the players, influence that is taking the fantasy factor out of the game and strangling individualism on the pitch. Certainly, the pace and tactical emphasis of the modern game has created a sport in which work rate has become highly prized.

He says, 'The coaches have too much power in dictating the way players must perform. "Play this way, or I'll drop you," ensures that the players will conform. This attitude is removing improvisation and creativity because some coaches do not value these qualities.' Such influence, had it existed in 1970 when Brazil won the World Cup, would have meant that Tostão and Pelé would not have been in the same side. At the time, the press insisted the two could not be on the same pitch together because they played in the same way. 'Intelligent players can always play together. I had the freedom to play the way I wanted. I could be in defence, midfield or going forward. These days, the coach stands there shouting at the players because they're not moving the way he wants. If players don't have their own personalities, how can they play? Some beautiful movements are lost.'

Worse, in Pelé's eyes, is the coaches' influence over the development of young talent. 'Sometimes the youngsters get the same treatment as the senior players! That way they won't improve, since they never experience the freedom to express themselves. Even in Brazil it is starting to happen, the way tournaments at under-17 or under-18 are exposing the kids to the same pressures as the seniors; they have to win, they have sponsors, and they can't play as they did before. It's win, win, win.'

While Pelé was at ease with the idea of an international trade in players, he does worry that the quantity of foreign players was affecting the development of youngsters throughout Europe. 'In one way it is good, youngsters are around the best players. But if there are too many foreigners, the youngsters then have to wait an extra two or three years for their chance and that restricts their development.' One wonders if the beautiful game might be that little bit more beautiful if Pelé had been persuaded to become a manager.

CHAPTER 16

FIFA, PELÉ AND MARADONA

'The people voted for me, but now they want me to share the prize with Pelé. I am not going to share the prize with anybody.'
Diego Maradona

When Diego Maradona left FIFA's award ceremony in Rome on 11 December 2000, before Pelé received his Player of the Century award, the animosity, frustration and anger that the Argentinian felt towards the Brazilian were out in the open for everyone to see. The ceremony had finally highlighted the feud between the two. Even events leading up to the ceremony were pure theatre.

Officials from football's world governing body had tried to defuse the embarrassing situation over who should be named Player of the Century by giving both three-time World Cup winner Pelé and Maradona an award each. FIFA originally planned to name only one Player of the Century with the winner being decided by a combination of votes cast on FIFA's website, through its own magazine and by a grand jury. But although

FIFA refused to confirm the figures, it was widely reported that a surge of on-line support from Maradona fans had the recovering cocaine addict leading with 78,000 votes ahead of Pelé on 26,000.

FIFA came up with a compromise solution that they felt would resolve their huge embarrassment if Maradona, after all his controversial brushes with authority, should win the vote. The award would therefore be split up into an Internet Player of the Century and a FIFA Jury Player of the Century. Effectively Pelé would be the choice of the football family, while Maradona could have the less-than-satisfactory distinction of winning the internet poll.

After originally threatening not to attend the ceremony when he heard of this compromise, Sepp Blatter, FIFA's General Secretary, had to personally persuade Maradona to turn up, who did so grudgingly. And so the build-up to FIFA's grand event in the Foro Italico was tarnished by the rivalry between the two stars, which had first appeared in 1998 when Maradona had bizarrely accused Pelé of having had a homosexual affair.

Before leaving Buenos Aires, Maradona said: 'The people voted for me, but now they want me to share the prize with Pelé. I am not going to share the prize with anybody.' He added: 'They are judging me on the twelve years I played in Europe, something Pelé did not do. Let's be serious – don't compare me with him any more.'

Maradona supporters protested throughout Argentina over FIFA's decision. 'Pelé and all of Brazil are crying because Maradona won the election,' sports daily *Olé* gloated.

In turn, Pelé's supporters blamed FIFA for conducting a web-based poll which was sure to be dominated by younger voters who remembered Maradona in action, but not Pelé.

When Pelé arrived in Rome he argued: 'Every generation produces its greatest players. I'm happy with the recognition I was given in the past. As early as 1958 I was awarded a title – O Rey (The King) – and that's enough for me.'

As tempers rose, Maradona described Pelé as 'overrated', and Pelé responded by saying there were several of his compatriots better than the Argentinian. In Rio de Janeiro and throughout Brazil there was outrage as Pelé hit back: 'Socrates, Rivelino, Romario, Tostão ... I think that if Maradona wants to speak with Pelé, he has to speak to them first.'

Maradona delayed proceedings by arriving late and then embracing numerous acquaintances, including a slightly embarrassed Pelé, following which both men were given a warm welcome. Maradona left the gala dinner after receiving the internet award and before Pelé received his accolade. Maradona bluntly declared, 'I want to go home' and promptly left with his wife, Claudia, and his agent.

Although no longer the grotesquely bloated figure of the previous year, the forty-year-old Maradona did not quite look in as good shape as the sixty-year-old Pelé, and that told the tale of the vast difference in lifestyles of soccer's two icons.

Pelé later diplomatically said: 'I would have liked Maradona to be there to join me on the platform, but he had already left.' Maradona had earlier thanked FIFA, adding he dedicated his trophy to: 'The Argentinian people, Fidel Castro, my wife Claudia and all the players in the world that I love and respect. The people voted for me. I feel good in my head, serene. I'm happy and proud.'

Pelé had been flanked in the audience by Beckenbauer and Platini, while Maradona sat beside his wife Claudia, unmissable with her newly bleached hair and lime-green mock fur stole.

Again Pelé was asked to respond. He said: 'It's no secret that we're not friends but Diego did well at Napoli and I respect him as a player. But if he thinks that makes him better than me, that's his problem.'

The two-week feud culminated with Maradona insisting on having the final word: 'I had the vote of the people – Pelé won by forfeit.'

FIFA realised that it was not a good idea to dabble with the vagaries of the internet and the peculiarities that it can throw up. Although their intention was to secure the will of the people, it backfired. Indeed, there had been suspicion that there was a campaign in Argentina to ensure Maradona gained the most votes as there was a big disparity between the results from the internet and from the readers of the magazine. Blatter announced that a new polling method would be found by 2004, when the world soccer governing body celebrated its centennial.

Two rows behind Pelé sat Alfredo Di Stefano, angry and puzzled by all the fuss, but with probably the most sensible view on the matter:

Who is the greatest player of the century? Just one player? For me, no one. Maybe Bobby Charlton. Or Puskas, or Gento. Or Michel Platini. I don't know. They are all different. It is impossible. Anyway, football is not a sport for individuals. It is a sport for teams and, in truth, the only prize they gave correctly tonight was to Real Madrid. Madrid is the club of the century and has always had great teams. It is unarguable. It is a genuine award for a club that has standing and meaning. To see these people doing this tonight, it is a piece of floss and nonsense. These kinds of awards mean nothing at all when this happens.

Clearly, FIFA were concerned about presenting a favourable image of the game, but the whole episode created universal condemnation in both Argentina and Brazil, where only days earlier both nations were in eager opposition on the pitch.

'Pelé wins on the big carpet,' declared Brazil's *Folha de São Paulo*, using a local expression for a match that has been won in the boardroom rather than on the pitch. 'At the last minute, FIFA created a trick to kick Maradona into touch and decorate Pelé as the best of the century.'

It added: 'The legendary Argentine midfielder is *persona non grata* in the corridors of FIFA.' In similar vein, Rio de Janeiro's *Jornal do Brasil* ran the headline: 'FIFA finds a political solution.'

In Argentina, where posters with the words 'wretched FIFA' had decorated a number of lamp posts on the morning of the ceremony in Rome, *Olé* emphasised that the two had hugged each other before the awards began. But the same paper, gloating a week earlier that Maradona would win the contest outright, added: 'The questionable aspect of this whole story was the way FIFA handled it when it became clear that Maradona would win the internet vote.'

In Colombia, the Bogata daily *El Tiempo* ran the headline: 'FIFA wash their hands of Pelé and Maradona.'

Brazilians were seething at the very notion that Maradona could have outvoted Pelé. Veteran sports commentator Armando Nogueira said Pelé and the late Garrincha were in a class of their own. 'Pelé and Garrincha filled my heart and soul,' he wrote, 'so much so that I won't allow comparisons. The two are simply incomparable.'

Nevertheless, despite their rivalry, Brazilians and Argentinians, who had been arguing all week over who should be named Player of the Century, were united in their condemnation at the way

FIFA had handled what was always going to be a contentious issue. In the end, nobody was satisfied.

CHAPTER 17

WORLD CUP 2002 KOREA AND JAPAN

At the time this was written, the first World Cup of the new millennium was rapidly approaching without Pelé's long-awaited successor in sight. Would the tournament in the Land of the Rising Sun finally shed some light on the reasons why no one had emerged to supersede Pelé as the World's Greatest Ever Player? Doubtful. Diego Maradona came close with his exploits in Mexico in 1986, and perhaps the tournament itself would reawaken Ronaldo's claims, enhance those of Rivaldo or strengthen those of the current world champions France and their mesmeric Zinedine Zidane. Meanwhile, there had been a call to retire the no. 10 shirt, currently worn by former World Footballer of the Year Rivaldo, as an everlasting tribute to Pelé. Precedents include Napoli's refusal to allow any player to wear the no. 10 after Maradona's departure and AC Milan's withdrawal of the no. 6 shirt on the retirement of Franco Baresi.

Brazilian football circa 2001 was in decline: its image had been tarnished by two corruption inquiries; crowd chaos at the league final play-off led to more than 150 fans being hurt; the national team had three managers within a year, while Brazil struggled to even qualify for the World Cup. Brazilian President Fernando Henrique Cardoso has been tempted to call up the triple World Cup winner for a return to the political arena. It was Cardoso who named Pelé as Minister of Sport in 1995 but after three years of trying to push through radical reforms, Pelé returned to the business of being a United Nations charitable ambassador, championing youth and anti-drugs campaigns. Cardoso said: 'Pelé is a symbol of Brazil across the world so when he wants to return to political and administrative life the door is open.'

Pelé will inevitably be high profile at FIFA's World Cup draw and at the final itself. He was UEFA's guest of honour at the Champions League final at the San Siro and he selected Bayern Munich's Oliver Kahn as the MasterCard Man of the Match after the goalkeeper's phenomenal penalty saves in the victory over Valencia in Milan. His selection of the Bayern Munich goalkeeper was quite ironic, as Pelé himself commented: 'Here it is, the first time ever that I'm actually choosing the best player and I give the MasterCard award to a goalkeeper! This is bit strange for me, because during my entire playing career I always killed the goalkeeper!' Pelé explained his decision: 'It was an even, tough physical game. Both teams were very, very tired at the end of extra time. I never like to see a match end on penalties, but in the end I felt Bayern Munich deserved to win because they tried more to go forward and score. The tone of the game changed dramatically with two penalties called within the first five minutes – both teams played a bit nervous.'

From his own experiences, notably scoring his special 1,000th goal from the spot, Pelé recounted:

The crowd at the stadium and fans watching all over the world, think that penalty kicks are easy to convert because it's just you against the goalkeeper. But honestly, it is very, very difficult, especially in a match like this one, where there is so much pressure to score and because these days goalkeepers prepare themselves much more for penalty kicks. The first, crucial save made by Kahn in the penalty shoot-out was fantastic! He was like a cat making that save and for that reason I selected him as the MasterCard Man of the Match.

Pelé did his homework before the final, studying videos of the semi-finals before giving his customary profusion of pre-match interviews in a variety of languages. For the benefit of the English media, he pronounced his opinions on Owen Hargreaves – the England under-21 midfield player that had made a huge impression in Bayern's triumph over Real Madrid when he stood in for the suspended skipper Stefan Effenburg. Hargreaves was the major talking point for the English media and Pelé's views were highly regarded as usual.

When it comes to the World Cup Finals, there is no more recognisable figure, no more sought after personality, than Pelé.

CHAPTER 18

PELÉ: THE WORLD'S GREATEST EVER FOOTBALLER

Pelé is still The Greatest, and may always be The Greatest.

Johan Cruyff described Pelé as, 'The only player who surpassed the boundaries of logic.'

Edson Arantes do Nascimento is the FIFA Player of the Century who holds the Guinness World Record of 1,283 for total career goals and no player is ever likely to beat that.

After all these years, decades, even generations, no one has usurped his throne at the pinnacle of the global game, the beautiful game, indeed he is the greatest player of all-time in world football, and only a handful of candidates have come close. And he remains at the top of the pile, despite the extraordinary exploits of current world stars: Cristiano Ronaldo, Lionel Messi, Neymar, and legends such as Diego Maradona and Johan Cruyff.

Cristiano is currently the World No. 1 and recently surpassed Pelé's seventy-seven for Brazil. However, the seventy-six-year-old Pelé challenged the Portuguese captain and Real Madrid megastar to go one step further. Pelé was happy to see Cristiano overtake his international goals record, but considered that the other man still had a long way to go before he could be even considered to be 'The Greatest.'

Ronaldo hit a hat-trick for Portugal in a 5–1 win over the Faroe Islands in World Cup qualifying, to take his international goal scoring to seventy-eight, the first of those a spectacular scissor-kick early on in the game. 'I saw the goal, it was really special,' Pelé told *Goal.com*, 'It was a really nice play.' Pelé's seventy-seven Brazil goals came in just ninety-two appearances, but he trumps Ronaldo as he also won three World Cups. Ronaldo, who helped his nation bring home the Euro 2016 trophy, managed seventy-eight strikes in 145 games for Portugal. 'Of course, these are different times,' Pelé said. 'But the beautiful thing about football is the goals. And I take this opportunity to send a big greeting to Cristiano Ronaldo for that victory.' In reference to his total career goals record, the three-time World Cup winner added: 'Now he has to score more than 1,283 goals!'

While Pelé shrugs off the 'Wannabe Greatest' from the modern era, he has the same answer for iconic players from other generations. Pelé insists that he and Diego Maradona are friends, despite a constant war of words over the years, but believes the two former World Cup winners should not be compared.

In his book, Maradona snapped back at Pelé for being critical of his accomplishments, while the Argentine also often plays down the achievements of his South American rival. When Pelé was speaking at a Snickers event that saw competition winners from over twenty countries to play with the legend, he gave Ben Hayward of *Goal. com* an exclusive interview on 5 September 2017 [extract]:

'I can't explain why Maradona is so concerned with that because I always say that he was one of the best in the world, and that's true. Now, we can't say that Maradona was a great header. He didn't score goals with headers. And we cannot say Maradona shot very well with both feet, because he didn't shoot with his right, only mainly with his left ... so from time to time, when people make comparisons, I make jokes about that. For me he was a great player, just that you can't compare Maradona with Pelé.' Pelé claimed it is all in good humour and says he and Maradona are close, despite the constant quarrels over the years. 'We are friends,' he said. 'We are always joking. I always say to him: "Maradona, you can be level with Pelé when you have scored more than one thousand goals." And he says: "I can't now, but it doesn't matter!"'

It has been my pleasure and privilege to have interviewed Pelé many times in order to compile an authentic and true picture of his life and times. The interviews have occurred around the world, but there have been many occasions when they have taken place in London.

The invitation that was to mean so much to me popped into my busy email, but despite the volume of electronic correspondence these days, this one caught my attention instantly. It was an invitation to Pelé's seventy-first birthday party on 26 October 2011. It might have been half term and the family were off for a break on the south coast, but my ten-year-old daughter Poppy (who had never heard of Pelé) and my football enthusiast wife Linda (a Chelsea fan) had to put up with me making a dash back home in mid-week, because an audience with the Great Man himself is rare enough, but on his birthday it was an invitation I couldn't decline, whatever the inconvenience. Well, this was a personal invitation for an audience with THE Greatest Footballer of all time. Who could refuse?

Not that it was the first time I'd talked to him – far from it. I had not only interviewed Pelé many times in the preparation of compiling his life story for this book, but also on many other occasions for various journals for whom I worked as the chief football writer, such as the *Daily Mirror* and the *Daily Express*. Even though I had come to know him well and had met him, oh, maybe twenty or more times over the years, I would never turn down an opportunity to 'chew the footballing fat' with the guy universally recognised as the best of all time. Of course some say this accolade goes to Diego Maradona, or Cristiano Ronaldo, or Lionel Messi. Not me. For me, Pelé is still No 1.

On this occasion I was to catch up with the three-time World Cup winner in Covent Garden, London, for the global launch of his new sports lifestyle collection. Pelé was in London for his seventy-first birthday and to launch a new range of Pelé Sport boots and iconic leisure clothes marketed as: 'Viva a Revolucao Bonita', meaning 'The Beautiful Revolution'.

After my journey back from Boscombe, near Bournemouth, I was off in search of a tiny road behind the Shaftesbury (Avenue) Theatre where Pelé was holding court all day to launch his new range of sports gear and was going to finish things off with a birthday bash at the same venue. Pelé spent the entire day facing the media, mainly TV cameras, but only specially invited journalists were present, and an invitation to this media gig was the hottest media ticket in town. As you would expect, Pelé's ranges of boots and leisure ware were on display, mostly in glass cases, or displayed prominently on a series of iPads.

During the first part of the day he played host to the fashion media and trade representatives, then he held court with a selected group of TV crews and journalists for one-to-one interviews – I was down on the list representing ESPN (the cable and satellite sports TV channel). Finally Pelé spoke at a special drinks reception with guests who included Rio Ferdinand, Michael Laudrup and the great man's England 1970 World Cup opponent Terry Cooper, formerly of England and Leeds United.

Brazil's leading all-time record goalscorer told his star-studded audience that he was delighted to be in England and hailed the country's top-flight division, saying: 'The English Premier League is the best league in Europe, better than La Liga.' When asked about who his toughest opponent had been, Pelé, who faced Bobby Moore and Giacinto Facchetti at the peak of his formidable powers, joked: 'Sylvester Stallone during the filming of *Escape to Victory*. He was very strong.' (In this World-War-Two film, in which he co-starred with Michael Caine, Pelé and others, the 'Rocky' star played an American POW-turned-goalkeeper.)

As a birthday present, Pelé was given a special lifetime award: a glittering, eighteen-carat gold-plated football boot. This was presented to him by Professional Football Association Deputy Chief Executive Bobby Barnes and the then Arsenal youngster Alex Oxlade-Chamberlain. Barnes said in his presentation speech:

> Alex is one of the best young players in the English Premier League. He made his debut at sixteen, and if he achieves a fraction of what Pelé did he will have a fantastic career. Everyone remembers Pelé's Brazil teams from 1957–70, and the World Cup victories of '58, '62 and '70. Only a few things are memorable from my childhood – the Apollo moon landings, Muhammad Ali's boxing fights ... and Pelé. On behalf of the PFA, we are delighted to present this award as a symbol of our esteem.

By the time I was allowed that precious access to the inner sanctum where Pelé was being filmed by a procession of media from all over the world, my slot was running about half an hour late. Actually, that wasn't too bad – in the past I've often had to wait an hour or even much longer beyond my time slot. But I was as bad as the rest. No matter how many Pelé signatured shirts adorn my wall, irrespective of how many times he has signed my book *Pelé: His Life and Times*, I still come back for more. Gerry Cox, an old Fleet Street chum, became at my request my unexpected 'cameraman'. After doing his day-job filming my interview (his cameraman hadn't turned up), he was given little choice as I asked him to do the honours and take a snap on his iPhone of me and Pelé.

From my personal perspective, this wasn't so much a routine journalistic assignment, but an opportunity for yet another chance to shake his hand and get him to sign my book about him. Although he hadn't seen me for a few years, and must have been presented to literally thousands of journalists since then, he still recognised a familiar face, and once he knew he was meeting a trusted 'friend', he embraced me the only way a Brazilian can, with genuine affection, a broad grin, and a large hug. One thing you notice when you meet Pelé is that he is not a large man, yet his hugs are pretty big and compensate for his lack of size. 'It must be six or seven years since I last saw you,' I hazarded a guess, 'and I can imagine you took a while to recognise me, as I've changed a bit, I'm a bit more grey, have a bit less hair, but you haven't changed at all.'

Pelé smiled and pointed to the jet black mop of hair on top of his head, saying, 'I keep the hairstyle the same, and if the hair is the same, I look the same, I will never change the hair!'

While he is generally recognised as the Greatest Footballer

of All Time, he has never, to my knowledge, been asked who have been his personal all-time greats, and his all-time greatest. When I did so, his answer was typical of him. Pelé doesn't believe that anyone has taken his 'world's all-time greatest' crown since he left the stage four decades ago. He was still No. 1 on his seventy-first birthday.

So Pelé believes he is still the greatest, and there won't be many who think otherwise. Some say Messi has overtaken Maradona, and that is the view of Ossie Ardiles. I have known Ossie for a long while, and he believes that Messi is the greatest footballer of all time. It's all a matter of opinion. Messi himself suggested that he could not judge whether Pelé was a better player than him, since he had never seen the former Santos forward play, to which Pelé replied that he would send him a copy of his movie!

While visiting the victims of the earthquakes in Japan, Pelé said that he would show Messi an account of his career. 'It is a normal thing when a player is compared [to a player from another time period], sometimes he is not interested in the comparison,' Pelé told *globoesporte*: 'If he really did not see me, I'll do what I once did with Maradona: I'll send him the video *Pelé Eterno* and then he will.' Back then, Romario felt the Barça goalscorer would only gain by watching the documentary. 'If Messi sees the video, he'll probably learn some things. You simply cannot compare him with Pelé. You cannot say he is the same when he has never won a World Cup. Messi has all the conditions to be the best one day, but first he has to overcome Maradona, Romario and then eventually Pelé.'

As for Pelé, he considered whether there has been anyone to take his place. He told me: 'I think another Pelé – that is a little difficult because my mother and father closed the machine! There are always excellent players. Maybe one day there will be some player who will play more games than Pelé did, or score more goals than Pelé did. But I think that is a little difficult.' Pelé declared Messi as the current generation's best, although he felt Neymar, from his own club Santos, had the capability of shortly surpassing the Barcelona great. His comment seemed to me as a dig at those who thought Messi was better than Pelé. His point was that Messi hadn't won one World Cup let alone three, nor scored as many goals as he had, nor played as long as he did. It is possible he could ... but he hasn't yet.

As for Pelé's own 'all-time greats' selection, Pelé told me, '[My No. 1] is difficult to say. I saw a lot of good players.' Then Pelé proceeded to deliver the list of his personal all-time greatest: 'Beckenbauer, Georgie Best, more recently Zico, and Maradona, well, he was a good player, then we have Platini, and of course Di Stefano, Zidane was for a long time the best player in the world. Sometimes you need luck, [to stay clear of injuries]. There is also a problem comparing players, such as Garrincha and Zico. Today there is no doubt Messi is the best player, maybe Neymar will be.'

I pointed out that he didn't mention even one English player. He went on to say how much he liked Wayne Rooney and Steven Gerrard but was at a loss as to why the England team have fallen short of its potential and while its players have risen to the ranks of the world's elite, they are always just a tier or two below. It must have been an oversight that he didn't mention his old mate Sir Bobby Charlton! Let's hope so.

Pelé told me:

I like Rooney because he always plays more with the heart than with technical. I like Rooney as he plays for the team. I would always have Rooney, a player like that, in my team. I don't only want players to play beautiful football all the time! For the team Gerrard is also a good player too. You can always mention a lot of players from different clubs and different countries, but today you have too many to make comparisons as to which players are the best. Five years ago, it was more simple. Zidane has been the best player for ten years, then came Kaká, but of course, he has been injured. But even now there are few to choose from to compare, and to select the very best. There is Cristiano Ronaldo with one style, and Messi with another style, they are both outstanding but you cannot compare as they are two different styles.

So why were English players not mentioned in the same breath as Ronaldo and Messi in the new generation of the best? Why is the style of English football taking such a battering? Pelé says: 'It is about more technique. Otherwise, Germany, England, Italy, they are almost the same in their football, so I don't know why England is not highly regarded any more. Perhaps it is because the players don't behave very well, then they say everybody is the same. Maybe it is the behaviour of the players; it is very hard to say.'

Pelé doesn't advocate an English coach for the English, even though the Brazilians wouldn't countenance a foreign coach for their national team. 'No, that doesn't matter. The whole game has become more cosmopolitan so it doesn't matter if England has a foreign coach. The level of football in England is the top, English football is the leader in the world. Maybe it is the behaviour of the players; it is very hard to say why.'

English football was mourning another failed England manager, Steve McClaren, at this time, so the question at the forefront of the debate was whether the national team would be better served by an English manager.

I introduced Pelé to Rio Ferdinand, who was also there to do an interview for his own website. Rio got Pelé to sign a No. 10 Brazil shirt. The Manchester United centre-half asked Pelé which was his toughest opponent. Pelé replied: 'Bobby Moore, and Beckenbauer. Moore because he was always the hardest to play against.'

Pelé was also asked who would be his dream strike partner, and he went for Neymar ahead of Messi. 'I would love to play with Lionel Messi. But Messi is an incomplete player because he can't use his head. Also I played football for twenty years; Messi has only played for several years. If there is one player in the world today I would love to play with it is Neymar.'

The great man felt that Ronaldo had overtaken Messi as 'the best player, the best scorer and the best forward' in the world when he attended the Confederations Cup in Russia a year ahead of the World Cup Finals. 'Two years ago I gave the [Ballon d'Or] trophy to him and it was an honour for me,' Pelé told reporters. 'The best player in the world? No doubt. As I have mentioned, I think that today there is no doubt the best player, the best scorer and the best forward is Cristiano Ronaldo.'

Pelé can also reel off ten names in as many seconds referring to who competed for that title in the past and was saddened that the debate these days is only between Ronaldo and Messi, and has been the case for some years. Pelé counts on his fingers as he goes through some of the greats:

George Best, Bobby Moore, Jairzinho, Bobby Charlton, Pelé, Zico, Beckenbauer, Cruyff, Zidane, Maradona. Now you say Cristiano Ronaldo and Messi – Cristiano Ronaldo and Messi. It's not too good for football. At the moment the best player in the world is Ronaldo. I admire him, if I had to set up a national team he would be my first pick.

But in the meantime I feel sorry because today and for the last five years, you just mention two big stars. Some years ago, you had a lot of players.

He cannot compare himself or Maradona with Cristiano Ronaldo partly because they belong to a different footballing generation, but more importantly because they both have different roles to his. 'Maradona, myself, it's a little bit different than him,' he explains:

> Cristiano is higher up the pitch, more central, more direct, more for scoring. But what is important is he is a player who decides the game. He is a player who scores goals. That's the same. But we cannot compare Pelé and Maradona with Cristiano because we were players who came from behind. We played deeper. He plays in front. He's more like [the Brazilian] Ronaldo. This you can compare. It's the same with Messi. They are two players with completely different styles. Messi is playing more from midfield; he is an excellent player and passer. But Ronaldo is more forward, the No. 9, the striker. He has a different style to Messi.

Gareth Bale and Neymar may emerge but, for Pelé, there is still something missing. 'You have Bale and Neymar, but they are not enough. You used to have two or three players in one team who were stars. Now there are that many in the world. It's a shame. The game deserves more great players.'

Winning not only major international tournaments, but also European and World Cups mark greatness, yet Pelé does not place as much faith in that argument as others, since these tournaments come with a slice of fortune, he says. He feels that winning the Champions League has grown in importance, especially when it comes to the annual vote for the world's best player. 'Ronaldo has to have some luck with him,' Pelé adds. 'It doesn't depend on him to win important tournaments and to be champions. He has time – maybe the next World Cup he could be there. No doubt.'

So what of Neymar now? Half a billion pounds! Yes, £500 million; the buy-out clause of £195 million and eye-watering wages of half a million pounds a WEEK on a five-year contract that took him from Barcelona to Paris St-Germain.

Imagine then what Pelé would be worth today. One-billion, perhaps? For sure he is twice the player that Neymar is right now or is ever likely to aspire to be.

Both Neymar and Pelé hailed from Santos, and a few years ago when I interviewed Pelé on video for ESPN, the elder statesmen of Brazilian football advocated that Neymar should spend at least one more year at Santos before moving on, at a time that he was being chased by Real Madrid and Barça. Neymar chose not to take Pelé's advice, but a move from one of the world's greatest teams to one of world's richest simply for the sheer volume of money was something that would not meet with Pelé's approval.

Pelé chose not to leave Santos despite offers from the world's greatest clubs to play in Europe, and during my many one-to-one interviews with him for this book he explained the reason for his reluctance to test his skills in Europe. Back then, Pelé maintained that Messi needed to overhaul his goalscoring record if he is to be considered the best player ever. Pelé bagged 1,283 goals in his career for Santos, New York and Brazil. Pelé responded to suggestions that the Argentine had already surpassed his achievements: 'Messi better than Pelé? To get there he needs to score more than 1,283 goals,' he said.

Neymar was the subject of a transfer tug-of-war between Real Madrid and Chelsea at that time when, Pelé remarked: 'Neymar has great talent. I hope Neymar doesn't end up like Messi, who plays so well for his club but does nothing for his country.' Asked whether Neymar can become the world's best, Pelé told me back then:

> Maybe Neymar is too young to be the best just yet. Messi has been around for a few years, while Neymar it has been just one-and-a-half, two years. However, already there is no doubt that Neymar is one excellent player, very skilful, very dangerous, very intelligent. He needs more experience, a little more time, right now he needs a little more of a base. He has a good future but to be the best we have to wait a little bit because he has only played for one year, one-year-and-a-half, though already the expectations are there.

Neymar might have moved again when he allowed PSG to evoke the £195 million buy-out clause. He wants to be the best, and being at the right club is crucial.

Pelé backed Neymar's decision to leave the shadow of Messi. Pelé hopes Neymar's new club can help him join fellow countrymen Rivaldo, Ronaldo, Ronaldinho and Kaká in winning a Ballon d'Or. As Jason Pettigrove reported for *marca.com* [3 September 2017] when he spoke to Carlos Alberto:

> At the moment the best player in Brazil is Neymar and I think the move for him was very good because there was huge competition with Messi at Barcelona. I think it's a good opportunity for him and he needed to move because

now he can really play and show what he's capable of. But it's also very dangerous when you get given that responsibility.

Carlos Alberto was asked if Coutinho needed to move to Spain to prove himself and added:

No. You don't necessarily have to change teams all the time to prove you are good. It all depends on taking your opportunities.

Returning to Neymar, Carlos said:

Neymar has a football at his feet which is all he needs. Coutinho is a player I think we should all look at too because he is excellent for his team. No doubts at the moment though that Neymar is the one.

As Alex Richards reported Pelé's thoughts (*Daily Mirror*, 8 September 2017):

But for him, I think it was the best thing because there was always the discussion, 'Neymar, Messi, Neymar, Messi'. Now, he will have the opportunity to be the big star. But for the Brazil national team, not much changes (Alex quotes from *goal.com*). Messi is an organiser and he also scores goals. Neymar is more of a striker. There is no doubt he has a great future ahead, but there are things he needs to improve on, in the next World Cups for example. Today, with different styles, Cristiano Ronaldo, Messi and Neymar are the best players in the world. There are other players, but the best in the world at the moment are those three.

Pelé is a one-off, not just for his 1,000-plus goals, his incredible skills, and for winning the World Cup three times, but also for his footballing philosophy that was the trademark of Brazil's best at their best – the intent to follow their destiny to play the beautiful game. Not for them the relentless pursuit of money that marks out the contemporary version of a beautiful game now tarnished by the lure of gold.

As Declan Taylor reported (*The Sun*, 12 September 2017):

> Anthony Joshua wants to become the Pelé of boxing after he met the Brazilian football icon at the GQ Awards. And AJ hopes to follow in Pelé's footsteps, and be remembered as a man of the people. Joshua said: 'I definitely want to be like Pelé, he's a lovely guy. Take football away and he's a good person – he connects with everyone. Everyone who I saw that met him is in awe of him and he just seems to connect with people easily.' It was the second time Joshua chatted with the great man. He added: 'I'm not sure if he's a boxing fan, but he is a fan of humanity and remembered me from the first time we met. The first time I came across him was in a London hotel when one of my friends called me up and said, "Pelé's in town, do you want to meet him?" You don't pass up the chance, do you?'

Pelé and Sir Geoff Hurst were among the honourees at the GQ Men of the Year Awards, where the Brazilian legend led the crowd in chant of 'Love, love, love'. Pelé was given the

Inspiration award by England manager Gareth Southgate, who said: 'In football there is one individual who stands above all that have gone before and after him, he scored over 1,000 goals, won the World Cup on three occasions, inspired his nation and the rest of the world to embrace the beautiful game.' He added: 'There has never been another footballer like him.' Arriving at the stage, Pelé said he prioritised attending the awards over getting hip surgery, telling the crowd: 'After playing thirty years of football, twenty-five in Brazil and the last five in the United States, I have to pay the bill.' Sir Geoff, who scored a hat-trick in the 1966 World Cup final, collected the Legend prize.

What makes the Pelé, the World's Greatest Ever, tick? What is his background, his beliefs, likes and dislikes? Meeting him several times, interviewing him in various locations around the world for the purpose of compiling his life story, was one of my greatest pleasures in my forty years in football journalism.

All the facets of his life are explored in depth in *Pelé – His Life and Times*, as I planned to produce the authentic and approved biography of someone I have always admired, respected and regarded as untouchable as the greatest footballer that ever lived.

At the 2018 World Cup Finals in Russia, Pelé's place as one of the father figures of world football remains, and his observations about the players' and the nations' chances will gain momentum as the tournament gets closer.

At the opening game of the FIFA Confederations Cup in St Petersburg, President Putin addressed the crowd moments before kick-off with a rousing speech as Russia went on to win 2–0 in front of more than 54,000 fans in the brand new space-age Krestovsky Stadium. 'When Putin and Pelé walked in, it certainly turned heads,' said the head of the New Zealand FA.

Brazil may be among the favourites to win the next World Cup, but Pelé knows it will take more than relying on Neymar and Gabriel Jesus. Neymar and promising young Manchester City forward Jesus will lead the line for the Seleção in Russia, as they seek to make up for the disappointment of a humiliating 7–1 loss to eventual winners Germany in the semi-finals on home soil in 2014. Asked if the presence of Neymar could make the difference, Pelé commented, in an article by *Omnisport* (*beinsports.com*, 19 June 2017):

'Listen, this is very difficult to say because today people mention one or two good players, but who won the game and [the] World Cup is the team. Individually it is difficult to say people [did it]. Sometimes one team have a better one [player]. For example, Barcelona have Lionel Messi, one player, but they have a lot of good players. To win the World Cup, or to win the game it has to be a nice team not just one player.... Of course, always we [Brazil] expect to win [the World Cup]. I think Brazil has good new players and the team has more experience because most of the players that play for the national team play outside [of Brazil]. This is important. What we need now is to get a nice team and let them play. I think it will be an excellent World Cup and I wish Brazil make the final.'

Pelé believes Neymar thrived upon moving to LaLiga in 2013. 'He improved a lot in Europe when he went to Barcelona, and I think he has a chance to be one of the great players at the next World Cup in Russia ... I think he will be one of the great players in the future.'

Of Jesus, who impressed upon his arrival at City last season, Pelé added: 'He's a good player too. The same as

Neymar, [but] he's just started. I think Neymar has a little more experience than him, but both have the same style of game. But they are both two forwards that will give Brazil success in the future.'

Pelé feels new Argentina coach Jorge Sampaoli will need luck to guide them to World Cup glory. Sampaoli was lured from Sevilla to take over as coach of La Albiceleste after Edgardo Bauza left them floundering in the CONMEBOL qualifying group. Pelé feels he may require some help from above!

As he said to *Omnisport* (*sportskeeda.com*, 18 June 2017):

'You know, he is a great coach, no doubt, he has vision,' Pelé said of Sampaoli. 'Argentina always has a good team. I think being coach – that's the reason why I'd never be a coach – because you need luck. Sometimes you have the best team with the good players and then you don't win the World Cup.'

As for whether Messi needs to win the World Cup to confirm his status as one of the game's greatest ever players, Pelé feels chance will also play a role. '[It] depends; I think this is a little bit like luck, at the same moment [as needing to win a World Cup]. To me he is a great player, as a midfield forward, to me, he's the best.'

Pelé, though, is no longer the world's most recognisable face of world football, with the emergence of social media and the obsession of the new generation with the likes of Ronaldo and Messi.

The new generation have seen precious little of Pelé in action other than mostly black-and-white clips of his goals and his World

Cup exploits, although more recently there has been a Hollywood biopic, *Pelé: Birth of a Legend*, premiering in New York.

Tarcisio Burgnich, who attempted to mark Pelé in the Mexico 1970 Final, said: 'I told myself before the game, "he's made of skin and bones just like everyone else." But I was wrong.' Costa Pereira, who kept goal for Benfica in the 1962 Intercontinental Cup, reflected: 'I arrived hoping to stop a great man, but I went away convinced I had been undone by someone who was not born on the same planet as the rest of us.'

Such is Pelé's stature in the global game, his endearing qualities have remained everlasting. His Brazil shirt worn in his World Cup finals' debut and a crown he got as King of Football went on display in Manchester in the exhibition *Pelé: Art, Life, Football*, which showed stages of his life courtesy of artists and photographers, including some never-before-seen objects such as his 1962 World Cup winner's medal. The exhibition at the National Football Museum in Manchester ran until 4 March 2018. The artefacts included the Brazil shirt he wore in his first game at the 1958 World Cup finals against the USSR, his 1962 World Cup Winner's medal and a crown he was given in a game against Chile. There was also the ball from a hat-trick he scored for New York Cosmos in the 1970s and a passport. Kevin Haygarth, interim director at the museum, said (reported by *halcyongallery. com*, 25 May 2017): 'We wanted to celebrate Pelé in a way which befits his vibrant and creative personality, and hosting a range of stunning imagery alongside significant items from his career certainly does this.'

Previously unseen photos of Brazil's 1966 World Cup squad relaxing in a rural Cheshire hotel went on show in an exhibition at the most unexpected location of the Lymm Hotel. The reason? It was the venue for the world's most glamorous football team, based there for the tournament, that remains the only time England won the World Cup. According to BBC News, 20 February 2016:

> The exhibition included images of football greats Pelé and Garrincha and their teammates at ease in the hotel grounds. Some of the shots were taken by then hotel manager Roger Allen, loaned by a private collector. Manager of the hotel in Lymm, Jamie McDonald, said: 'My granddad never stopped talking about meeting Pelé. I'm told the players were very approachable, some even borrowed bikes to go round the village.' The arrival of the most famous footballer on the planet attracted scores of autograph hunters. Glenda Bowers, who was fifteen at the time, recalled: 'My friend and I hung round outside all the time. We got loads of autographs of the Brazilian team. I must have had Pelé's a dozen times. I think when I got married my mum threw them out!'
>
> Also on display were more personal items, including Pelé's training kit, which he gave to the hotel laundryman. Exhibition organiser Alan Williams said: 'A press photographer wanted to photograph Pelé throwing something to the laundryman. So he threw his training kit, which he allowed him to keep. The man didn't have any interest in football but his family have kindly loaned it to us. Another item is a picture of one of the bar staff, Bessie Vale, with Pelé. She has kept the photo in her purse for the last fifty years.'

While the locals loved the arrival of the boys from Brazil, the tournament was disastrous for the team as they failed to get past the group stage. Pelé vowed never to play in a World Cup again – although he broke this pledge four years later – after suffering repeated kickings in all three group matches at Goodison Park.

The exhibition, *BrazilLymm66*, ran for four days in aid of funds for a Lymm Heritage Centre, and was opened by Roger Hunt, one of the stars of the triumphant England team.

Ronaldo might argue, with some foundation, that Pelé is still the most recognisable face of football given the Portuguese captain's astronomic social media status; the Real Madrid superstar amassed over 163 million followers on Twitter (56m) and Instagram (107m) combined, putting him way out in front of any athlete in the world. In comparison, Neymar has 110 million followers on social media (Twitter: 31m and Instagram: 79m). For a long time the Barcelona star had the largest number of followers on both social media sites until 2015.

Pelé commands a modest 2.5 million Twitter followers. But, of course, his generation is not so attuned to social media as current fans are, nor are they so reliant on that form of communication. John Motson recently referred to the final day of the Premier League season with vital issues still at stake, saying that fans would be 'tuned in to their transistor radios!' Not really Mottie, not with their smartphones always within easy reach.

But, assessing social media numbers is not the best way to judge Pelé's global stature.

Certainly Ronaldo and Messi have dominated the global awards, but Pelé would have done the same had there been so many of them in his heyday, what's more he alone would have dominated them.

On the eve of the last European Championship, two of the greatest players in the history of the game came together to take part in a one-off five-a-side match in Paris. So often at loggerheads, Pelé and Maradona put their differences to one side for Hublot's Match of Friendship at the Palais Royale in Paris to mark the Euros. They embraced during the five-a-side exhibition game, demonstrating their friendship. Pelé and Maradona played the roles of coach as two teams of former stars went head-to-head in the palace garden the day before France played Romania at the Stade de France in the opening game of the Euros. Former England captain Rio Ferdinand, ex-Holland midfielder Clarence Seedorf, former Spain and Real Madrid defender Fernando Hierro and Italy's World Cup-winning defender Fabio Cannavaro took part.

As Aaron Flanagan wrote (*The Mirror*, 9 June 2016):

'I want to thank Pelé; we know who he is and who he will always be. We need icons like him,' Maradona declared to the audience.

Pelé responded warmly:

'The most important is the message of peace. Many thanks to my friend Maradona for this opportunity and a big round of applause to the players who have been here today. This is a moment of peace.'

FIFA decided the player of the twentieth century in 2000. This was when the world body organised an online vote which Maradona easily won (see earlier). But, as detailed in previous chapters, FIFA thought the online users at the time were too young and so the vote was skewed in Maradona's favour. It then organised a vote by readers of the *FIFA* magazine and cast by an international jury.

This time Pelé won by a landslide. FIFA decided to split the award and named Pelé and Maradona as the two greatest players of all time. In the French capital, Pelé asked Maradona if he knows his compatriot personally, according to John Downes (*Mail Online*, 9 June 2016), prompting Maradona to comment:

> [regarding Lionel Messi] 'He's a really good person, but he has no personality. He lacks character to be a leader.' Pelé then responded: 'Ah, I get it, he's not like we were back in the days. In the 70s we [Brazil] had really good players like Rivellino, Gerson, Tostão. Not like Argentina now, which depends only on Messi. He [Maradona] is saying that Messi is a good player, there's no doubt about it, but he has no personality.'

Pelé was nine when Brazil lost the 1950 World Cup Final to Uruguay. Brazil required just a point against Uruguay to lift the World Cup at the Maracana. By now his family had relocated from Minas Gerais to Bauru in Sao Paulo state. Pelé and his enraptured father Dondinho left home that day surrounded by a posse of friends listening to the match on the radio, hearing that A Seleção were 1-0 up. The nine-year-old returned from a kickabout to discover that Brazil had become victims of an upset.

According to the FIFA website (11 May 2017):

> 'It was the first time I saw my father cry,' recalled Pelé. 'I was brought up thinking that grown men didn't cry, but he was devastated. It was the first time I ever saw my father cry, and all because of that defeat,' Pelé commented on the FIFA web site in 2014. 'I remember saying to him: "Don't cry, Papa. I'll win the World Cup for you."'

Pelé later admitted it had been a spontaneous and futile attempt at raising his father's spirits. 'I just came out with it because I didn't know what else to say,' he reflected. Yet eight years later, a prodigious seventeen-year-old fulfilled that promise bagging a brilliant brace – his fifth and sixth goals of the tournament – in an emphatic 5–2 win over hosts Sweden. The Swedish players were in awe. 'After the fifth goal I didn't want to mark Pelé any more. I wanted to applaud him,' said midfielder Sigge Parling.

'Pelé is obviously infantile. He lacks the necessary fighting spirit. He is too young to feel aggression and respond with appropriate force. In addition to that, he does not possess the sense of responsibility necessary for a team game.' So read a now-infamous report compiled by Brazil's team psychologist, Dr Joao Carvalhaes, ahead of the 1958 World Cup. His verdict was decisive and unambiguous: the seventeen-year-old should not feature. Nor, indeed, should Garrincha.

... As Pelé recounted: 'Fortunately for me and Garrincha [Brazil coach Vicente], Feola was always guided by his instincts rather than experts. He just nodded gravely at the psychologist, and said, "You may be right. The thing is, you don't know anything about football. If Pelé's knee is ready, he plays."' That knee, and the injury he had sustained in a pre-tournament practice match, proved an even more immediate danger to the youngster's participation in Sweden than Carvalhaes' dire warnings. But Feola took the gamble and was repaid handsomely.

'It was impossible not to applaud Pelé's brilliance,' admitted no less than Swedish King Gustaf VI Adolf afterwards.

The youngster was 'overcome with emotion.' 'My first thoughts were about my family,' Pelé wrote in his autobiography. 'Did they know that we were champions? I wanted to speak to my parents but there were no telephones, so I kept on saying, "I've got to tell my dad, I've got to tell my dad." I only managed to speak to him in the following days, using an international radio. I can remember saying things like: "Did you see me with the Swedish king? Over," and "I shook the king's hand. Over."' When they were reunited, Pelé recalled: 'I saw my father cry again ... this time with happiness.'

As Paolo Amaral, Brazil's fitness trainer in 1958, recalled (courtesy Mark Lomas, *espn.com* and *fifa.com*): 'He could shoot with his left, with his right, and he had such vision that as soon as he got the ball, he already knew what he was going to do with it. He was extraordinary.'

The teenage sensation went on to claim a variety of World Cup records, and twelve of his record seventy-seven Brazil goals came at the game's most celebrated tournament.

Manuel Rosas was the little-known Mexican who, prior to 1958, held the record as the World Cup's youngest goalscorer. Rosas was eighteen years and ninety-three days when he bagged a brace, which included the first penalty converted at a World Cup, in a 6–3 defeat to Argentina at the tournament's inaugural edition in 1930.

That remained in place for twenty-eight years until Brazil faced Wales in the 1958 quarter-finals. The Welsh qualified through a play-off against Israel, but remained unbeaten in the first round and – even without their injured talisman, Juventus star John Charles – provided Brazil with their toughest match of the tournament. After sixty-six goalless minutes, Pelé, two days on from his World Cup debut against USSR and still 126 days away from his eighteenth birthday, received the ball on his chest, and, with his back to goal, the youngster pulled off an audacious turn to leave Mel Charles, John's brother, trailing. Stuart Williams raced in to cover, but Pelé had seen his chance and flicked out his left boot to send the ball flashing into the bottom corner. Overcome with joy, he raced into the net, picked up and kissed the ball before being mobbed by teammates. The seventeen-year-old went on to hit a brilliant hat-trick against France in the semi-finals before adding a memorable brace in the 5–2 win over Sweden that secured Brazil's first world title.

As Pelé recalls (*fifa.com*, 21 November 2016):

'[Against USSR] I had missed two attempts at goal that I would surely have buried had I been more relaxed ... After our celebration dinner, I went back to my room and replayed in my mind every move, every kick. I wasn't too pleased with my performance – I could have played better. I'd tried to chip Yashin at one point and realised that was pure cheek on my part. That was something I'd have to work on. The Wales game took place just two days after my first. Jack Kelsey, the Welsh goalie, was in great form and his team were forceful in defence. The USSR game had been tough and it was important for Brazil because we qualified top of the group. But on a personal level, I consider the game against Wales my most important of the tournament. And the goal was, perhaps, the most unforgettable of my career. Wales marked very tightly at the back and I remember getting the ball, turning and squeezing it into the corner of the net. I consider it the most important goal I've ever scored. It boosted my confidence completely. The world now knew about Pelé. I was on a roll. The 1958 World Cup was my launching pad. I was on the front pages of newspapers and magazines all over the world. *Paris Match* ran a cover story immediately after the victory, saying there was a new king on the block. The name stuck, and very soon I started to be called King Pelé. Or, more simply, the King.'

Cliff Jones recalls (*fifa.com*, 21 November 2016):

We didn't know anything at all about Pelé. The ones we were focused on were Garrincha and Didi. This young kid, seventeen years of age, playing for Brazil ... who was he? We didn't know. But we found out. You didn't have to be an expert to know, half-hour into the game, that this kid was very special. He broke the team's heart getting that goal, knowing we were so close. We took Brazil all the way, and I still think to this day it could have been a different result, if big John [Charles] had played. John was our main man – like Gareth Bale is in the present Welsh side. He would have caused Brazil problems they'd never faced before.

In June 2012, Pelé was awarded the Olympic Order by the International Olympic Committee – the movement's highest honour. He was named 'Athlete of the Century' by the IOC in 1999 despite never competing at a Games because professional players were barred from doing so during his day. Also in 2012 Pelé was awarded an honorary degree from the University of Edinburgh for his 'significant contribution to humanitarian and environmental causes', having worked as a United Nations ambassador for ecology and the environment.

PELÉ: HIS LIFE AND TIMES

The University announced on their website (*ed.ac.uk*):

Pelé, considered by many to be the greatest footballer of all time, has received an honorary University degree. The degree celebrates Pelé's significant contribution to humanitarian and environmental causes, as well as his sporting achievements – including winning the World Cup three times with Brazil, as well as being named as FIFA's joint player of the century and the International Olympic Committee's athlete of the century. Since his retirement from football, Pelé has been Brazil's Extraordinary Minister for Sport and was appointed a United Nations ambassador for ecology and the environment in 1992. Pelé received his degree – his first from a European university – at a reception, held at the Victoria & Albert Museum in London on 9 August, which showcased both the sporting and cultural achievements of the University of Edinburgh. Also in attendance was recent Olympic gold medallist and University alumnus Katherine Grainger. Pelé was also presented with a University football strip.

Since retiring in 1977, he has taken up ambassadorial roles both in and outside football, and was involved in politics as Minister of Sport in his home country for a three-year period from 1995.

In 2013, he received the FIFA Ballon d'Or Prix d'Honneur in recognition of his career and achievements as a global icon of football. Pelé holds the record as the youngest player ever to play in, and score in, a World Cup final. Pelé won his first World Cup winner's medal at the age of seventeen. He also holds the Guinness World Record for goals scored in a career, with 1,283. He played for Brazil's World Cup winning teams of 1958 and 1970, scoring in both finals, and was in the squad which won in 1962. With Santos he twice won the Copa Libertadores and Intercontinental Cup. He went on to become the face of soccer in the US, as the NASL looked for a sporting breakthrough in the mid-1970s.

In recent years, Pelé has suffered ill-health, but showed his remarkable fighting spirit by recovering from a number of setbacks. When he was not well enough to light the Olympic flame, I felt compelled to bring his incredible and unrivalled life and times story up to date. Knowing him as well as I do, it would have been heart-breaking for him to pull out of the cauldron-lighting ceremony of the Olympic Games. The honour of lighting the Olympic cauldron is usually given to the highest profile athlete in the host country, and Pelé would have considered it the highest possible honour, and he would have backed out only if he was seriously unfit to take part. Similar Olympic duties were previously carried out by other sporting greats such as Muhammad Ali and Cathy Freeman.

Pelé had a new hip fitted in 2012 and has had several other health issues since. The hip replacement operation slowed his walking, evidence by him being spotted ambling into a room with the assistance of a stick. He also spent two weeks in hospital for a urinary infection in 2014 and had prostate surgery a year earlier. The three-time World Cup winner had also been suffering from muscle pains. 'I'm not in physical condition to take part in the opening ceremony,' he said. He wrote to the organisers of the three-hour opening ceremony spectacular to tell them that his health did not allow him to perform the duties he had been asked to in front of the 78,500 crowd in the Maracanã. His withdrawal from the climax gave a role to Barcelona megastar Neymar.

In a statement released just hours before the ceremony,

Pelé said: 'I'm not physically able to attend the opening of the Olympics. Only God is more important than my health. In my life, I've had fractures, surgeries, pain, hospital stays, victories and defeats. And I've always respected those who admire me. The responsibility of the decisions are mine, where I have always tried not to disappoint my family and the people of Brazil. And, as a Brazilian, I ask God to bless all who participate in this event and it is a great success and finish alone!' Pelé added that it was 'my own decision' to withdraw. He apologised to the Brazilian people and added: 'As a Brazilian, I ask God to bless all those who participate in this event.' Pelé signed off the statement with his full name Edson Arantes do Nascimento. Pelé's spokesman Pepito Fornos added: 'He is walking with a cane. The problem is that if he sits in a chair you need a winch to get him out of it. His doctor thought it best that he continues physiotherapy, that he rests and we hope that he will be able to appear at the [Olympic] closing ceremony.'

Earlier that week, Pelé said he was asked to light the cauldron by the organisers; however he had 'an international commitment with an English company'. He added that if he could change his travel plans it would be an 'honour' to carry out the task.

Later, Pelé was spotted using a metal-framed walker to get around, which his agent compared to him having a new piece of 'sporting equipment'.

According to Steven Wade (*usatoday.com*, 18 November 2016):

'He is calling this his new soccer shoes with wheels,' his agent, Jose Fornos, told *The Associated Press* in November 2016. A widely circulated newspaper photograph of the then 76-year-old Pelé using a walker gained lots of attention in Brazil. Fornos said Pelé used the walker regularly – or a cane – since hip surgery almost a year ago to correct the displacement of part of a right hip prosthesis done in 2012. He also underwent back surgery in 2015 for what was described as a 'nerve root decompression.' Fornos said Pelé's left knee was now the problem. The right knee is also reported to be problematic, and of course the right leg and hip. Everybody is worried about this. But that's life. For him it's not good, but you have to become accustomed to these things.' Fornos repeatedly made light of the Pelé's physical condition. 'We hope in the next few months he is ready to play,' Fornos said. 'Now he's on the bench.' In an interview with the Sao Paulo newspaper *O Estado De S.Paulo*, Pelé described his health as 'very good.'

Pelé was booked for a number of personal appearances in England, so with the usual promotional circus it was time to refresh all of his usual views about English football as well as around the world. Pelé loves England, loves the football and loves the opportunity to talk about our national game. But having seen him in action around the world in similar promotional media interviews, he normally gives the same sort of message, adapted to the country he's in at the time.

He told Jim White (*The Telegraph*, 7 April 2016):

'We will talk about sport, about my life,' he says of the black-tie nights. 'The most important thing is to be with some old fans, and to see some of the new generation, the new fans of football.' He is, he says, really looking forward to having his picture taken with young English fans, mixing with the selfie generation.

... He was here last year at a London art gallery, opening an exhibition of pieces inspired by him a year earlier.

That day he expressed a hitherto unspoken enthusiasm for Arsenal. He watches their games from his home in Sao Paulo and long admired the Arsène Wenger way. So much so, it is the modern club he would most like to turn out for!

[earlier in the piece] Just think of those playing in England, he suggests: 'My memories are of Georgie Best, Bobby Charlton, Bobby Moore, and not forgetting Banks – Gordon was a proper great. And that was just in England. All around the world it was the same, brilliant Germans, Dutchmen and of course Brazilians. Today you have just three great players in the world, Messi, Ronaldo, and maybe Neymar. Maybe. But in that time there were so many.'

... 'I think one of the problems is that the players used to remain longer in the team they started with, in the country they were born. Before, the players belong to their club; they had the chance to grow there. Now the players belong to the impresarios, the agents, their personal managers. We have this problem in Brazil, the best players start to play, then immediately comes the impresario, they pay a little too much, and hoping to make money straight away, they push them too early. They don't have time to develop.'

... 'There is one, Johan Cruyff, what a gentleman,' he said of the then recently deceased Dutch maestro, whose greatness has never been in question. 'I had the opportunity to be a friend of his beyond the field. He was one of the best players in the world, ever. Cruyff, the ultimate midfielder. He was fantastic.'

Shortly before the Olympics, Pelé released a song called 'Esperança' [Hope]. Pelé said he was inspired by what he describes as 'the feeling of hope and happiness' generated by the Games. Just look at the horizon for a new hope dawning, he sings. 'Open your eyes to the future where another sun will shine.' But it was panned by the waspish Jonathan Liew, who wrote in *The Telegraph* (20 July 2016):

> Pelé claims to have written it himself to coincide with next month's Rio Olympics. He also sings and raps on the record, accompanied by a children's choir, an off-the-peg bossa nova beat and a wimpy guitar solo that sounds like it was coaxed from the guitarist at gunpoint.
>
> The lyrics read like they were generated at random by a 1970s computer fed a series of Olympic-themed keywords. The flame is lit and ready to fire, it begins, a line that means less and less the more you look at it. Soul and heart here in Brazil. The nations of the world ready to celebrate. Love, and much peace. Put it this way: we suspect Pelé's invitation to the Ivor Novello awards may end up getting lost in the post.
>
> ... Pelé's Olympics single is that it is not actually that bad. If you are into bossa nova, empty sentiments and septuagenarian rappers, you will love it. It is neither accomplished enough to be a proper song, nor interesting enough to be a genuine novelty song. Which raises a pertinent question: why?
>
> To answer that question, you need to understand Brazil's curious ambivalence towards its greatest ever footballer. His feats on the pitch, bookended by those two World Cup triumphs of 1958 and 1970, are largely

unarguable. But to a younger generation it is his second incarnation – as a statesman and largely self-appointed father of the nation – that is less palatable.

This is not simply about his his collection of questionable opinions, of which the assertion that Nicky Butt was the outstanding player of the 2002 World Cup was not even the most contentious. Pelé's home country has long since stopped taking his public pronouncements seriously, whether in speech or in song. It was Romario, another great Brazilian footballer, who perhaps put it best a decade ago. "Pelé when silent," he said, "is a poet."

No, it is the growing feeling that the Brazil that Pelé increasingly seems to embody – a Brazil of samba football, bikini bottoms, world peace and other Lovely Things – exists largely in the imagination. This was most starkly evident during the Confederations Cup three years ago, when widespread anger against the government spilled over into a series of demonstrations across the country. Pelé's response was to tell the protesters to pipe down. "Let's forget all this commotion," he said, claiming that the protests were harming Brazil's image abroad.'

Liew's acid-tongued attack on Pelé was clearly well wide of the mark.

Pelé never played in an Olympic Games. 'I won a lot of tournaments and scored more than 1,000 goals, won three World Cups, but I could not play in an Olympic Games,' he said in one interview. 'I like to joke that the only reason Brazil has never won a gold medal at football is because I didn't play!' He flippantly talked about slipping on a pair of shorts and making a comeback for the Games.

After the Olympics, Pelé was quoted as saying: 'The Olympics went very well. Brazil welcomed the world with open arms and showed everyone our special way of life in work and play. I waited my entire life to see Brazil win a gold medal in football and now my dream has come true.'

Pelé has a colourful private life. He was married for a third time in a private ceremony to businesswoman Marcia Cibele Aoki, who was aged fifty at the time and Pelé seventy-five, in the resort of Guaruja, near Sao Paulo. The couple had been in a relationship for six years. The news was released on Pelé's social media channels and Brazilian television showed parts of the ceremony. In Pelé's words on a social media page, Aoki is his 'definitive love' in Portuguese. Pelé and Marcia were due to marry two years earlier, but were forced to postpone the ceremony after he suffered a series of health problems. They add: 'The Brazil all-time leading goalscorer met her at a party in New York in the 1980s. They only began dating when the pair bumped into each other in a lift in a Sao Paulo apartment block that they both lived in.' Pelé was married to first wife Rosemeri Cholbi for twelve years – they share three children together. His second union to singer Assiria Nascimento lasted fourteen years and they have two children.

Pelé moved his family to New York, where he'd make the Cosmos famous and become the best paid athlete in the world. On 10 June 1975, the New York Cosmos announced Pelé was joining the club. He signed a three-year $2.8-million contract, even though he was thirty-four-years old and had not played competitively for eight months. He scored thirty-seven goals and thirty assists in three years, winning the 1976 NASL MVP and leading the team to the 1977 Soccer Bowl title. He made his debut on 15 June against the Dallas Tornado at Downing Stadium in New York with a goal and an assist in the 2–2 draw. Ten million tuned in to watch CBS's live broadcast of Pelé's debut match – a record American TV audience for soccer. His career ended on 1 October 1977 against his former club, Santos, in front of a sold-out Giants Stadium. The Cosmos's home attendance tripled in just half the season Pelé was there. By the time he retired in 1977, average attendance for the league had almost doubled from 7,642 to 13,558. The Cosmos set several attendance records during Pelé's three years with the club: 9 April 1976 – 58,128 (NASL), 9 June 1977 – 62,394 (U.S. Soccer), 14 August 1977 – 77,691 (North America).

The New York Cosmos's 1977 NASL roster was one of the most star-studded in world soccer. It had a strike partnership of Pelé and Giorgio Chinaglia, Brazilian 1970 World Cup legend Carlos Alberto at the back partnering Franz Beckenbauer, more glamorous South Americans ... and ex-Aston Villa reserve Steve Hunt flying down the wing. The idea of playing with Pelé was a unique selling point which Hunt could not refuse, even though it meant being separated from the wife he had so recently married.

This roster represented Pelé's role in establishing football in America. If the NASL was good enough for Pelé, who could turn it down? Hunt enjoyed three seasons with the iconic Cosmos and this year recalled those remarkable times, including sharing a dressing room with Dutch great Johan Cruyff, and a training-ground fight with former Italy striker Giorgio Chinaglia. Mr Hunt is the recently appointed manager of ninth-tier Cowes Sports and spoke to Neil Johnston (*BBC Sport*, 4 August 2017):

'Playing for New York Cosmos was like travelling in a rock and roll band,' the sixty-one-year-old told BBC Sport. 'There were always celebrities in the dressing room after games. I've always been into my music and Mick

Jagger came in after one particular game. I heard him say "Where's the Englishman?" All he wanted to talk about was the match. All I wanted to talk about was the Rolling Stones.'

Off the pitch, the Cosmos were the hottest tickets on the New York social scene, thanks to some clever early examples of cross-marketing by their owners, Warner Bros. Cosmos games were frequently attended by rock stars, film stars, politicians, and celebrities, leading to Hunt having conversations with Mick Jagger and Henry Kissinger in the locker room, as well as attending the famous *Studio 54* nightclub on a semi-regular basis.

Neil Johnston continues his interview with Steve Hunt:

So how did the £125-a-week 20-year-old with only a handful of top-flight appearances for Aston Villa land a place in a team of World Cup winners in 1977-78? The Cosmos were looking for a left winger and Hunt, regarded as a player with a big future, fitted the bill. 'It was a choice of playing at Preston on a damp November night or going to Bermuda to link up with my new teammates for pre-season training,' he said. 'Cosmos doubled my wages but I didn't go for the money. Pelé, who was in his last season as a player, was there and they said they were getting Beckenbauer. These stars were coming to the end of their careers, I was just starting mine.'

... As well as clashing with Chinaglia, he also swore at three-time World Cup winner Pelé during a match. 'Pelé was annoyed I hadn't passed to him and said something in Spanish. I responded by flashing two fingers in his direction. Immediately my number went up on the board. They were not impressed and I was subbed. I was in the company of great players and I had to grow up very quickly.'

The above incident happened during the middle of a nationally televised game against the Tampa Bay Rowdies. Hunt went on to play two games for England under Bobby Robson, making his international debut alongside Gary Lineker against Scotland in 1984.

For Pelé, it was an important move for many more reasons. It was a chance for a new start and it was badly needed. The great man's past was catching up with him. Rumours of his infidelity were frequent and some were proved to be true. In 1993, Sandra Arantes do Nascimento was recognised by the courts as his daughter after DNA evidence confirmed Pelé's thirty-year-old affair with Anizia Machado, a housemaid. She released a book, *The Daughter the King Didn't Want*, before dying of cancer in 2006.

Long before such facts emerged, the home his son Edinho grew up in was broken. 'As soon as we got to New York, my parents separated, so I was just raised by a single mother with my sister in a small apartment,' Edinho says. 'Very typical. I think in retrospect it's the only place I could have been brought up as just another person, without the association to my father.'

Edinho had little contact with his famous father as a child. 'Maybe birthdays, or some special occasion, just once or twice a year. He'd get the date and not show then, though, so there was a lot of letting us down as kids. I kind of created an aversion; I didn't like my father. And then he made my mother cry, so he was the villain, the bad guy.'

His son had the chance of a big career in the game; as a goalkeeper.

Edinho played for four clubs, Santos, Portuguesa Santista, São Caetano and Ponte Preta, before retiring from professional football in 1999, at the age of twenty-nine. He was hired as Santos's goalkeeping coach on 9 February 2007, and later became the team's assistant coach. But it all went terribly wrong, because Edson Cholbi Nascimento ended up as a convicted criminal.

On 21 June 1970, Pelé won his third World Cup final at the Azteca in Mexico City, cementing his legacy as the greatest footballer of all time. Sixty-seven days later, his wife, Rosemeri dos Reis Cholbi, gave birth to their first son, Edinho.

Ewan Mackenna wrote this account of Edinho's troubles for the *Bleacher Report*, on 16 March 2017:

> 'There was an order for my head to be handed over on a platter when I was in prison, and it's very common on the inside,' Edinho tells Bleacher Report. 'All this brings me back to how fortunate I was. Really, I'm very grateful. It's why I'm sure the Lord was always by my side, protecting me. Those things that have been happening recently were happening when I was inside too.'
>
> ... Edinho was sent back to jail to serve a sentence of 12 years and 10 months on drug-trafficking and money laundering charges. Six days later, a higher court in the capital of Brasilia decided he should be free until what will be his final attempt at an appeal, as he continues to maintain his innocence.
>
> ... As a boy, Edinho played basketball, baseball and football. By the time he went away to boarding school upstate, he could skate and was playing ice hockey. At nineteen, he arrived at the Vila Belmiro – the same Santos stadium his father used to star in – as a highly rated young

goalkeeper. 'Being Pelé's son helped,' Santos journalist Ted Sartori tells Bleacher Report. 'I doubt if he wasn't Pelé's son he'd have gotten an opportunity just like that. He was short for a goalkeeper. Sometimes he could be great, unbeatable; other times it was the opposite. Naturally, he suffered the pressure of being Pelé's son too.' ... [Edinho recalls:] 'Up until that moment I never had to deal with who he was and who I was as a result, and then immediately, I had to deal with it. From one day to the next I became Pelé's child. As soon as I got here to Brazil, I realised how much pressure I was going to face and was up against. So I focused very much on that and dedicated myself, and it all became motivation. ... People always would say, "He's just at Santos because of his father; he's never going to make it." It becomes inspiration and part of the challenge.'

... It was the early hours of 24 October 1992. Edinho tells me he was behind the wheel when, a couple of cars in front of him, a retired man, Pedro Simoes Neto, was knocked off his bike and would subsequently die. Edinho pulled over, telling his friend to get to a pay phone and call an ambulance while he checked the victim. As a crowd gathered, Edinho decided to move on. But the scene in his rear-view window as he drove away would haunt him for 13 more years. 'About two months later I was notified that I was being accused of being in a street race, and that's what became the case against me. There were a lot of unscrupulous people involved that created a situation where there was none. Obviously, because of my father and who I am, I became that target. That wasn't something I was prepared for; I didn't do anything wrong, so there was no reason to be worried.

But in Brazil the justice system is very fragile and easy to manipulate...' The 1990s should have been about his time at Santos. 'That year, 1995, when they got to the final [of the Campeonato Brasileiro], the referee robbed them, which stopped an extraordinary thing happening with the son of Pelé winning with his old club,' Juca Kfouri, one of the most prominent football writers in Brazil, recalls. 'But Edinho came a long way. The name helped at the start, but you can't say that he didn't make his own effort, because to get from the reserves to the first team and get his place, that took huge dedication from him.'

That time, though, was remembered for Edinho's legal issues. In February 1999, after seven years of legal battles, a judge declared him guilty of manslaughter by reckless driving. He says: 'I come here [Santos], I'm famous, I'm an athlete living quietly, and this all happens.'

Returning to the *Bleacher Report*:

Edinho's instant appeal in 1999 meant his six-year prison sentence was put on hold.... 'It's very clear now that the way I grew up, that was for a reason. Everyone expected me to flip out, but the fact I took it in stride was surprising to many, but it makes all the sense in the world to me and people who knew me and how I grew up. But still people thought "he'll break; he's just Pelé's son."'

In July 2005, thirteen years after the fateful night, Edinho was cleared at the long-awaited retrial. But on the retraction of the original verdict, he was returned to jail in handcuffs and would spend six months there, facing a fresh charge of trafficking and money laundering.

... Tres Coracoes is a small agricultural city of around 80,000 people; But while the surroundings may be coffee country the town itself is all about football. After all, this is where Pelé was born. There's a statue of him; the museum across the street from it documents his time and his many visits here. The main square is named after him; on Rua Edson Arantes do Nascimento, his restored family house sits. There, Pelé was raised in a small room shared with his brother – his parents in another small room, his grandparents in yet another. During the day, his grandmother would cook, while his grandfather gathered sticks to take to the street and sell for a few coins.... 'It's just part of my family's heritage,' Edinho says. 'But I got to know my grandfather, Dondinho, here in his later years. Very sweet, very serene. I know he liked his little whiskey at the end of the day when older, and I can associate that to his serenity. He's the oldest reference to my family.' From the front door of that house, down the hill, you can see the small stadium where Dondinho once played and where Edinho recently took over coaching duties at local club Tricordiano.

... The 1999 verdict shook his reputation, but he responded with vigorous declarations of innocence and the lodging of an appeal. Edinho decided to push on with his coaching education, invited back to his family's spiritual home of Santos by former Real Madrid manager Vanderlei Luxemburgo. 'My introduction onto a top-level staff, and it was an eight-year trajectory, from (early) 2007 to (late) 2014,' Edinho says. 'It was a learning experience...'

... After just two games in charge at Tricordiano, Edinho's association with the club abruptly ended – the result of financial problems. This followed his brief spells coaching at Mogi Mirim and Agua Santa, making a body of work hard to measure.

... Edinho still feels he has a lot to offer as a coach. 'Brazil is very far back as far as the evolution of the game tactically and technically. Of course, as individuals, we've always been at the top, but collectively, it has stopped in time; and that's where I feel I can contribute, with my sports culture from America. I've a lot of experience with coaches in different sports. I'm composed of all those philosophies.' Tricordiano clearly saw his value, as their marketing manager, Ze Roberto, told Bleacher Report before things imploded: 'Edinho is a big marketing tool for us. It could make us more well-known because of that name. And we've Pelé now as honorary chairman too.'

... There remains one very happy memory for Edinho from his fleeting spell at Tricordiano. When he signed his contract, a photograph was taken of him with the club staff and his father. Looking at his son, Pelé has pride in his eyes. Finally, everything became clear for the boy whose father was once distanced from him. 'As I became an adult and an athlete, I realised he [Pelé] was never really mine; he was the king of soccer,' Edinho says. 'I realised I had to share my father with the world. So from the frustration of not having a father in my mind growing up, I became thankful of the privilege of being the son of that great man. Even though being his son entailed me sacrificing him as my father, as I grew up, I realised how important that was, and it let me take my guard down and approach him again and try to cultivate our relationship again. Suddenly, I got to know him as a person – to realise how simple of a human being he actually is. He was just a simple boy who was a genius at his art, that became what he was, what he is, and that was difficult for him.'

Edinho says he now understands the sacrifices his father made in 'the name of his greatness.' The anger was gone, and a new openness came in their relationship. 'Immediately we were healed, and sometimes now the roles are reversed, and he's the son and I'm the dad,' he says.

When Edinho arrived at Santos, his teammates started calling him 'prince,' the son of the king. The more he disliked it the more it stuck, and the more he become proud of it.

The son of Brazil's most famous man ended up back in jail with a drugs gang and worse still, facing the most brutal cartel in the Brazilian penal system. His father used to make him cry, but his father cried in an emotional embrace before the son was taken away.

Ronaldo Duarte Barsotti de Freitas, better known as Naldinho, was introduced by a player they both knew, and the pair became friends.

Returning to the *Bleacher Report*:

[Edinho says] 'He is the son of an ex-football player, Pitico, who played with my father. My father helped his father go to Mexico to play after they were together at Santos. He referenced him, and he had success there. His entire family grew up with my father like a god. Literally. They'd light candles and pray to him every day because all their success in life came after the experience my father helped give him.'

In 2005, a police operation saw a lorry load of Naldinho's associates locked away, including Edinho, who police said was the link between the financial and military wings of the cartel. ... Edinho maintains his innocence: 'We literally were associated by phone taps; that's the only physical evidence. They are also completely abstract but manipulated and edited to create the context where I could be accused. If you take it and listen, there's nothing that incriminates me. I'm not proud of my relationship with him, but I stand by everything I've done in my entire life. I'm not ashamed or embarrassed of anything because I was completely entrapped. A victim.'

Edinho was arrested on charges that he was laundering money for Naldinho's drug empire; a tape emerged on Record TV. In it he says, 'I'm guilty, that's no secret; I'm prepared to face two or three years.' Edinho says the reporters were put in the room by the police chief to frame him. Edinho initially served six months in 2005, a lot of thinking time in solitary confinement.

As the *Bleacher Report* continues:

He remembers his father's reaction – the tears when he hugged him for the first time after he was put away. 'Completely supportive but caught off guard,' he wrote. 'He was always supportive, but at the very first moment, he was definitely a little sceptical. But as soon as he understood the corrupt nature of the situation, he doubled his support and has been nothing but supportive to this day.' Pelé has continued to protest his son's innocence, in 2006 being particularly vocal when commenting 'There is not a shred of evidence against my son.'

Pelé was admitted to hospital for the third time in eight months. He spent two weeks in hospital and then underwent prostate surgery in May, then in July he was admitted to a hospital in Sao Paulo. Mirtes Bogea, a press officer for the Albert Einstein hospital, confirmed Pelé was a patient. Pelé's personal assistant Jose Fornos Rodrigues later told Reuters that he had undergone a procedure to decompress a nerve root in his spine. This was the third time Pelé has been hospitalised since November. He spent two weeks at the Einstein facility with kidney problems, and in May he underwent prostate surgery in the same hospital. Doctors said he would continue his recovery at home, needing to rest for about a week. He also needed to undergo physiotherapy to recover some of the muscle mass that he lost during the time he spent in the hospital. 'It was really a scare,' Pelé said in a news conference broadcast live on Brazilian television. 'What happened was a surprise to me. I was worried, of course, but I never had any fears about dying.'

The three-time World Cup champion said he was doing fine and joked that he would be ready to play for Brazil as one of the three over-twenty-three players at the 2016 Olympics in Rio de Janeiro. 'Thanks to God everything is fine now. I have recovered,' Pelé said. 'I'm already preparing for the Olympics.'

Pelé spent several days in an intensive-care unit while undergoing haemodialysis to help support his only kidney. Doctors said Pelé, who had one kidney removed when he was still a player, had to be more closely monitored because of how his body reacted to the infection, but his life was never in danger. Doctors said his transfer to an intensive-care unit was needed because there was excessive inflammation in his body caused by the infection, which is not uncommon, but he always responded well to the antibiotic treatment. The infection stemmed from surgery to remove kidney stones which were diagnosed after Pelé had to cancel an event at his museum in Santos because of abdominal pain. The surgery was successful and he was released from the hospital just a few days after the procedure, but he had to be readmitted after a new medical evaluation showed signs of the infection.

Pelé recorded a video message from his hospital room to thank his fans around the world for praying for him during his illness. 'I was moved with all the messages that I received from all over the world. I didn't know so many people were paying attention to my situation.'

Pelé said he spent most of his time in the hospital watching local football and writing songs, including 'One that will remain a secret for the Olympics.' Pelé, who recorded a few songs many years ago, had a guitar with him in his hospital room. He said that although he wasn't overly concerned while in the hospital, the illness made him start reflecting a bit more about life. 'During a career of thirty years and while travelling all around the world, I had never gone through something like this before,' he said.

Then came the announcement that Pelé was selling off his memorabilia. 'Having donated a significant portion of my collection to the City of Santos, I have decided to allow fans and collectors to own a piece of my history as well,' commented Pelé. 'I hope they treasure these artefacts and share my story with their children and generations to come. I will also be donating a portion of the proceeds from the auction to Pequeno Principe [Little Prince], the largest paediatric hospital in Brazil.'

From elaborate crowns and ceremonial daggers, model ships and jet fighters, to clocks, dishes, and freedom-of-the-city keys from various municipalities, it included his three World Cup winner's medals, a one-off Jules Rimet trophy made for him after Brazil's famous triumph in Mexico in 1970. That World Cup replica was the most expensive item, with an estimated price tag of £281,000 to £420,000. The medals were expected to fetch up to £141,000, and the ball he scored his 1,000th goal with was estimated to sell for £28,000 to £42,000. Beverley Hills-based Julien's Auctions handled the sale, which even included old passports and driving licences.

Among the 1,500 lots that were auctioned was a pair of black football boots worn by Pelé in the film *Escape to Victory*. In the film he starred alongside Sylvester Stallone and Michael Caine, as well as World Cup-winning captain Bobby Moore.

Pelé was seen near the end of the film wearing these boots as he scored with a dramatic bicycle kick to equalise for the Allied team. 'I understand the film has a bit of a cult following in the UK, and these boots are certainly out of the norm,' says Dan Nelles, sports specialist at Julien's Auctions. 'I think there will be great interest in this highlight from his film career.' They were in the auction catalogue with an estimate of $6,000 to $8,000.

Were health or business reasons behind the great sell off?

Bill Wilson has some ideas, and reported just prior to the auction (BBC News, 31 May 2016):

'There are many reasons, there are clearly some personal ones that he alone knows about,' Dan Nelles, sports specialist at Julien's Auctions, tells me. Pelé himself says: 'It was a difficult decision to make but it takes a lot to properly care for these artefacts, and I felt I could do much more good by sharing these items with the world, as well as helping my causes that are important to me.'

Mr Nelles adds: 'He had a lot of the property in storage, and it wasn't seeing the light of day, which this auction now allows. Also, he wasn't sure what of it his family wanted to keep, and he didn't want it [the collection] to fall by the wayside. And the Pequeno Principe paediatric hospital in Brazil, which he supports, will receive a proportion.' Mr Nelles says that the auction house's 'conservative estimate' was that the sale will make £2.5m to £3.5m, but that 'the bidding would determine the final price.'

'There are so many wildcards in the auction, the Jules Rimet trophy, his World Cup medals, soccer boots, which means that ideally we are looking at three times that conservative estimate, and maybe as much as 10 times. There are also a great number of game-worn items from his career ... Although the auction is in London, we will not just be selling to UK customers, as the auction will be streamed live on our website for overseas bidders to take part,' he adds.

Pelé was a huge media attraction at the time and speaking at the Mall Galleries, he advised Marcus Rashford heading to the European Championships in France: 'Don't be afraid.' Pelé was called up to his national team when he was only sixteen, and won his first World Cup a year later. Rashford, then eighteen, was playing Under-twenty-one football a year earlier, but he too enjoyed an incredible rise. 'It doesn't matter about age. It is important to be prepared. Never, never, never be afraid. Don't be afraid.' Pelé knows there are far more pressures in the modern game but backed Rashford to deal with it. 'In my time I didn't have so many pressures with the TV, the radio the communications. Now there is a big pressure. But if he has a good support from the team I think he has to have confidence and trust himself.'

Pelé was shocked at how much was raised. His 1958 winner's medal was estimated to be worth between £70,000 and £140,000, but sold for £200,000. His medal from the 1962 World Cup in Chile was sold for £140,800. The boots worn in *Escape to Victory* sold for £8,025 despite an estimated price of between £4,200 and £5,600. The *L'Equipe* athlete of the century trophy with book went for £20,480, his 2007 *Fifa* presidential award fetched £30,720 and a 1,000th goal tribute crown with book sold for £162,500. Small items such as 'Pelé 2015 best in the world wood plaque' sold for much more than expected at £1,225, 'Pelé 2014 Brazilian Football Confederation One-hundredth anniversary medal' for £425 and a 'Fifty years of the first Intercontinental Cup title plaque' at £225.

* * *

From the *New York Times* and *USA Today*, to the lead item on the BBC Sports website, to every media outlet from the UK across the globe; the big sports news was reported in January 2018, that seventy-seven-year-old Pelé's latest illness prevented him from attending an awards night in his honour in London.

Coincidently, prior to the announcement, I had been with Glenn Hoddle, whose London-based agents 10Ten also represent Pelé in the UK. Glenn told me over lunch that his planned interview with Pelé for his *Mail on Sunday* column had been shelved, as Pelé wasn't coming to London. Curiously, there was no mention of Pelé being taken ill! Ossie Ardiles emailed me asking if I was attending the Pelé tribute dinner, and I told him that I doubted whether he would attend. When the news broke it seemed hardly a big surprise.

The Football Writers' Association announcement read: 'In the early hours of Thursday morning, Pelé collapsed and was taken to hospital in Brazil where he has undergone a series of tests, which appear to point to severe exhaustion. He remains on fluids while doctors monitor his recovery. Thankfully, there is no suggestion of anything more serious than exhaustion and everybody at the Football Writers' Association wishes Pelé a swift and full recovery. Understandably, his medical situation prevents him from travelling to London for the Football Writers' Association Tribute Night on Sunday evening at The Savoy. But after discussions with Pelé and his team, he has insisted the event should continue, not least because many of Pelé 's friends are travelling from overseas to be with us on Sunday. While it is incredibly sad Pelé cannot attend the function, the FWA are grateful that all those who have been asked to pay tribute on the night - Gareth Southgate, Cliff Jones, Gordon Banks and Steve Hunt - are determined to help make the evening a memorable one. Pelé 's team have also asked that we film the event and send a copy to Brazil in the knowledge it will lift the Great Man's spirits to see his friends are thinking of him and sending their best wishes. With that in mind, we want to do Pelé proud and make Sunday night as memorable as possible. It goes without saying, Pelé has an open invitation to any of our functions once he regains his health and we are already discussing the possibility of him joining us in May for the Footballer of the Year Dinner.'

It was a hugely disappointing black-tie affair for so many of football's greatest ever legends, and the sponsors.

Then, came something of a bombshell. Pelé's representative in Brazil described it as 'fake news' that the great man was in hospital suffering exhaustion. 'He just didn't want to make a long and stressful trip to London, in and out of who knows how many planes and airports,' said José Fornos Rodrigues, known as 'Pepito'. 'That's all.' Pelé 's family members said when approached by Brazilian media that they were unaware he had been hospitalised. 'I don't know who invented that news. He went to and from Rio de Janeiro this week by car and it was stressful, a tiring trip. He didn't feel bad. He's at home doing physical therapy,' José Fornos Rodrigues told EFE. 'A round trip to London would have been even more exhausting. He's fine. He didn't travel because it was going to be to exhausting to go and come back shortly afterward. He is at his home in Guaruja with his family. Resting and doing physiotherapy.' São Paulo's Albert Einstein Hospital, where Pelé undergoes routine tests and evaluations, denied he had been admitted.

Fornos said Pelé had reduced his scheduled appearances recently so he could receive more therapy for his hip. 'Pelé used to make two long trips every month, those that put him in a plane for more than 10 hours, but now we cut that to one. Doctors say he shouldn't travel one time after the other.'

Pelé appeared in a wheelchair in Moscow in December for the World Cup draw, an indication that his days of globetrotting for personal appearances were over, if not curtailed.

The FWA told me that their reporting of Pelé's illness came from 'impeccable sources' and that they did not accept it was fake news at all. The *Daily Mail* reported that Cambridge University were due to present him with an honorary doctorate the day after the tribute evening, but they too were left disappointed.

On Tuesday of that week, Pelé made fun of the walker he used at the opening ceremony of the Rio state championship. 'I decided to come in with this,' Pelé joked. 'God gave me those new boots and I decided to show them.'

The Savoy Hotel event went ahead with Gareth Southgate, in his toast to the FWA, stating that Pelé created so many iconic moments in football history. 'To have watched his performances, to see the impact he had on the world stage was incredible. You could see the enjoyment he took from the game, as well as the ability that he had. To have gone on to have been an incredible ambassador for the game in the way he has as well speaks volumes for the impact I think he has had, not only on football community, but right across the world as one of those rare iconic figures. You can travel to any part of the globe and people know who he was. Players of my generation, we didn't watch Spanish football or Italian football as the modern generation do, so how did we learn about the game? We watched old football, videos of old games. You can travel to any part of the globe and people would know who he was. Talk of Pelé and the beautiful game, enjoyment and freedom obviously brings me to England this summer. I am, of course, incredibly proud to be leading my country to a World Cup. When you see the incidents like Gordon's save that are replayed time after time – it is what I am always saying to the players, 'you have an opportunity every time you play for your country to make moments of history which people will always remember'.'

Cliff Jones, the former Tottenham and Wales winger, talked about facing Pelé in the 1958 World Cup, when the Brazilian was an unknown kid. 'Our manager Jimmy Murphy had warned us about the great players we'd be facing, such as Garrincha. But we had no idea who this seventeen-year-old kid Pelé was. We soon found out. He scored the goal that beat us, three in the semi-final and two more in the final. We knew then we were watching someone special.'

Pelé's former New York Cosmos team-mate Steve Hunt spoke about playing alongside the great man in the final year of his illustrious career. 'I was 20 years old and playing for Aston Villa reserves when the chance came to play in America. When I was told my team-mate would be Pelé , I said 'Where do I sign?' When

I met him the first day, I was greeted by a huge smile and the biggest hug imaginable. He was the warmest, friendliest guy I could have hoped for. I played in his last competitive game ever, and after we won 2–1, we carried him on our shoulders, which was the greatest moment of my life. He was a genius as a player and also one hell of a human being.'

Hugh McIlvanney, who covered the great Brazil sides when Pelé was at his peak, made an eloquent case for the 1970 World Cup winning team being the greatest side in the history of football: 'There can be no failure to recognise that the very incarnation of the glories of Brazilian football then, and forever, was and is Pelé.'

Patrick Barclay, FWA Chairman, paid tribute to the national committee for their work in organising the evening, thanked title sponsors William Hill for their support, and gave thanks to Boadicea the Victorious for their table gifts of luxury perfume. They were joined by members from the National Football Museum, who brought some precious artefacts from their Pelé exhibition, including the shirts he wore in 1958 and 1970.

Banks accepted the FWA tribute award on Pelé's behalf. He recalled his famous save from the group match against Brazil in Guadalajara. 'When I saw him in London, he said: "Gordon, I go all over the world and people talk about the goals I scored, but when I come to England, all they talk about is that save."' Banks, at the time, did not quite realise what an iconic moment it would become. 'I have leaped over there to reach as far as I possibly could and anticipate how high the ball was going to bounce up from the hard surface. As I got over it and I got my hand to it and the ball takes my hand back, honest to God, I thought it was a goal. I hit the floor and turned around, I saw the ball bounce behind the goal, and I said: "Oh, Banksy, you lucky t***."'

Yet, only a few months later, Pelé attended the first yearly convention hosted by CVC in Dubai. He attended the convention as a global ambassador of Emirates Airline. CVC is Brazil's largest tour operator overseas and represents 1,200 stores across the 27 states in Brazil. As the official airline of the convention, Emirates showcased Dubai's latest tourism attractions and services along with promoting the cosmopolitan city to Brazilian travellers. Clearly this visit involved commercial and sponsorship-led commitments as an ambassador for Emirates. Pelé posted tweets on board Emirates A380 flight in the first-class section. He first visited the UAE in 1973 when Santos played with Al Nasr and he last visited Duba in January 2014.

England's most famous goalkeeper turned eighty on 30 December, 2017. To celebrate the life of Gordon Banks, Radio 5 live's *Sportsweek* produced an in-depth interview with the World Cup winner. 'That save in 1970? It was all about the bounce' England headed to Mexico in 1970 to defend their title as one of the favourites. They led West Germany 2–0 in the quarter-finals, but lost 3–2. The tournament was won by Brazil, who defeated England 1-0 in a memorable group game. During it, Banks seemed to defy physics by somehow managing to save a header from Pelé , tipping it over the crossbar. 'I'll be remembered for that one. When we arrived in Mexico it was red hot, so whenever we trained or practised we were wet through. The sun was out all the time so the turf was rock hard and of course when we started shooting sessions the ball seemed to be kicking up quite high. I thought I'd better get some more practise in here - get used to it kicking up. That is exactly what happened. I saw Pelé racing to the edge of the box. I had a quick look before their winger Jairzinho crossed the ball – Pelé had got in front of Alan Mullery. Jairzinho centered the ball, but I could not come out for the cross. I knew from the penalty spot it would have to be a fantastic header to beat me. But the ground was hard so I thought I should get off my line and as I dived I had to anticipate how high it was going to bounce. I got a hand to it, the ball actually hit the top of my hand and looked as though it was going into the top of the net. As I hit the floor I saw that the ball had missed the goal. At first I thought 'you lucky so and so' but then I realised it has been a bit special.

'I've met Pelé many times since and we often have a chat about it. He thought he'd scored.'

CHAPTER 19

PELÉ: THE WORLD'S VIEW

Various people made interesting comments about Pelé, so here are a selection. We'll start with Wayne Rooney. Pelé tweeted a selfie with Wayne at a charity event when the striker was still captain of England and Manchester United. Rooney responded on Twitter that 'it had been a "huge honour" to meet him.'

Here are the rest:

'The greatest goal I ever scored was a one-two with Celeste – we named him Edson Arantes do Nascimento.'

Dondinho, Pelé's father

'I told myself before the game, 'he's made of skin and bones just like everyone else'. But I was wrong.'

Tarcisio Burgnich, the Italy defender who marked Pelé in the Mexico 1970 Final

'On this special date when you celebrate your seventy-fifth birthday, allow me to offer you my best wishes of health and happiness. I sincerely hope you find some time to spend a wonderful day with your family and friends. I thank you for everything that you have done for football, and I would like to convey to you my sincere friendship and respect."

Issa Hayatou, Acting FIFA President

'My name is Ronald Reagan, I'm the President of the United States of America. But you don't need to introduce yourself, because everyone knows who Pelé is.'

Ronald Reagan

The difficulty, the extraordinary, is not to score 1,000 goals like Pelé – it's to score one goal like Pelé.'

Carlos Drummond de Andrade, Brazilian poet

'The greatest player in history was Di Stefano. I refuse to classify Pelé as a player. He was above that.'

Ferenc Puskas

'In some countries they wanted to touch him, in some they wanted to kiss him. In others they even kissed the ground he walked on. I thought it was beautiful, just beautiful.'

Clodoaldo

'After the fifth goal, even I wanted to cheer for him.'

Sigge Parling of Sweden on a 5–2 defeat by Brazil in the 1958 FIFA World Cup Final

'I arrived hoping to stop a great man, but I went away convinced
I had been undone by someone who was not born on the same
planet as the rest of us.'

Costa Pereira on Benfica's 5–2 loss to Santos in the 1962
Intercontinental Cup in Lisbon

'Pelé was the greatest – he was simply flawless. And off the pitch
he is always smiling and upbeat. You never see him bad-tempered.
He loves being Pelé.'

Tostão

'When I saw Pelé play, it made me feel I should hang up
my boots.'

Just Fontaine

'Pelé was so focused on winning the Trophy. It was like he knew it
was his destiny. He was like a child waiting for Santa Claus.'

Mario Americo, Brazil's masseur, on Mexico 1970

'Pelé was one of the few who contradicted my theory: instead of
fifteen minutes of fame, he will have fifteen centuries.'

Andy Warhol

'You may be right. But you know nothing about football and I've
seen Pelé play.'

Brazil coach Vicente Feola to the psychologist who said
Pelé was too immature to play at Sweden 1958

'Pelé was the only footballer who surpassed the boundaries
of logic.'

Johan Cruyff

'His great secret was improvisation. Those things he did were in one moment. He had an extraordinary perception of the game.'

Carlos Alberto Torres

'I sometimes feel as though football was invented for this magical player.'

Sir Bobby Charlton

'Pelé played football for twenty-two years, and in that time he did more to promote world friendship and fraternity than any other ambassador anywhere.'

J.B. Pinheiro, the Brazilian Ambassador to the United Nations

Malcolm Allison: 'How do you spell Pelé?'
Paddy Crerand: 'Easy: G–O–D.'

British television commentators during Mexico 1970

INDEX

INDEX